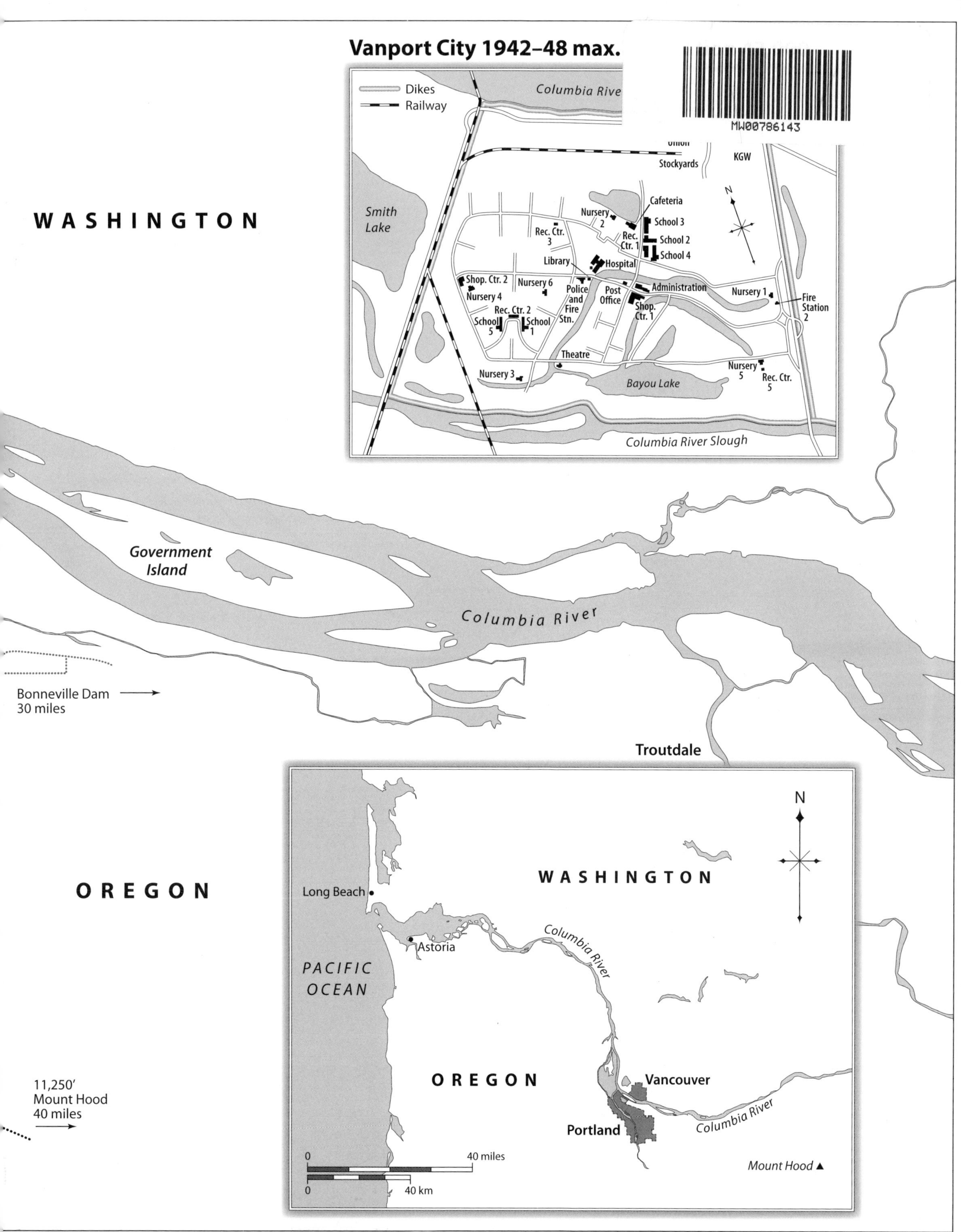
Vanport City 1942–48 max.
Dikes
Railway
Columbia River
Union
Stockyards
KGW
Smith Lake
Cafeteria
Nursery 2
School 3
Rec. Ctr. 3
Rec. Ctr. 1
School 2
School 4
Library
Hospital
Shop. Ctr. 2
Nursery 6
Nursery 4
Police and Fire Stn.
Post Office
Administration
Nursery 1
Fire Station 2
Shop. Ctr. 1
Rec. Ctr. 2
School 5
School 1
Theatre
Nursery 3
Bayou Lake
Nursery 5
Rec. Ctr. 5
Columbia River Slough
WASHINGTON
Government Island
Columbia River
Bonneville Dam 30 miles
Troutdale
OREGON
11,250′ Mount Hood 40 miles
N
WASHINGTON
Long Beach
Astoria
Columbia River
PACIFIC OCEAN
OREGON
Vancouver
Portland
Columbia River
0
40 miles
0
40 km
Mount Hood

LIBERTY FACTORY

LIBERTY FACTORY

The Untold Story of Henry Kaiser's Oregon Shipyards

Peter J Marsh

Seaforth
PUBLISHING

This book is dedicated to my parents – Frederick and Ellen May Marsh – who married in October, 1939. He joined the army and later saw action in North Africa, she worked in the Royal Arsenal, and told me stories.

Half-title: Wartime US Maritime Commission poster urging shipyard workers to speed up production.

Title spread: A row of Victory ships under construction at the Portland yard of Oregon Shipbuilding Corporation (OSC)

First published in Great Britain in 2021 by
Seaforth Publishing
An imprint of Pen & Sword Books Ltd
47 Church Street, Barnsley
S Yorkshire S70 2AS

www.seaforthpublishing.com
Email info@seaforthpublishing.com

British Library Cataloguing in Publication Data
A CIP data record for this book is available from the British Library

ISBN 978-1-5267-8305-9 (Hardback)

ISBN 978-1-5267-8306-6 (ePub)

ISBN 978-1-5267-8307-3 (Kindle)

Pen & Sword Books Limited incorporates the imprints of Atlas, Archaeology, Aviation, Discovery, Family History, Fiction, History, Maritime, Military, Military Classics, Politics, Select, Transport, True Crime, Air World, Frontline Publishing, Leo Cooper, Remember When, Seaforth Publishing, The Praetorian Press, Wharncliffe Local History, Wharncliffe Transport, Wharncliffe True Crime and White Owl.

Typeset and designed by Stephen Dent
Printed and bound in China by 1010 Printing Ltd

CONTENTS

PREFACE

'We shall need a great mass of shipping in 1942, far more than we can build ourselves, if we are to maintain and augment our war effort in the West and in the East ... Here is the answer which I will give to President Roosevelt: Give us the tools, and we will finish the job.'

Winston Churchill, 9 February 1941

When historians look back on President Roosevelt's famous 'Arsenal of Democracy' – the massive militarization of American industrial capacity from 1942 – the city of Portland, Oregon in the northwest of the USA is rarely considered an important player. Far from the centres of political power and business, and lacking any naval installations, Portland was an unlikely site for the construction of the biggest emergency shipyards on the west coast. World War II never physically touched Portland, or its neighbour across the Columbia River, Vancouver, Washington. There were no battles or enemy incursions in the area – except for a single salvo from a Japanese submarine into Fort Stephens on the northwest tip of Oregon.

But this was the time when the entire country, unanimously turned itself into a giant national war machine, providing material support of every kind to the Allied forces around the globe, and the Portland-Vancouver area made an enormous contribution by producing large numbers of merchant and naval vessels that they desperately needed to defeat Germany and Japan. By 1943, around 150,000 people were working in the region's three giant yards built by the industrialist Henry J Kaiser and four smaller independent yards.

The Kaiser organization was based in Richmond, California where its first shipbuilding complex was created at the end of 1940. The second centre in Portland at the confluence of the mighty Columbia River and its tributary the Willamette was established in the second wave of emergency shipyard expansion and was not expected to compete with Richmond in output. After all, Portland was 100 miles from the sea and lacked the marine trades and tradition of the San Francisco Bay Area. Nonetheless, Henry Kaiser established two big shipyards in Portland and a third across the Columbia River in Vancouver, Washington, and made his son Edgar the general manager. What this father-and-son team achieved was nothing short of miraculous, and these yards were acclaimed by the country's top naval and government officials as the best performing in the nation, year after year. Through their combined efforts, these three Kaiser yards and their army of workers launched over seven hundred and fifty ships and saw themselves as vital parts of a nationwide military machine supporting the country's armed forces in Europe and the Pacific, and taking immense personal pride in their contribution.

This achievement has been all but forgotten by Oregonians, who must travel 600 miles to the south to the San Francisco Bay to learn about the Kaiser company's war effort. This is where Kaiser began building his short-lived wartime shipbuilding empire and there the history of his shipyards is alive and well. Thanks to the large number of historic sites and naval bases nearby, this was the natural location of the 'World War II/ Rosie the Riveter National Historical Park' established in 2000 by an act of the US Congress, and managed by the National Park Service. The park includes four of the Kaiser's World War II health service buildings, a memorial garden and a research centre, and celebrates the activities of the women shipbuilders at the nearby Richmond shipyards.

In addition, two of the handful of surviving Liberty and Victory ships in the world have been preserved by local veterans' groups as historic monuments and are moored in the Bay. The Victory ship is the SS *Red Oak Victory*; the Liberty ship is the SS *Jeremiah O'Brien* that was built in New England, and attended the 50th anniversary of the D-Day landings in 1994.

The National Park's literature explains this area's claim to fame in this way: 'The four Kaiser Shipyards in Richmond produced 747 ships during World War II, more than any other shipyard complex in the country ... making them 'the most productive shipyards in history'. However, any visitor who reads a little further will also find this curious fact: 'All of Kaiser's shipyards together produced 1490 ships, which amounted to 27 percent of the total US Maritime Commission fleet of 5777 merchant ships.' These impressive numbers beg a very obvious question: where were the other half of the Kaiser ships built?

Nowhere in the park's guides or website is there an answer to this important question. Fortunately, one can easily be found

than twins
...ink. Read
births in
magazine.

The Oregonian

We...
Thursday
42 degr...
Friday fo...
weather

...t Portland (Oregon)
...as Second-Class Matter

PORTLAND, OREGON FRIDAY, DECEMBER 15, 1944

CITY EDITIO...

Last of 30 Attack Transport Vessels From Oregon Yard Heads Down River

...RTLAND Last of Oregon Shipbuilding corporation's attack transports, the U. S. S. Lavaca, was delivered Thursday to the maritime commission. The vessel, 30th of the class built at the yard, gracefully went down river after "aloha" ceremonies which streamers of confetti were tossed at the outfitting dock at the yard.

Above: A typical front page of *The Oregonian* as it appeared during the war.

in the footnotes to many maritime histories of World War II: it is, of course, Portland, the unfashionable small city that won a place in the 'major league' of the war effort. The Kaiser company's own history and US Maritime Commission records reveal that these three NW yards also achieved construction records that have never been surpassed, and show how they routinely out-performed the other seventeen emergency shipyards, including those in Richmond.

OSC – often known as Oregonship from its telegraphic address – was the first of the Kaiser yards in this region. It was to become a veritable 'Liberty Factory', building 322 Liberty ships, 99 Victory ships, and 33 Attack Transports. The second Portland yard was Kaiser Swan Island, which built 147 T2 tankers. Kaiser Vancouver's output of well over 100 ships of five different types included the only fighting ships of the Kaiser company's output: the 50 escort aircraft carriers (CVEs) that played an important role in the defeat of Japan and the U-boat war in the Atlantic. Between 1941 and 1945 three smaller Portland shipyards also distinguished themselves for speed and quality of construction, and were so proficient in building small naval vessels, they led the nation in delivering numerous minesweepers, subchasers and landing craft of all sizes and types. The total output of the seven shipyards in the Portland-Vancouver area was well over 1100 merchant and naval ships, equalling or exceeding the total built in San Francisco Bay. Should anyone wish to challenge this statement, I will throw in the 3000 lifeboats and 440 landing craft built by Gunderson Brothers to tip the scales.

The Kaiser organization also broke many social barriers to achieve those amazing production records: it was here that Henry's son Edgar Kaiser recognized the potential represented by women who were demanding equal opportunity to work in the shipyards. In the spring of 1942 the first two women welders took their place next to the men. The Kaiser yards began training thousands of women in shipyard skills to the extent that they would soon comprise one third of the workforce. The next year, Edgar opened the world's first large-scale child care centres, open 24 hours a day, allowing as many as 1000 mothers to work in the shipyards knowing their young children were well cared for. The Kaiser shipyards also welcomed thousands of migrants from the mid-west and southern states who journeyed to the Pacific Northwest in search of work in the war industries. They even attempted to stop the notorious racial discrimination that was typical of everyday life in Oregon at that time, although they had more success in California than in Oregon. The Kaiser family wielded immense economic and political power and when Edgar Kaiser personally decided to solve his workers' housing problems, he bypassed local authorities and rapidly constructed 'Vanport', the second-largest city in Oregon, which housed as many as 44,000 shipyard workers. To keep the workforce healthy, the Kaisers created the first company-wide healthcare insurance plan and built their own hospitals.

These progressive social measures still stand out today as far ahead of their time, but were not enacted purely in a philanthropic spirit. They were necessary to retain and encourage as many as 100,000 employees to stay in the three Vancouver-Portland (that I abbreviate to Van-Port) shipyards and maintain the incredible pace of production. However, it is hardly surprising that the nation has forgotten these grand achievements when the city of Portland itself has no memorials, no signs, and apparently no awareness of the important part the city played in the war effort.

San Francisco is a world-famous city with a unique history dating from the gold rush of 1849, its bay is by far the biggest harbour on the west coast and is a major naval base, so it is understandable that they should consider themselves the centre of the war effort on the west coast. But I do feel that the National Parks Service could do a better job of presenting the 'other half' of the Kaiser story and the efforts of 'Wendy the Welder' (Rosie the Riveter built planes not ships!).

The Bay Area did do Portland one very big favour: a group of US Navy veterans preserved another World War II ship, much smaller than the great cargo ships of that era, but equally important in its military significance. It is only 158ft long and does not even have a name, but the USS *LCS(L)-102* on Mare Island in Vallejo is the last of its type, with a proud heritage and a fascinating history. This 'landing craft support' was based on a standard landing craft, but converted into a deadly gunboat loaded down with every offensive weapon it could possibly carry. Its mission was to lead the way and clear the beaches in the amphibious landings on Pacific islands heavily fortified by Japan.

A total of 130 of these gunboats were built in a race against time to minimize casualties among the soldiers and Marines who risked their lives during the landings. Three shipyards in the USA were given the task of building these gunboats nicknamed the 'Mighty Midgets' as quickly as possible. Two of those yards were in Portland, and together they launched 83 of them. Though rarely acknowledged, the USS *LCS(L)-102* is one of those Portland-built boats, making it the only surviving World War II vessel built in Portland. It was in fact launched by the Commercial Iron Works, once located in Portland's newly redeveloped Southwest Waterfront District and another of Portland's historic World War II shipbuilding sites that has been completely ignored.

Lawrence Barber, marine editor of *The Oregonian* newspaper, faithfully recorded the city's wartime scene day-by-day and the archive material he had preserved was the primary source for this book. I am also indebted to George Kramer for permission to quote from 'It Takes More than Bullets', a research paper he wrote for the Housing Authority of Portland. His title comes from a slogan that Kaiser's shipyards used during a United War Chest bond-buying campaign. The Kaiser Foundation's online archive and the American Bureau of Shipping (ABS) booklet *Workhorse of the Fleet* by Gus Bourneuf Jr were also valuable sources.

However, these contemporary records were often overlooked by the specialists who have written accounts of World War II shipbuilding, and by social scientists who continue to study the part played by women, and the development of Portland in the twentieth century. Between 1940 and 1945, Portland transformed itself in many significant ways and gained national

Above: Larry Barber, marine editor of *The Oregonian* newspaper, whose files provide the main source for this book.

Left: Larry Barber's first boat, *Little Shaver*. Despite the peaceful scene, the boat wears the Coast Guard Auxiliary markings introduced after Pearl Harbor. Yacht clubs on the west coast organized their members into CGA fleets that patrolled their local waters and ports. Small vessels were required to register and were given a reference number to identify them as friendly.

recognition for the skills and diligence its workers brought to their vital wartime tasks.

In this book, I hope to revive interest in this period and increase the understanding and appreciation of Portland's truly remarkable wartime achievements. My intention is to tell the story of all Portland and Vancouver's forgotten shipyards, large and small, and honour the part their workers played in the nation's defence industry with all its hardships, dangers and small victories. My intention is to show the war years almost day-by-day as seen by Barber and other contemporary observers, with explanations where necessary – and occasionally my own opinion.

························

ACKNOWLEDGEMENTS

The primary source and inspiration for this book was the personal photo archive and papers of Lawrence Barber (1901–1996), a photo-journalist who began reporting on the Portland maritime scene in 1932 when he was made the marine editor of *The Oregonian* newspaper. In 1940 he began covering the activity of the Kaiser organization in the city, and became the paper's lead reporter on the war effort in the region's numerous shipyards.

The author met Barber when they both wrote for a local boating publication in the early 1990s. Barber allowed him to view the large collection of photographs he had preserved, covering the period from 1930, when sailing ships still loaded wheat, to the 1960s, when the steam-powered sternwheel tugs began to disappear from the local rivers. After his death in 1996, Barber's widow Elizabeth invited the author to catalogue the photo collection and eventually gave it to him for preservation and further use.

George Kramer wrote a definitive history of Portland's wartime housing estates in World War Two for the Housing Authority of Portland, titled *It Takes More Than Bullets: The WWII Homefront in Portland, Oregon*. He and the Housing Authority generously gave the author permission to use this work for reference and guidance. (George has a BA in history, a Master's Degree in Historic Preservation from the University of Oregon, and over thirty years' experience in the field of historic preservation in Oregon.)

The Oregon Historical Society has put the entire run of Kaiser shipyards' newspaper *The Bo's'n's Whistle* online, thanks to the efforts of Lincoln Cushing, archivist and historian for Kaiser Permanente, and an expert in Kaiser's World War Two shipyard history. This material gives a highly detailed view of daily life and work in the three Portland-Vancouver shipyards 1941–1945 and provided valuable background to this book. https://digitalcollections.ohs.org/the-bosns-whistle

Kaiser Permanente is the health care system that was pioneered in the Kaiser shipyards in Richmond, California and Portland, Oregon during the war. Today, it has become one of the nation's largest not-for-profit health plans and maintains an extensive history archive online that covers many aspects of the Kaiser corporation's wartime activities. https://about.kaiser-permanente.org/our-story/our-history

The city of Portland Archives & Records Center provided the 1942 Trolley Map of Portland used in the map on the endpapers, and other historic documents used for reference.

My thanks also to Al Venter, the South African writer specializing in contemporary military history who has had over 50 books published, and recommended me to Pen & Sword. And also to Floyd Holcom, the owner of the restored Pier 39 in Astoria, dating from 1875, who provided me with an office with a view of the Columbia River, where over 1100 newly-launched ships passed by during World War II.

INTRODUCTION

EUROPE'S DESCENT INTO WAR 1938–1940

Historians generally agree that the root cause of World War II is found in the severe terms exacted by the Allies in the Treaty of Versailles after the defeat of Germany in World War I. The Wall Street Crash of 1929 and the Great Depression that followed also played a part in driving Germany to elect Adolf Hitler as Chancellor in 1933. He embarked on a vast national program of propaganda and social control as he eliminated all opposition. This allowed him to begin re-armament and revive the economy, paid for by huge federal deficits.

In the USA, the same economic issues helped to elect Franklin D Roosevelt, the Democratic party candidate, and he became president in 1933. His New Deal was also an attempt to end the Great Depression by spending public funds to create jobs in public works and amenities, but there was no appetite for additional military spending. Outside of the established two-party system, there were other popular figures who opposed FDR and rose to national prominence mainly by finding scapegoats for the disastrous economic situation in various ethnic and political groups.

Many of the unemployed were drawn to these causes, which also attracted some famous public figures. Charles Lindbergh had gained worldwide fame as the first person to fly solo nonstop across the Atlantic in 1927, but was also a committed fascist; Henry Ford was a public supporter of Hitler as early as 1930. Organizations like the German-American Bund and the American Liberty League advanced fascist policies as a counter to union protests and labour unrest. Throughout the 1930s, Roman Catholic priest Father Charles Coughlin preached rabid pro-fascist sermons on the radio and reached millions of listeners, his audience size rivalling the president's fireside chats.

In Great Britain, the Labour Party government believed an austerity budget would solve the national financial crisis, but were unable to win support and collapsed in disarray in 1931. The general election resulted in a landslide victory for the Conservative party, who formed the coalition National Government with the Liberals and some Labour MPs. They also resisted the demands to increase spending to escape the Depression, and pursued their austerity policies on the country from 1931 until 1940, although this completely failed to combat the mass unemployment in the industrial areas.

In October 1933 Hitler withdrew from the Geneva Disarmament Conference of the League of Nations. While FDR cut the military budget in the USA by a third, the governments in Britain, France and the USSR were constrained even more by the terrible losses of the Great War to follow a policy of German appeasement. On 16 March 1935 Hitler announced that he would re-arm Germany and begin conscription to create an army of more than half a million – in open violation of the Treaty of Versailles signed in June 1919 in Paris.

Then came the Nuremberg Laws of September 1935, stripping German Jews of their citizenship. In 1936, when Italian dictator Benito Mussolini's invasion of Ethiopia led to only ineffectual protests by the British and French governments, Hitler marched 3000 troops into the demilitarized zone in the Rhineland, again in violation of the Versailles Treaty. In July 1936 the Spanish army launched a coup d'état, which started the Spanish Civil War. The League of Nations was now seen to be powerless in the face of more provocations by the fascist governments whose confidence in their military ability continued to grow.

Hitler then signed agreements with Japan and Italy, and sent military supplies to the Nationalist army of General Francisco Franco in Spain. In 1937 Lindbergh was living in Europe to escape the American press, and happily accepted the invitation from Reichsmarshal Hermann Göring, the head of the Luftwaffe (German air force), to inspect the new generation of German warplanes like the Messerschmitt 109, probably the world's most advanced fighter. Göring presented him with the Cross of the Order of the German Eagle. (This was a time when the British and French operational fighters were still biplanes, not radically different from those employed in World War I.)

In 1938 Germany began making increasingly aggressive territorial demands on the surrounding countries, threatening war if these were not met. On 12 March 1938 Hitler ordered the *Anschluss* or occupation of Austria. The campaign against the Jews began immediately after this invasion, and Hitler next targeted Czechoslovakia, under the policy of *Lebensraum* ('living room', in effect space for Germany to expand). This forced other European governments to react, and led to an international attempt to intervene in the crisis.

Above: Wartime British poster underlining the importance of seaborne trade to the survival of the United Kingdom.

In September 1938 British prime minister Neville Chamberlain flew to Munich to meet Hitler and Mussolini, with the French Prime Minister Édouard Daladier in attendance. They all signed the Munich Agreement confirming the German annexation of Czechoslovakia's province of Sudetenland, which followed the policy of appeasement. When he returned to England, Chamberlain famously announced that he had secured 'peace in our time' to crowds delighted that war had been averted. He was invited by King George VI onto the balcony at Buckingham Palace before he had reported to Parliament, which broke one of the unwritten rules of the British constitution.

There was strong opposition to appeasement by a group of MPs, but Chamberlain encouraged and bullied the press and the BBC to censor coverage of his opponents. This included the news of 15,000 people in Trafalgar Square protesting his return from Munich, a Gallup poll that showed 86 percent of the public believed Mr Hitler was lying about his territorial ambitions, and knew about continuing persecution of Jews by the Nazis.

Six weeks later, on 9 November 1938, a young Jew killed the Third Secretary of the German Embassy in Paris. The next day, Nazi Party members began the pogrom of '*Kristallnacht*', where hundreds of Jews were killed and thousands more imprisoned. Despite the warnings in Parliament by Winston Churchill, daily life continued unchanged in London. World-famous psycho-analyst Sigmund Freud fled Vienna and joined a growing refugee community in the capital of the British Empire.

In the last year of peace, the upper classes seemed to be untroubled by the growing war clouds on the horizon. The children's garden at London Zoo was opened by Robert and Ted Kennedy, two of the young sons of United States ambassador Joseph P Kennedy. Great Britain and the US contested the first Amateur World Series in baseball. (Britain won every game.) Britons continued to follow the progress of patriotic attempts on speed records: a streamlined steam locomotive, the *Mallard*, reached a world record speed of 126 mph, while on Coniston Water, Sir Malcolm Campbell set the world water speed record in *Bluebird K4* with a speed of 141.75 mph.

The majority of Americans also continued to live in a state

of denial, with many politicians opposed to any involvement in Europe and blatant anti-Semitism arising in the state department. This had a devastating effect on 900 Jewish refugees who arrived in US waters on the SS *St Louis*, but were denied permission to land in Florida on 4 June 1939 after already having been turned away from Cuba. Forced to return to Europe, many of the passengers died in Nazi death camps.

THE GERMAN INVASION OF POLAND – THE WAR AT SEA BEGINS IMMEDIATELY

At 4:45 am on the morning of 1 September 1939 the German blitzkrieg ('lightning war') on Poland began when Hitler's armoured divisions crossed the Polish frontier. In support of British treaty obligations to Poland, Prime Minister Neville Chamberlain gave the Germans 48 hours to withdraw, then declared war. On the same day, he brought Churchill back into government as First Lord of the Admiralty. A few hours later, a U-boat torpedoed and sank the British liner SS *Athenia* off the coast of Scotland. The ship was en route to Montreal, Canada with 1400 passengers on board – 112 lost their lives, including many Jewish refugees and 28 Americans.

Attacking an unarmed passenger ship without warning was a war crime, so this led to German fears that the incident would bring the US into the war. Reich Minister of Propaganda Joseph Goebbels, who had spent a decade manipulating German popular opinion, immediately started spreading 'fake news' on the world stage by claiming that the *Athenia* had been sunk by the British to win over public opinion in the USA. This theory was supported by American isolationists, including some leading political figures. It was also the harbinger of the total war to come, where attacks on civilians would become standard tactics.

This marked the start of what became the 'Battle of the Atlantic', when German submarines began causing appalling losses to British shipping and the Royal Navy. At the start of the war Germany's fledgling U-boat fleet comprised fewer than fifty active submarines, but in relative terms the British had even fewer destroyer escorts to counter them. U-boats were to inflicted terrible losses on British shipping – they had sunk more than 200 Allied cargo ships before the end of the year, and at various times came close to starving Britain out of the war. This began a running battle – the longest of the war – that would continue until Germany surrendered in May 1945.

While war raged at sea, a curious state called the 'phoney war' reigned over Europe for nine months until May 1940. That was when a surprise German blitzkrieg thrust through Belgium and the Netherlands into northern France, forcing the Allied armies into headlong retreat, including the British Expeditionary Force (BEF) which fell back towards Dunkirk. In a separate but simultaneous campaign, Norway surrendered to German forces on 10 May 1940, and Prime Minister Chamberlain resigned. Winston Churchill took over the premiership and within days he was faced with his first crisis of World War II when the British army was trapped on the beaches at Dunkirk. After the capitulation of the Belgian and French armies, around 500,000 men were stranded, but the German army was told to halt for three days for reasons that have never been completely explained.

This short break in hostilities between 26 May and 4 June gave sufficient time for the BEF to organize a defensive line and the British War Department to call out an armada of fishing boats, ferries and small naval ships to evacuate Dunkirk. More than 338,000 men were rescued, among them 140,000 French. One positive outcome of this disaster was the realization that if the Allies forces were ever to return to Europe it would probably be across a similar beach, and that an entirely new type of ship would be necessary to accomplish that – the 'landing craft', most of which would be designed and built in the USA.

In a speech on 10 June 1940 reacting to this situation Roosevelt argued 'Some, indeed, still hold to the now somewhat obvious delusion that we can safely permit the United States to become a lone island … in a world dominated by the philosophy of force. Such an island may be the dream of those who still talk and vote as isolationists. Such an island represents to me and to the overwhelming majority of Americans today a helpless nightmare of a people without freedom – the nightmare of a people lodged in prison, handcuffed, hungry, and fed through the bars from day to day by the contemptuous, unpitying masters of other continents.'

Then on 22 June Marshall Pétain, the French commander, signed an armistice with Germany taking France out of the war and into German occupation. The German submarine fleet was now able to operate freely from reinforced basins in western France, radically shortening the distance to the Atlantic shipping lanes. The war against merchant shipping stepped up a gear and before long Germany was sinking more ships than Britain could build – and by a wide margin – limiting the transport of vital supplies of food, fuel and arms from North America.

THE ISOLATIONIST MOVEMENT IN THE USA

The war would probably have been lost if FDR had not agreed to meet Britain's appeal for ships, but much of the US print media was still in favour of a negotiated peace with Germany. The *Reader's Digest* was owned and published by the pro-Fascist and anti-labour DeWitt Wallace. The *Chicago Tribune*, the Hearst and Gannett newspaper chains, the Scripps-Howard Syndicate, and the *Washington Times-Herald* all supported the Fascist cause, and The Citizens National Keep America Out of War Committee was active in many cities.

President Roosevelt himself denounced William Randolph

Above: A North Atlantic convoy, seen off Newfoundland in July 1942.

Hearst, the United Press Syndicate and the *Chicago Tribune* for their support of Hitler. But back in the USA from Germany, Lindbergh continued to use his reputation to praise Hitler and the Luftwaffe and champion the isolationist cause. He was active as the spokesman for the America First Committee, one of whose slogans was 'No Convoys'. Only with the attack on Pearl Harbor on 7 December 1941 did Lindbergh decide to support the president's position.

The German army had failed to crush the Allied forces at Dunkirk, but Britain now stood alone against the Nazis, separated by only 22 miles of water from the French coast. Hitler now ordered his air force and navy into action. Herman Göring began the air war over southeast England that became the Battle of Britain as a prelude to an invasion by an armada of river barges. Fortunately, this invasion, code-named Operation Sea Lion, was doomed to failure because the German High Command had never planned for an amphibious operation on this scale nor taken into consideration the rough conditions likely to be encountered on the Channel crossing. (That was one reason why they failed to identify the huge D-Day fleet as it was assembled in southern England in 1944.)

Americans were well informed about the 'European situation' at this time: journalist William Shirer reported from Berlin for CBS from 1933 and accompanied the German army's Blitzkrieg across northern Europe in 1940. By December, the Gestapo were investigating Shirer's work; but he was warned and escaped just in time. Edward Murrow famously reported from London during the summer of 1940 as the Battle of Britain raged over southern England.

By this time, it was well understood that Britain's fate depended on the survival of its merchant fleet – the largest in the world – with around one third of the total tonnage afloat. Even in peacetime the country was dependent on merchant shipping for the import of food, equipment and raw materials, and its needs for imported military aid only added to the demand during the war. During the war, approximately 185,000 seamen served in the Merchant Navy, including

40,000 from Asia and the British Empire; and over 30,000 were killed at sea, a death rate that was higher than in any of the armed forces.

THE U-BOAT - THE NEW TERROR WEAPON

It was the German navy's growing fleet of submarines, commanded by the highly experienced Admiral Karl Dönitz, that was given the task of stopping the convoys and 'bringing Britain to its knees'. The production of U-boats increased, more crews were recruited, and French workers were conscripted to build three impregnable submarine bases in western France with massive concrete walls and roofs that could resist any known form of bombing attack.

Britain required more than half a million tons (about fifty ship-loads) of imported material per week in order to be able to survive and fight, and the vital supply line from North America was now under daily attack by organized groups of U-boats, known as 'wolf packs'. By the end of 1940, over 150 U-boats had been commissioned and the submarine wolf packs ruled the waves. They were devastatingly successful and had sunk over 270 Allied ships; there seemed to be no way to counter them. Britain's survival was balanced on a knife edge. In July Churchill had to cable Roosevelt that the British had lost eleven destroyers in ten days and urgently requested help. In August, US Ambassador to the UK Joseph P Kennedy reported from London that a British surrender was 'inevitable' unless the USA provided a wide range of aid. A national survey found that two thirds of Americans now believed that a German-Italian victory would endanger the United States.

By the end of summer 1940 the American people were already aware of preliminary activity by the federal government in case the nation should suddenly become embroiled in the war in Europe. On 16 September the first peacetime program of compulsory military service in the USA became law with substantial opposition in both houses. All males between the ages of 21 to 35 were required to register for the draft. A lottery system would determine who would be called into service.

In September 1940, as the Battle of Britain intensified, US Secretary of State Cordell Hull agreed to the transfer of fifty mothballed World War I era US destroyers to the Royal Navy to help defend the vulnerable North Atlantic convoys. In exchange, the US was granted the right to establish naval or air bases in the British Empire. Most of the antiquated ships required extensive overhaul because they had been out of use for many years. Churchill disliked the deal but the nation's reserves were already spent, and he hoped this would lead to more assistance. This partnership did officially become 'Lend-Lease' on 11 March 1941 despite strong isolationist voices from respected figures such as Senator William Borah and Charles Lindberg.

Below: A large proportion of the British merchant marine was made up of traditional tramp steamers with triple expansion steam engines, like the SS *Dorington Court* seen here. However, this ship was to play an important part in the evolution of the Liberty ship.

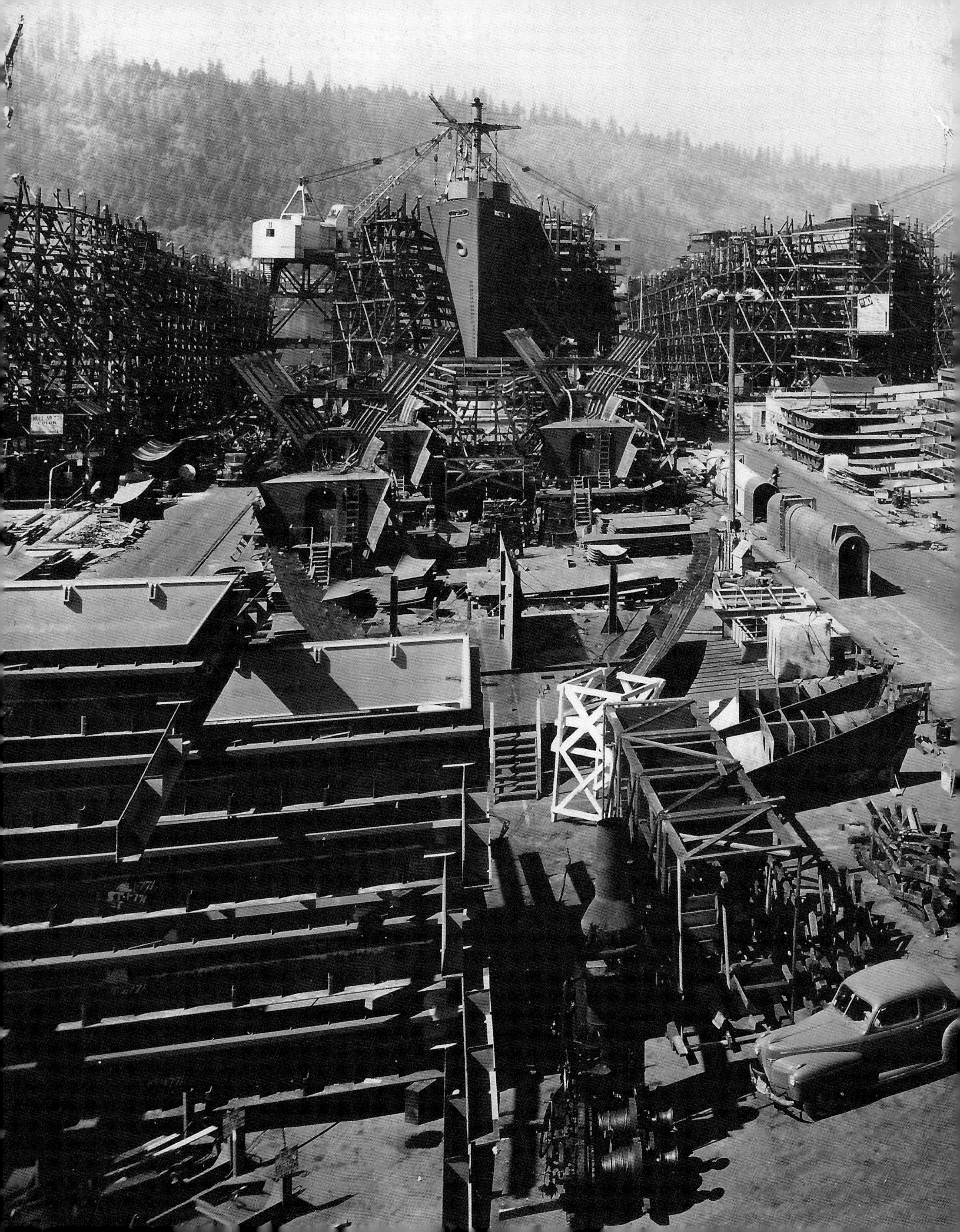
HULL № 770
COLOR

Part One
The Emergency Shipyards

1

HENRY KAISER AND THE LIBERTY SHIP

Henry Kaiser came to public prominence as a leading light in the consortium building the giant hydro-electric dams that were the cornerstone of Roosevelt's New Deal to revive the US economy and alleviate unemployment during the Depression. These projects made the Pacific Northwest familiar territory to him, but with the dam-building era coming to an end in 1938, and the clouds of war gathering over Europe, Henry Kaiser had become a leader in the national debate around isolationism. The papers dubbed him the 'patriot in pinstripes'. By the autumn of 1940 the country was already aware of preliminary activity by the federal government in case the nation should suddenly be pulled into the war in Europe.

Exactly how Henry Kaiser could serve the country in this new political era was not clear, but there was no question that he would find a way to utilize his considerable talents and resources. His only connection with shipbuilding was as a junior partner with the Todd Shipbuilding's president John D Reilly in the revival of the Seattle-Tacoma Shipbuilding Corporation to construct five standard C1B cargo ships early in 1940. Kaiser's men had years of experience building in concrete, so had laid the foundations for the new facility. Reilly had already recognized that this yard would need further expansion to serve the US Navy's need for new fighting ships. This was Kaiser's introduction to the US Maritime Commission.

This independent government agency had been created by President Roosevelt in 1936 to direct the renaissance of America's merchant shipping industry. The Commission adopted a long-range building program of 50 new ships a year for the next 10 years. America's moribund shipyards slowly came back to life and modernization and expansion began to produce more naval and merchant ships in case of war in the Atlantic or Pacific. In 1940 the question of how and when to replace the merchant fleet became an issue in the intense debate all over the national government about the role the USA should play in the war in Europe.

Previous pages: OSC in September 1943, when a record 24 Liberties were launched and delivered. Spurred on by the slogan '22 depends on you', workers beat the month's goal by two ships. Note that the pre-assembly areas all contain different parts of the ship. In the central area stern frame castings are being finished under the roof, and three more stand ready for installation in front of a stern section. (See Chapter 3)

Todd Shipbuilding's president John D Reilly was planning to enlarge the existing Todd yard in the northeast of the country in Portland, Maine. This led Kaiser to suggest to his dam-building partners in the Six Companies group that they consider entering the shipbuilding business. There was still a lot of vacant land on the northeast side of San Francisco Bay where they could use their experience to drain and grade the shoreline and hire some experienced marine superintendents. Neither of these proposals was based on any firm orders, but they relied on the likelihood of hostilities increasing and driving a government demand for more ships than the existing yards could handle. It was what we might call a 'trickle down economic theory'. The answer came sooner than they expected when the British Merchant Shipbuilding Mission arrived in Washington DC in September 1940. This consisted of half a dozen highly experienced ship-builders whose task was to obtain cargo ships, by any means possible. They were authorized to order 60 of them and had their own design for a standard tramp ship, based on the SS *Dorington Court* – recently launched by J L Thompson & Sons Ltd, of North Sands, Sunderland in north-east England. This was a traditional type of coal-burning steam ship that that had been in world-wide use since the end of the nineteenth century, and was the type of vessel that had carried US aid to the Allies in World War I, making it decidedly outdated by 1940. However, it could carry about 10,000 tons of cargo, significantly more than the older hulls, at a modest speed of 11 knots.

It was not the design that was the problem but the fact that every established yard in the USA was now working full-time on navy ships following the Naval Expansion Acts passed by Congress, and cargo ships under the1938 Long Range Program, and was booked far into the future. Since failure was not an option for the British mission, they persisted, showing their plans of the prototype to maritime organizations and shipyard owners. When Admiral Land of the Maritime Commission realized they were likely to return to Britain empty-handed, he mentioned that their last chance might be the Todd yard, which was expanding with the help of Henry Kaiser and his dam-building associates.

It is highly unlikely that Land thought this lead would prove productive, but Kaiser had kept his office near the capitol and spent most of his time on the east coast lobbying for more aid to the UK. The British team were convinced by the response from Reilly and Kaiser that they could build 30 ships each in their proposed yards in Maine and California. The need to create the yards from bare ground was a minor issue; the main point was the modification of the British design to suit the mass-production methods they intended to use. Kaiser's lack of shipbuilding credentials was only of minimal concern: Kaiser and his partners were recommended by FDR and had a proven track-record of taking on challenges that others thought too difficult, then succeeding beyond anyone's wildest expectations.

It could be argued that the British really had no choice, given their desperate situation, but the proof that Kaiser and his partners could get the job done was to be seen in the three mighty dams – Boulder, Bonneville, and Grand Coulee – the Six Companies had completed over the last decade. The fact that Kaiser insisted he was going to weld these ships not rivet them and pre-fabricate much of the structure represented a second huge gamble. In Britain, this approach previously had only been considered for small wooden craft like the 112ft Fairmile B motor launch, which mass-produced all the structural parts in well-equipped workshops, then delivered them to small boatyards for assembly.

But as the president had stated, 'business as usual' was not going to get the job done. This new welded version was given the name 'Ocean' class, while the Canadian government was persuaded to commit to delivering another 30 riveted ships that would be called the 'Fort' class. One of the engineering features of the original design that had been carefully considered was the traditional 2500hp triple-expansion coal-fired steam engine, which it was hoped could be quickly cast, machined and assembled in large numbers by one or more large American foundries. This came under the authority of the Maritime Commission, which had no objections in terms of allocation of materials or labour, since it did not involve the companies supplying the modern steam turbines and diesels for the US Navy.

Note that none of these players had any awareness that the very basic hull and engine of the Ocean class would within a year have evolved into the Liberty – the cargo ship often judged one of the biggest keys to the Allied victory. It was this casual introduction that would lead to the establishment of the two Kaiser shipbuilding centres on the west coast that many historians believe turned the tide of the war in the allies' favour. Note that Portland, Oregon was not mentioned during these discussions.

While a few cities with established yards were already participating in the new wave of mercantile and naval shipbuilding, the prospect of the winds of war in distant Europe causing a tidal wave of industry to surge up the Willamette River to Portland, Oregon must have seemed highly improbable. With a population of 300,000, it was the biggest city between San Francisco Bay and Puget Sound, but had always taken a back seat, politically and economically, to the big ports of Seattle-Tacoma to the north and California to the south.

Above: Henry Kaiser, an entrepreneur of vision, who grasped the opportunity the war in Europe provided.

Oregon's economy depended heavily on the timber industry, which had earned Portland the nickname of 'Stumptown' in the Depression. It had been in an economic slump for a decade, which was not helped by its reputation for racism and corruption. The city's leaders could not possibly have imagined that the area was about to be transformed into a shipbuilding powerhouse. Remarkably, it met all of the Maritime Commission's important geographic, economic and military criteria for an additional shipbuilding centre on the west coast. In outline, these were:

Security: in the event of war with Germany and/or Japan, the mouth of the Columbia River was guarded by three forts with long-range guns and a minefield, and the city was 100 miles from the sea to deter attack by carrier-borne aircraft.

Transportation: Portland was at the crossroads of north–south and east–west rail and road links, and it was only 40 miles downstream from the Bonneville Dam, which began generating huge amounts of electricity in 1938.

Economy: the area was *not* a centre of wartime industry, although it had an industrial base with small shipyards, iron works and logging equipment suppliers; so it already had a nucleus of skilled and manual workers who were looking for work and could provide the early workforce for a new Kaiser shipyard.

Below: Before the Liberty came the Ocean class, 60 cargo ships built to British order and Henry Kaiser's first involvement with shipbuilding. Half of these were built in Portland – but Maine not Oregon. This is *Ocean Traveller* ready to be undocked.

Property: There was plenty of vacant shoreline suitable for shipbuilding on the Willamette and Columbia Rivers that was close to residential areas where workers might find housing.

EDGAR KAISER'S VISIT GIVES PORTLANDERS HOPE FOR WAR WORK

There is no record of where or when Rear Admiral Emory S Land mentioned to Henry Kaiser that he should take a look at Portland in case FDR kept insisting on the need for more ships. The first news about the Kaiser Corporation's interest in Portland was published in *The Oregonian* newspaper by Lawrence Barber, the marine editor, after rumours he overheard in October 1940. The following are his first references to the subject:

1 November 1940. His first column on the topic was based on rumours about emergency shipbuilding coming to town when four members of the British Shipbuilding Mission visited the city.

20 November. Barber returned to the subject, writing 'A leading San Francisco builder and financier was connected with the British plan that involved an order for 120 ships for Britain and the US to a standardized specification.'

29 November. The number of ships had been cut to 60 with Portland thinking it had a good chance of getting 30 of them.

3 December. 'Edgar Kaiser, Henry Kaiser's son and right-hand man, was revealed to be in Portland discussing plans with city council, unions, banks etc.'

19 December. 'John D Reilly, president of Todd, announced that contracts totalling $100 million had been signed for the construction of 60 Ocean class ships to be constructed in the two new shipyards that he and the Six Companies would build over the winter.'

20 December. Their bubble was burst when Portland city leaders learned the British order would be split between two yards that existed only on the drawing board: one in Richmond, California and the other in Portland, Maine. The latter added insult to injury by being the original town that gave its name to Portland, Oregon in 1845 when two pioneers tossed a coin to decide between the names 'Portland' and 'Boston'.

But the Depression was finally over for the people of Richmond 600 miles to the south; they were to become an official 'emergency shipbuilding centre' and construct 30 cargo ships for the British government, which would pay Kaiser about $2 million per ship, plus a contribution of $7 million to the cost of the yard. In Portland (Oregon) this news was received with dismay, and the disappointed population endured another austere Christmas.

THE DESIGN DEBATE: THE ALL-AMERICAN C2 OR THE BRITISH-AMERICAN OCEAN/LIBERTY

There was no doubt in California that Kaiser's team would soon get steam up at the Richmond operation, just as they had at the dams. But the same could not be said of the Maritime Commission, where confusion reigned at the end of 1940 over the most crucial maritime design decision of the war era: what type of cargo ship were these emergency yards going to build for the USA?

This may sound absurd in retrospect, but the evidence is undeniable that there was an ugly amount of infighting on the commission. It ranged from a polite lack of agreement to a bare-knuckle contest among the civil servants and navy brass about the design of the new emergency cargo ship. This threatened to derail the president's attempts to aid Britain without becoming a combatant against Germany, and reflected the political infighting in the Congress and the population at large over the part the USA should play in the war in Europe.

This tense situation had surfaced because all the senior officers had begun their careers around the time of the First World War – when FDR was the Assistant Secretary of the US Navy. The government had initiated a huge emergency shipbuilding program in 1917–18 to produce around 3000 ships to supply the American troops that had been sent to Europe to ensure an Allied victory in the Great War. The planners assumed that the war would last for several years; when it ended on 11 November 1918, only 470 ships had been delivered, most of them too late to be of any use.

The US Shipping Board elected to continue the program to strengthen American merchant shipping in the post-war world – a disastrous decision that led to a very predictable outcome. When the construction finally ended in 1922, over 2300 ships had been completed, including about 400 wooden vessels, most of which saw no service and were eventually burned to extract their metal fastenings. This still left the US merchant fleet among the largest in the world. After a short-lived economic boom, the Great Depression struck and hundreds of the surplus ships were laid up and fell into disrepair.

American shipbuilders only launched a handful of general cargo ships in the next two decades as the glut of neglected vessels cast a shadow over the American shipping industry. Most of the 20-year-old ships with steam-powered piston engines were obsolete and many were barely fit for sea. The exception were ships like the 448ft x 58ft Hog Island* class, which consisted of 123 ships with modern turbine-power that were all delivered after the armistice. They showed their worth in 1940, when they joined the first convoys to supply the UK.

However, memories of the overall shipbuilding debacle continued to haunt the Maritime Commission, and public records reveal that the Maritime Commission seemed more interested in how the chosen ship would perform *after* the war rather than *during* the war. In his defence, Vice-Admiral Land was well aware that if or when Germany was defeated for a second time, there would probably be another wave of surplus

* The USMC had pioneered mass production of ships at the Hog Island shipyard in Philadelphia, PA with 50 slipways. It launched 122 ships to the standard Hog Island design that measured 380ft long, with a 54ft beam and 24ft draft, powered by twin 2500 hp steam turbines for an impressive top speed of 15 knots with 7800 tons of cargo. Ironically, the Hog Islanders were routinely called ugly because they had a straight sheer (deck line) and bow and stern were almost identical under the dazzle camouflage. (It was hoped this might confuse U-boats trying to aim their torpedoes.)

Many also served in World War II and 58 were sunk. Another of the early designs was the *Mundelta* class – length 385ft, speed 10.5 knots, capacity 5000 tons. Five were built, two were sunk in World War II, and two continued working until 1960. Naval architects considered these to be the best ships that came out of the American shipbuilding boom of 1917 to 1920.

Left: The Kaiser companies' expertise in earthmoving and large-scale construction was developed in the dam-building projects of the 1930s. It was put to good use in the preparation of the emergency shipyards. This view shows the pile-driving for the foundations of the second Kaiser yard, across the Colombia river from Portland in Vancouver, Washington.

ships to manage. He naturally favoured the three standard cargo designs, the C1, C2 and C3, that the commission had developed in the late 1930s under his supervision and in consultation with the major shipyards.

By December 1939 five of the smaller 418ft C1B design were under construction at the Seattle-Tacoma Shipbuilding yard. Land's choice for FDR's proposed emergency shipbuilding program was the standard C2 cargo ship: 460ft long with a beam of 63ft, powered by a modern steam turbine that gave it an operating speed of 15.5 knots and top speed closer to 20 knots. Now he was suddenly faced with an alternative: the Ocean class that the British delegation wanted to build in the USA.

Much has been written about this design by writers with no seagoing experience and no interest in naval architecture. They revel in repeating the 'Ugly Duckling' label that was attached to the ship right at the start in January 1941. Senators and admirals used it routinely to denigrate the proposal and try to embarrass the president. This putdown continued through the summer, until the first Liberty Fleet Day in September, when the name Liberty began to replace it. Note that the Ocean design itself was never called 'ugly', as that would have offended the British, who already had enough to worry about what with Hitler bombing London every night. Neither was there any explanation of the features that made it ugly, but Larry Barber himself was still using it 40 years later. This may be an early example of 'fake news' picked up by the media.

In fact, the Ocean and the Liberty were simply 'low-budget vessels with a high-volume hull designed for speedy construction'. That's not a criticism – it perfectly describes all the 10,000 cargo ships plying the oceans today. Some seamen find the Liberty more modern-looking and more functional than the C2, with its low freeboard and tall stack giving it a turn-of-the-century look, when designers were still influenced by the low profile of the last sailing ships.

As for the much-maligned traditional triple-expansion steam engine that propelled the 60 Oceans and the 2700 Liberties, yes it had reached its maximum efficiency in the late 1800s, but so had the steam locomotive. That did not bother the American railway companies, who relied on steam locomotives for long-distance haulage during the war. The Ocean class could have had a bigger steam engine from the General Machine Corp of Ohio. It could even have had twin engines, but there simply was no time to even consider these alternatives.

The British group understood that 'desperate times call for desperate measures' and a U-boat was just as capable of torpedoing a ship steaming at 11 knots as one motoring with a diesel engine at 14 knots. British and US officials understood that the ships would be considered a success even if they only made a single, completed voyage with vital cargo to the UK. The more complex and efficient steam-turbine and the new marine diesels were all reserved for new warships for the Royal Navy and the US Navy, so there was no alternative.

A durable steam engine could be quickly manufactured by many American foundries without any extra training –as happened in Portland (see chapter on the 'obsolete' engine below). It was reliable, forgiving, and simple to maintain, if somewhat labour-intensive. The proof of this is that there were very few instances of Liberties losing power in mid-ocean. Nonetheless, it appears that Land was not yet ready to accept defeat.

To use a nautical metaphor, he could have felt his superior American C2 design was in a sea battle with an inferior design

Left: This aerial photo of OSC shows the full extent of the 'Liberty Factory' shipyard as it was to become, from the eleven ways on the lower left to the vast parking lot at right of centre, with six ships in the water and fitting out.

Left: OSC's elegant Administration building. It was destroyed by fire on the morning of 7 November 1944 requiring a temporary re-location of the yard's 19 administrative offices. It was rebuilt in just ten weeks.

from Britain. and was being 'out-manoeuvred' on his watch without firing a single shot. He ordered the USMC Technical Division to undertake an immediate search of their archives to see if a design for the Emergency Fleet Corporation in World War I might be suitable. But into the winter of 1940, the tide was slowly turning against the C2 and in favour of an American version of the Ocean class as the wartime workhorse.

Despite the urgency of the situation, Land continued to delay the final decision until the end of the year. Gus Bourneuf Jr's excellent technical review *Workhorse of the Fleet* written for the American Bureau of Shipping, noted that Admiral Land's autobiography, published in 1955, hardly mentioned the building of the Liberty ships, and had no entry under 'Liberty' in the index. The British delegates remained undeterred by the criticism of their design and hired Gibbs & Cox Inc of New York as consulting naval architects.

The scope of their work covered every detail of the Ocean class hull because their original 80-sheet set of blueprints was practically unusable by American engineers and craftsmen. They were drawn in first-hand projection, whereas American engineers had always used third-hand projection. A second issue was that they were drawn specifically for riveting, which required an overlap on every part, while the Todd-Kaiser partners were going to weld the ships and attempt to pre-fabricate many parts. The plans also lacked many important details, measurements, and clearances, relying on traditionally-apprenticed and trained British craftsmen to interpret these points.

By the start of 1941 the land for the two new yards in Maine and California was already being levelled and filled in anticipation of the first blueprints for the 'Anglo-American' Ocean class being ready for use. There was no mention of Portland, Oregon even at this relatively late date. Land was seemingly unaware that, like it or not, this ongoing planning for the British order had given that design a flying start in this two-horse race with the C2, and was becoming the only practical option for the emergency program. The final decision to go with the British design – with numerous modifications – was only accepted by Land with great reluctance, and signed off on the last day of January 1941. Congressional approval of Public Law No 5, which covered the appropriation of the necessary funds, was passed on 6 February. An architect's agreement was drafted and signed the next day at the naval architects, Gibbs & Cox

PRE-FABRICATION – THE REVOLUTION IN SHIP CONSTRUCTION

During World War II, Gibbs & Cox was a leader in the shaping of the US maritime forces both naval and commercial, and was responsible for the plans of two thirds of all the ships being built for the war effort. At the peak, they had 2000 draftsmen sprawled over thirteen floors of a building in Manhattan. Over 5400 ships were built to their designs; the Liberties were just a small part of their output that included destroyers, destroyer escorts, light cruisers, landing ships and amphibious assault vessels, minesweepers, icebreakers, tankers and tenders.

After extensive consultations with industry leaders, Gibbs & Cox had been given a long list of changes by the Maritime Commission to suit American shipyard practice, which was different in almost every way from Britain. These began with two major decisions: to build the ships in sections away from the slipway using mass-production methods as much as possible;

and to replace time-consuming riveting with arc-welding at almost every joint. The most visible change was the move to a single, midship house to accommodate the crew, which placed the house closer to the engine room.

The construction method would be nothing short of revolutionary. Until 1940 most ships were built, one at a time, in a single yard, with many of the technical details left to the experience of the men on the shop floor. This mass production of ocean-going ships required a huge shift in conventional thinking, a technical leap that history shows was most likely to happen during a war. Gibbs & Cox formed a second team for the Liberty working in parallel with the conversion of the Ocean plans and continuing the re-design to fully implement the goal of pre-fabrication of the emergency ship.

Another major change was below the waterline where some of the curvature of the hull in the bow, stern and bilge was eliminated to cut down the amount of rolling and furnacing needed to shape plates. This also had the advantage of providing more hold space. Riveting was retained in some yards for attaching the frames to the skin. Below decks there were numerous substitutions in mechanical systems like switching from coal to oil as the fuel, replacing three Scotch coal boilers with a pair of water-tube boilers, and specifying all fasteners with American threads.

A factor that is harder to visualize was the need to supply precise measurements for every part. This was absolutely necessary for inexperienced Americans who may never have worked with steel before – there was to be no guess-work on the shop floor. American engineers had evolved their own language, technical symbols and abbreviations since the industrial revolution. This included the type of threads, measurements of tubes and pipes etc. The result was the original plan set of 80 sheets was expanded to over 500 to ensure that there was no question about the finished product and how it could be efficiently fabricated. These plans also covered all the equipment and accessories that would be produced away from the yards and many of the thousands of fastenings that would be needed.

Beyond the design work supporting the war effort, Gibbs & Cox was responsible for the central procurement of all materials and equipment. At its peak, the firm issued 10,000 blueprints a day, representing 26 acres of blueprints per month, and 6700 purchase orders representing contracts for about $1 million worth of materials per day. They centralized material and equip-

Left: Henry and Beth Kaiser pose in front of a model of the new Liberty ship while their son Edgar points to the rigging. The fourth person is a Maritime Commission inspector.

ment procurement, and design-for-production features that became the foundation of modern shipbuilding techniques.

Standardization enabled centralization of the procurement process at Gibbs & Cox and made it possible to track every order between hundreds of small factories and any of the eighteen emergency yards. This was achieved by phone calls or letters, the only forms of communication available. The use of fully-interchangeable components came directly from the automobile industry and made it possible for a yard to order or fabricate all the parts for a given ship in advance. It also allowed all the suppliers of tens of thousands of separate parts needed – from the 2500 hp steam engine down to the door handles – to be produced in factories all over the USA and sent to any of the Liberty yards, because every ship was identical.

Getting all the shipyards on the same page would create efficiencies, speed and economies across the board. It would make it possible to get identical parts and components from a broader array of manufacturers, who in turn could make fewer products to supply more customers. The oil-fired water-tube boiler was based on a tested Babcock & Wilcox product. On the west coast, the Western Pipe & Steel Co, of Los Angeles and the Puget Sound Machinery Depot, Seattle undertook to make the boilers. It also enabled the Liberty ships to be repaired in remote locations with spare parts from the other ships in port, or taken off ships that were beyond repair after enemy attacks, a practice often referred to as 'cannibalization'.

The hull lines from which every other drawing derived had to be faired full-size by hand on the floor of the mould loft of the Newport News Shipbuilding & Dry Dock Company. By the time the Gibbs & Cox team had re-drawn the plans to their satisfaction in June 1941, the first keels had already been laid in fourteen shipyards and the plan set had grown to 550 sheets. However, there is no mention in Barber's accounts of any delay waiting for the modified plans to arrive.

Classification was by the American Bureau of Shipping – the US equivalent of Lloyds Register – who would have representatives in every yard. ABS discovered that the scantlings tables the British used were oversize compared to American rules, so the design was classed at 10,865 deadweight tons of dry cargo, an increase in capacity of 430 tons. One change they recommended was the reduction of the number of different plate thicknesses, which simplified the purchase and shipping of steel from the mills to the shipyards.

Below: A Liberty ship at full speed off the mouth of the Columbia on a windy day.

2

PORTLAND BECOMES 'THE LIBERTY SHIP CAPITAL OF THE WORLD'

'But all our present efforts are not enough. We must have more ships, more guns, more planes – more of everything. We must be the great arsenal of democracy.'

US President Franklin D Roosevelt
in a radio address on 29 December 1940.

On the first day of 1941, a few American ports were already participating in the stepped-up shipbuilding program, but Portlanders could only watch and wait. Four days after the holiday, families gathered around their radios to listen to an important speech from the White House that would come to affect their hometown in ways that would involve every one of them.

On 29 December President Roosevelt, recently re-elected to an unprecedented third term in office, broadcast his famous appeal to the American people to dedicate all their efforts to national defence. He waded even deeper against the isolationist tide and strongly cautioned against America becoming 'a lone island in a world dominated by the philosophy of force'. For almost 37 minutes, he spoke about the need for the nation to support Britain in the conflict with Germany, while in Asia, Japan had swallowed up large parts of China. ... 'We must have more ships, more guns, more planes – more of everything. We must be the great arsenal of democracy.'

'If Great Britain goes down,' he warned, 'the Axis powers will control the continents of Europe, Asia, Africa, Australia and the high seas. ... It is no exaggeration to say that all of us, in all the Americas, would be living at the point of a gun.' The president vowed that America would 'extend to the opponents of force the material resources of this nation' with the policy that would become known as Lend-Lease, even though America was still technically neutral in the European conflict. In response, Charles Lindbergh testified before the US Congress and recommended that the United States negotiate a neutrality pact with Adolf Hitler.

Author's note: In the summer of 1943, Larry Barber took the time to type out a short history of the first three years of the Kaiser Corporation in Portland. It ran to twelve pages, but appeared to have sat untouched for 75 years in one of his folders with faded newspaper clipping of his reports. They form a unique first-hand record and are the basis for this chapter. The quotations are his words, the remainder is my attempt to add some background.

30 December. FDR's speech was reported on the front page of The Oregonian as the first Kaiser yard on the west coast was emerging from the mudflats in Richmond, on the east side of San Francisco Bay. Barber and his readers must have been wondering what part Portland would play in this national effort in the new year.

1 January 1941. The headline in *The Oregonian* announced: 'FDR announces plans for 200 vessels ... Portland takes new hope.' The President and the Defense Department had decided that the threat posed by Germany and Japan was now so great that the United States needed to double its shipbuilding facilities to produce 200 cargo ships within a year. The new facilities would follow the 'Government-Owned, Contractor-Operated' (GOCO) model used during World War I. Apparently, the young Kaiser shipbuilding organization had been informed it had the go-ahead to start preparations to open a second operation in Portland.

11 January. The night edition of the paper proclaimed: 'Maritime Commission announces plans for three shipyards, Portland, LA, Houston ... Portland awarded 31 ships costing $57,000,000, just north of Terminal No. 4 on 98 acres with 1800 feet waterfront acquired by lease and purchase. Plant to cost $4,700,000 with eight slipways. RR spur tracks, whirley cranes from Coulee Dam.'

12 January. More details were made public: 'It will have eight 740ft ship ways and plans are being made for the launching of four ships from each way, or 31 ships in all, with prospects for additional ships being ordered later.'

13 January. 'Grading started right on heels of surveyors who staked out location of buildings etc. Drilling of test holes started.'

Larry was in a unique position in 1941 to be an eye-witness to the revolution in shipbuilding that took place in the St Johns district on the northwest edge of Portland. It had a few industrial businesses on the waterfront but the biggest employer was the Portland Woolen Mills, the largest wool processor west of the Mississippi River, with several hundred workers. The landmark of St Johns was – and still is – the elegant St Johns Bridge, the longest suspension bridge west of the Mississippi River when it opened in 1931.

Like the bridge, the new shipyard would be the first of its kind, designed to eliminate the hold-ups and flaws of the traditional system and build ships faster and more efficiently than ever before. By mid-January, the work to prepare the site was proceeding around the clock under illumination from tall light towers, a system Kaiser had perfected at the dams. St Johns was beginning the transformation into an industrial centre that would launch over 460 large ships in five years.

THE 'LIBERTY FACTORY' GROWS BESIDE THE WILLAMETTE RIVER

14 February 1941. 'OSC announces purchase of 87 acres, enlarging site to 165 acres. Permits construction of 2200ft outfitting slip, just north of NW Oil Co plant … to be moved bodily to new location.

Kuckenburg Construction Co will move 190,000 yards of earth from eight slipways … and 200,000 yards from outfitting slip. Dock commission prepares to fill site to 26ft above sea level using port dredge *Clackamas* and 30ft pipeline.'

March. In Portland, the planning and organizing continued unabated as the site-preparation teams continued working around the clock.

13 March. 'Construction of Administration building and mold loft under way.'

18 March. 'Mr. A Mechlin here as res plant engr USMC (resident plant engineer US Maritime Commission). Worries about labor and housing shortage, and highway bottlenecks.'

27 March. 'OSC purchases 11 acres from Miller estate, and announce plans for three more ways … talk of further enlargement to 16 ways.'

FDR declares 'unlimited national emergency' and orders 112 additional emergency ships, more ways and second Richmond yard.

4 April. 'Great future enlargement of shipbuilding program seen in Washington. 36,000 (wooden) piles supplied for ways, crane ways and foundations at OSC. Piles floated in rafts from many Willamette and Columbia River plants. Nine pile-driving rigs put down 750 a day.'

18 April. 'USMC formally announces 12 more ship orders for OSC. The 43 to be built here are part of 312 *"Ugly Ducklings"* [*sic*] ordered from seven shipyards. They will be 416ft long, 57ft beam, 37ft depth of hull, 6800 gross tons. Engines 2500 hp steam.'

In just three months, Kaiser's expert road-building teams had levelled 183 acres of muddy ground in North Portland, and his dam-builders had poured foundations for the slipways, fabrication and administration buildings. By May they had transformed the wasteland into a modern shipyard with one slip ready for the keel of the first ship. However, Richmond had a head start and the keel for the first Kaiser ship, the British *Ocean Vanguard,* was laid on 14 April 1941. This set the scene for the rivalry that would run without a break for the next four years as these two locations with the same owner tried to prove their superiority.

1 May. *The Oregonian* carried the news that Bethlehem-Fairfield shipyard of Baltimore, Maryland had laid the first keel of the new class of emergency cargo ships. This was the biggest emergency yard, built adjacent to the company's naval shipyard at a cost of $35 million.

2 May. 'Poole & Fairfield hold contract for 10 whirley cranes.' Other contracts are for tug and barge service, stone for riprap (riverbank protection), roof trusses, pile driving etc.

Before they could really start work on the first ship, the yard needed the first slipway completed. This was formed by two walls of wooden staging, each about eighty feet tall and 500 feet long, enclosing a concrete-and-timber floor 80 feet wide that angled down to the water at the rate of one-half inch per foot, the minimum slope necessary to allow gravity to move a completed ship into the water – with a liberal application of grease!

Barber lived in North Portland, only a short drive from the site, so could stop by as often as he pleased without using up many of his precious gasoline coupons. He could make an educated guess about what the plant might mean to the city, but no one outside the Kaiser management could have dreamed that this desolate field downstream of the bridge was where records would be broken so often from the day the first keel was laid. To imagine that a company that had never constructed a single ship would expertly take Henry Ford's great industrial breakthrough – the production line – and apply it to shipbuilding would have sounded incredible for the rest of the year. Then the Kaiser workers began to re-write the book on shipbuilding.

19 May. The keel for the *Star of Oregon* was laid on 19 May 1941; followed the same day by the keel for the *Meriwether Lewis*. Oregon governor Charles Sprague, Rear Admiral

Howard Vickery of USMC and other VIPs attended the ceremony. The admiral stood on a raised platform and officially announced that from this day the 'Ugly Duckling' was to be called the 'Liberty Ship'. (The largest and most important class of cargo ships in nautical history now had a name that reflected its importance, but would anyone use it?) Then Vickery signalled for the first keel plate to be lowered into position. 'It's up to you fellows in Portland to roll ships out of here at the rate of 45 a year. I know you can do it and I do not mean start next February,' he told about 1000 workers. Edgar Kaiser responded to this challenge by saying: 'Boys, you've heard what they told us. It's our job and we're going to put this ship out and do it fast. Let's go!'

Fittingly, this occasion was held on the exact centenary of the launching of the original *Star of Oregon*, a 50ft wooden schooner built by local pioneers to carry their crops to the gold-mining boom town on San Francisco Bay. (It was traded for 350 head of cattle, and never returned to the Columbia River.) Another emergency yard in California, California Ship Corporation in Los Angeles, celebrated the keel laying for its first Liberty a week after Portland, when they began building the SS *John C Fremont*.

Above: Laying first keel plate on the first Liberty, 19 May 1941. The event was celebrated by 1000 workers, guests and Kaiser officers.

Barber noted that Vickery had stated later in the visit that he did not believe the Kaiser yards could possibly match the experienced Bethlehem-Fairfield operation in Baltimore, Maryland on the east coast. Ultimately, construction of the 30 Ocean class hulls in Richmond and the first Emergency Cargo hull in Portland (later called the Liberty) began at almost the same time and proceeded in parallel.

The US version was designated EC2-S-C1 (EC for Emergency Cargo, 2 for its length between 400–450 feet, S for steam engines, and C1 the design type). Whether they were to sail under the stars and stripes or the red ensign was still not clear. The official press release added that those that were to operate under the American flag would be known as the 'Liberty Fleet', but the class title of Liberty ship was not applied until the first ships had been put into service.

21 May. News from Washington DC: the workers heard the news of the loss of the SS *Robin Moor*, one of the many 'Hog Island' class of ships from 1919–21 that played a part in the next war. It was sunk by *U-69* in the South Atlantic en route to South Africa with a general cargo, after the passengers and crew were allowed to board lifeboats. This was a needless provocation by Germany that only reinforced the need for wartime preparation in the USA.

24 May. FDR gets bad news from London: the Royal Navy loses an iconic warship, the battlecruiser HMS *Hood*, the biggest, most powerful naval vessel in the world from 1920 to 1940, in a classic sea battle in the Denmark Strait with the *Bismarck*, Germany's single modern battleship, launched in 1940; 1400 British sailors died when a shell went through the deck and hit the magazine causing the entire ship to explode – only three men survived.

27 May. More news from London: After the most intensive search for an enemy ship in naval history, the pride of the Kriegsmarine, the mighty *Bismarck*, had been sighted in the western approaches to the Channel and hit in the stern by a single torpedo during a strike by Royal Navy Swordfish (an open cockpit biplane) from the aircraft carrier *Ark Royal*. The impact jammed the rudder and the crew could not regain steerage rendering them an easy target. The great warship was finally surrounded and sunk by an entire fleet of British ships and planes. Over 2000 German sailors lost their lives, and in Britain this was seen as just retribution for the sinking of the *Hood*.

This loss of Germany's finest, most powerful battleship confirmed to Hitler the need to move on to a new phase in the war and a complete change in strategy. He would turn his atten-

Left: Workers in the shaft alley on first Liberty

Right: Scene on deck of first Liberty shows the experimental nature of Kaiser's new production system.

Below: Lowering a complete hatch coaming into place on the first Liberty ship. This would soon become a routine operation.

tion away from capital ships and air raids and rely on his U-boat fleet to bring Britain to its knees. (The U-boats sunk 125 merchant ships in the month of May alone.) He also instructed his army to direct all its strength against a new enemy in the east – the USSR.

27 May. Washington DC: President Roosevelt would have been informed of this success when he woke in the White House, and prepared for a day full of important announcements and a speech broadcast to the nation. The sinking of the *Bismarck* undoubtedly influenced his speech, and was the second example of the vulnerability of even the most powerful battleships in the world to air attack.

The President announced a state of unlimited national emergency in response to Nazi aggression and reprised his famous remark from a speech 1933 during the Great Depression: 'The only thing we have to fear is fear itself.' In the evening, he gave a defiant 45-minute 'fireside chat' on the radio

Above: This wooden 'barn door' at the stern of the SS *Star of Oregon* was added to the standard drag chains as an extra device to stop the ship from reaching the far bank of the Willamette River.

to persuade isolationists that his philosophy of aid to Europe was in America's self-interest. He also announced that he had signed the Declaration of Unlimited National Emergency and raised the order for cargo ships to approximately 500 for 1942 and 700 for 1943.

Remarkably, while the Oregon Ship Corporation was hiring hundreds of new men every week, the Bonneville Power Administration (BPA) had invited folk singer Woody Guthrie to come to Portland and compose songs for a film about the benefits of the Bonneville dam and the Columbia River irrigation project. He produced 30 songs in 30 days, including 'Roll on Columbia' – a hymn to the mighty river that is still sung today. The worsening world situation caused the BPA to postpone the filming and the songs were only heard when Guthrie began performing them in working men's clubs in New York city a few months later. He eventually signed on as a messman to work in the galley and serve meals on a Liberty ship the next year.

6 June. 'Dredging completed at OSC.' The US seized 80 cargo ships in American ports that were owned by the Axis nations. FDR ordered the Pacific Fleet to move from San Diego to Pearl Harbor as a response to Japanese aggression in SE Asia.

9 June. 'Six Portland firms negotiate with Gibbs & Cox, purchasing agency of USMC, to build cargo winches, steering engines, swinging engines, anchor hoists, pumps etc for Liberty ships.'

19-20 June. 'USMC conference on standardization of steam engine production, foundry reps inspect prototype engine.'

22 June. Hitler attacks the USSR (Russia) in Operation Barbarossa, a move that would change the course of World War II and the final outcome. Lend-Lease was extended to the Soviets, and Portland became the leading western port where military, railway, and food shipments were loaded for Vladivostok.

26 June. 'OSC has four keels down against three at Calship and two at Bethlehem-Fairfield.'

6 July. 'Interest in Portland yard told [rumoured]. Todd holds 50 percent, remainder divided among 10 western construction companies. Kaiser holds 12.5 percent.'

11 July. 'FDR asks for 566 more ships and 48 more shipways, 3000 men now employed at OSC; 9500 scheduled by 1 Oct. Admiral Land congratulates Edgar Kaiser on fast work, setting the pace for the other emergency yards.'

16 July. '*Bo's'n's Whistle* makes debut with a 12-page bi-monthly publication.' This news magazine would cover all the activity at OSC – ship launches, production awards, bond drives, sports and social events.

10 August. 'Plans for four cafeteria inside yard announced. Each to seat 200 diners. Now 4800 employees and adding 100 a day. First ship grows slowly, has reached top of bulkheads and ready for first deck.'

12–14 August. The new British battleship HMS *Prince of Wales* transported Prime Minister Winston Churchill across the Atlantic for a secret meeting with President Franklin D Roosevelt in Newfoundland. After a three-day conference, the Atlantic Charter was signed, outlining US and UK democratic aims for the post-war world, including the British Empire.

16 August. The first American-built Ocean class vessel ordered by the UK, *Ocean Vanguard,* was launched in Richmond, about two months earlier than scheduled. The work on the Ocean design contract for the UK proceeded so well on both coasts that five Ocean class ships were launched on one day at Todd's yard in Portland, Maine. The last nine Ocean ships were all launched one week apart in the summer of 1942. With the last ships all in the water and ready for fitting out, the ways were now empty – but not for long. Henry Kaiser took this opportunity to buy out Todd and his Six Company partners. He renamed the California yard after his Permanente cement factory as the 'Permanente Metals Corporation'.

23 August. These launches were all completed ahead of the first British-built Ocean class ship, SS *Empire Liberty,* launched in Britain on this day by the Thompson yard in Sunderland.

11 September. 'Another report that eight more ways to be

Below: An aerial view of the launch of Portland's first Liberty ship, the *Star of Oregon* on 27 September 1941. Eight of the eleven ways were already occupied by this time. Note the huge parking lot in the background.

The launch celebration for the first OSC Liberty, SS *Star of Oregon*, on 27 September 1941 included this floor laid specially for the event. The crowd was estimated at 25,000 people; time to completion was 226 days.

STAR OF OREGON
ASSEMBLY OFFICE
ERECTION OFFICE

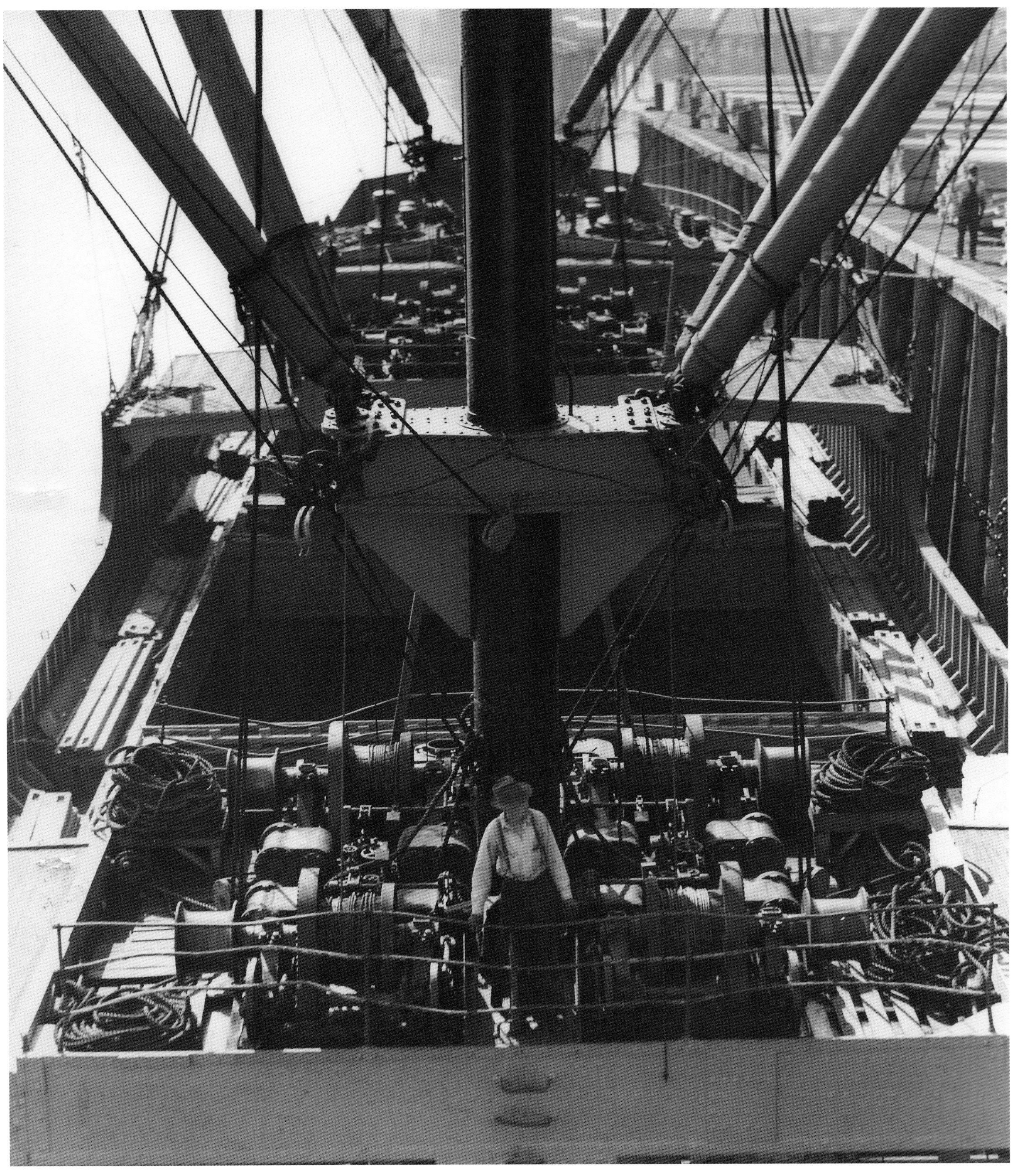

Above: Each of the three masts on the Liberty ship was surrounded by steam winches that operated the cargo booms.

added to OSC. OSC only added 3 more ways for a total of 11, all occupied.' On the east coast, Bethlehem-Fairfield was expanded to 16 ways later in the war.

By September, the US Navy had been operating the 'Neutrality Patrol' in the approaches to eastern Canada for several weeks – a secret strategy that might not have won public approval. A fleet of old destroyers escorted the Allied convoys between Iceland and Newfoundland. FDR had been actively supporting Britain for over a year, and was now attempting to maintain the policy of 'freedom of the seas' on the North Atlantic. Critics claimed this was warfare in all but name.

11 September. At an America First Committee rally in Des Moines, Iowa, Charles Lindbergh accuses 'the British, the Jewish, and the Roosevelt administration' of leading the United States toward war. He is widely condemned for this speech.

27 September. The first national 'Liberty Fleet Day,' when 14 Liberty or Ocean class ships were launched in yards all around the United States. 'They included the SS *Star of Oregon* – the first Liberty Ship launched on the west coast in front of 7000 workers and their families. It was only 45 percent complete.' The title of first in the water went to the SS *Patrick Henry*, at the Bethlehem Steel shipyard in Baltimore, Maryland, where FDR gave a speech in the morning.

Here are excerpts from that talk that was broadcast to the other yards and played later in the day.

> My fellow Americans, this is a memorable day in the history of American shipbuilding – a memorable day in the emergency defense of the nation. Today, from dawn to dark, fourteen ships are being launched – on the Atlantic, on the Pacific and on the Gulf and among them is the first Liberty ship, the *Patrick Henry*.
>
> While we are proud of what we are doing, this is certainly no time to be content. We must build more cargo ships and still more cargo ships – and we must speed the program until we achieve a launching each day, then two ships a day. The ship workers of America are doing a great job. They have made a commendable record for efficiency and speed. With every new ship, they are striking a telling blow at the menace to our nation and the liberty of the free peoples of the world.
>
> They struck fourteen such blows today. They have caught the true spirit with which all this nation must be imbued if Hitler and other aggressors of his ilk are to be prevented from crushing us. The *Patrick Henry* renews that great patriot's stirring demand: 'Give me liberty or give me death.'

Note that this was ten weeks before Pearl Harbor.

15 October. The *Ocean Vanguard* was delivered to the UK in Richmond, giving them first bragging rights in the contest with OSC.

17 October. The *Gleaves* class destroyer USS *Kearny* was attacked by a U-boat while escorting Convoy SC 48.

19 October. SS *Meriwether Lewis* launched at OSC, making it the first yard to launch a second Liberty. (Delivered in 1942 in 253 days.)

26 October. 'SS *William Clark* becomes third Liberty launched, watched by Henry Kaiser on his first visit to OSC. Carried first engine from WISCO.' Admiral Vickery was again present and challenged workers to match the pace set by Bethlehem-Fairfield. (Lewis & Clark were the two famous army officers who led the Corps of Discovery Expedition in 1802–5 to explore the US territory west of the Missouri River. They crossed the Rockies, and followed the Columbia River to the sea. Their achievement gave the young nation a stake in the distant Oregon territory, which led directly to European settlement.)

27 October. (Navy Day) President Roosevelt addressed the nation over the radio. *Ocean Vanguard* delivered in Richmond.

28 October. 'Admiral Vickery and Joseph Schmeltzer, chief of emergency shipbuilding department, visit three local shipyards with foundries able to build steam engines for the ships: Willamette Iron and Steel, Commercial Iron Works and Albina Engine. At a dinner Vickery admitted for the first time that the Kaiser Portland plant was the best organized and best managed on his tour.'

31 October. The *Clemson* class destroyer USS *Reuben James* was torpedoed and sunk by *U-552* while escorting Convoy HX 156 with a loss of 100 lives. This aging four-funnel ship was the first United States Navy vessel sunk by hostile action in World War II. Neither the Congress nor FDR considered this was ground for a declaration of war on Germany.

6 November. 'USMC allocates funds for additional buildings and facilities at OSC, including 855ft x 250'ft assembly hall, the first of its kind in the shipbuilding industry.' This was a major improvement, since Portland gets a lot of rain in winter.

16 November. 'SS *Robert Gray*, fourth Liberty ship, launched.' (Delivered in 1942 in 256 days.)

The fourth Liberty was named after the sailing ship captain who was first to enter the Columbia River in 1792. The 318 Liberty ships that followed were all named for people who had some connection with Oregon, some famous some not.

23 November. 'SS *John Barry*, fifth Liberty ship launched.' (Delivered in 1942 in 220 days.)

THE THREAT FROM THE LAND OF THE RISING SUN

So far, this brief history of OSC in 1941 has focused on Germany as the enemy, and the need to support Britain, but the USA had also been facing a growing threat from Japan. Under the leadership of Emperor Hirohito, Japanese soldiers had occupied Manchuria (1931) and part of China (1937); Japan continued its aggression by invading Korea and Taiwan. In 1940 Germany and Italy signed the Tripartite Pact with Japan in Berlin, providing mutual protection against attack by Britain or potentially the USA on Japan's new colonies in 'Greater East Asia'.

After the French surrender to Germany, the French colony of Indo China (now Vietnam, Cambodia and Laos) was left undefended and was an easy target. Japanese forces crossed the border on 15 July 1941, primarily to stop arms imports into

Below: Bottom plating for the second Liberty SS *Meriwether Lewis* was laid the same day as the *Star of Oregon* on the next way. Note the painted label denoting position of each plate.

China, which they were also invading, causing terrible casualties and war crimes like the Nanking Massacre. This prompted the United States to step up the diplomatic war on Japan by freezing its assets in the US on 26 July, followed by an embargo on oil and gasoline exports on 1 August. Next came the official closure of the Panama Canal to Japanese ships, which accelerated Japan's occupation of Southeast Asia where it could find critical raw materials like oil and rubber needed by its industries.

The Imperial Japanese Navy's strike force of six aircraft carriers was at that date the most powerful in the history of naval warfare and could launch an attack with up to 360 planes. Undefeated in Asia, the Japanese leaders had been planning an attack on the US since early in 1941. The forward base of the US Pacific Fleet at Pearl Harbor in Hawaii was to be the target. The Hawaiian Islands were first visited by Europeans in 1778 when the British ship commanded by Captain Cook arrived on his third and last voyage of exploration. The islands are 2000 miles from the US mainland and about 4000 miles from Japan, which made them a very risky long-range target in the minds of the top brass in the US Navy. Most of the ships of the US Pacific Fleet were moored in a confined area, and hundreds of the Navy's planes were parked on airfields nearby.

PEARL HARBOR ATTACKED

7 December. 'Pearl Harbor attacked.' 'SS *Thomas Jefferson*, sixth Liberty ship, launched by Mrs Beth Kaiser as sponsor. Last public launch at OSC. In future will be highly restricted. No more big crowds.'

Below: Launch of second Liberty, SS *Meriwether Lewis*, 19 October 1941, showing staging erected around ways. Time to completion was 253 days.

The Pacific Fleet was an easy target for the well-trained Japanese pilots. The air attack by 350 planes started at 8am and killed 2403 service members and wounded 1178 more, and sank or badly damaged six battleships, three destroyers and hit many other vessels. The Japanese planes also destroyed 188 US Navy and Army Air Corps aircraft on the ground. Japanese losses were light: 29 aircraft and five midget submarines lost, and 64 servicemen killed. Fortunately, all four US aircraft carriers were at sea and escaped damage, while important strategic targets like the fuel storage depots, power station, dry dock and repair shops were not harmed. The general mobilization that came with the declaration of war enabled the US Navy to rebuild and recover much more quickly than the Japanese expected.

The recovery was helped by the large amount of cement stored in silos near the harbour. The US Navy had contracted with the Permanente Cement Company in northern California to supply cement for their Hawaiian facilities. Around 400,000 barrels had been shipped in bulk in a couple of months by the cement carrier SS *Ancon*, which was moored in the harbour after unloading. 'Permanente' of course was a trademark of Henry Kaiser and the old ship he bought to transport the cement was his first venture into shipping.

8 December. 'Portlanders Resourceful After Grim News of Pearl Harbor.'

That was the headline of a front-page article in *The Oregonian* newspaper the morning after the attack detailing plans to protect against air raids and invasion. By the next day, Portland residents were coming to the 'grim realization that the mouth of the Columbia River is the closest point on the mainland to Japan.' Interceptor planes were dispersed to strategic airfields in the region and all military leave was cancelled. Guards were doubled around local military installations and airports and posted on bridges as the fear of invasion spread through the population.

The Japanese ambassador delivered the declaration of war to the US government an hour after the attack, which was followed by air attacks on US bases in the Philippines, Guam and Wake Island, and on British forces in Malaya, Singapore, and Hong Kong. At 12:30 pm Roosevelt delivered his six-minute address to a joint session of Congress and a nationwide radio audience. This is still remembered as his most famous speech: 'Yesterday, December 7th, 1941 – a date which will live in infamy – the United States of America was suddenly and deliberately attacked by naval and air forces of the Empire of Japan. The United States was at peace with that nation and, at

Right: The outfitting dock was where the Kaiser method reached its peak of activity with a bare hull being transformed into a finished ship ready for sea. The whirley cranes were originally used at the Grand Coulee Dam.

the solicitation of Japan, was still in conversation with its government and its emperor looking toward the maintenance of peace in the Pacific.' He went on to say, 'No matter how long it may take us to overcome this premeditated invasion, the American people in their righteous might will win through to absolute victory.'

10 December. Two days later, the Royal Navy was hit hard by the Japanese. The British battleship HMS *Prince of Wales*, launched January 1941, and the battlecruiser HMS *Repulse* were sunk in the South China Sea by land-based Japanese Mitsubishi twin-engine bombers. This was the first time that capital ships had been sunk solely by air power on the open ocean.

29–31 December. The momentous year in Portland ended with the trials and delivery of the first Liberty ship on the west coast. '*Star of Oregon* starts trial run, returns 30 Dec, is delivered 31 Dec – a few hours after the *Patrick Henry* Bethlehem-Fairfield's first ship. This was 7 months and 11 days after keel laying (226 days) and 3 months 3 days after launching. Assigned to States Line and 32-year old Captain E T Thomas.'

WAR IN THE PACIFIC EXPANDS

In the two weeks that followed Pearl Harbor, Japan's army and naval forces scored numerous victories over American, British, and Dutch forces in the Western Pacific. They invaded Burma, Borneo, Hong Kong, the Philippines, and took the US base at Wake Island before Christmas. In January 1942, the British withdrew into Singapore and were soon under siege. In February, Singapore surrendered. The Japanese invaded Java and Sumatra in the Dutch East Indies; this new empire was euphemistically called the 'Greater East Asia Co-Prosperity Sphere.'

Below: This launch picture was taken from a crane as the ship blew its steam whistle. Note also the busy lumber yard across the river in the NW Portland industrial area.

WAR IN THE ATLANTIC CONTINUES – OPERATION DRUMBEAT

FDR's call to 'build ships faster than the Germans could sink them' originated from the dreadful losses of shipping that happened at this time. Admiral Karl Dönitz, the capable commander of Hitler's U-boat fleet, began planning submarine attacks on the USA as soon as Germany declared war on the United States in December 1941. He called it Operation Paukenschlag ('Drumbeat'). On 13 January 1942 German U-boat attacks officially started against merchant ships along the Eastern Seaboard of North America. They were ordered to stay submerged during the day and ambush merchant ships at night.

From then until early August, Nazi U-boats dominated the waters off the east coast, sinking fuel tankers and cargo ships with impunity, often within sight of shore. The ships were easy prey as the U-boats could spot them easily at night against the lighted cars, buildings, streetlights and billboards along the coast. Merchant ships continued to operate with all their lights on, and the U-boats could even use American lighthouses for navigation. In less than seven months, U-boat attacks would sink 233 ships in the Atlantic Ocean and the Gulf of Mexico, including 129 tankers – over 20 per cent of the nation's tanker fleet – almost equal to the entire output of the Kaiser Swan Island yard in Portland.

The U-boats killed 5000 seamen and passengers, more than twice the number of people who perished at Pearl Harbor. This was over one quarter of all Allied merchant ship losses in the war. The US Navy lied to the public about the terrifying U-boat attacks and the news media agreed to government censorship, which helped to hide the military's incompetence in protecting shipping and the lives of merchant seamen. There were 19 U-boats operating on a daily basis along the coastline; the US government was under pressure, and at something of a loss, to counter the serious threat.

At the time, the US Navy was fully occupied dealing with the war in the Atlantic and Pacific and unprepared for a coastal campaign. Finally, after many of the vital fuel ships supplying the Northeast were sunk, the oil and gas industry informed the US War Department that the burgeoning war economy would grind to a halt from a lack of fuel in only nine months. After April 1942 the situation slowly started to improve, and *U-85* became the first German submarine sunk by an American vessel, the USS *Roper*. A blackout of the coast was finally ordered by the government, and the navy reluctantly began organizing a convoy system. Ships were restricted to movement only during daylight and under full convoy escort, and U-boat

Above: First Liberty ship SS *Star of Oregon* heads out on its 200-mile trial run to Astoria and back.

attacks fell to 26 on the east coast. Military air defences were also getting stronger, and on 7 July, in the first Army Air Corps success, a bomber sank *U-701* with two hits. On 19 July Dönitz withdrew the U-boats to seek easier pickings elsewhere and the Allies managed to destroy 9 U-boats by the end of 1942.

The 19 July order marked the end of Operation Drumbeat, but U-boat attacks in the western hemisphere did not end completely. The submarines moved to the Caribbean and the Gulf of Mexico, attacking fuel tankers and freighters. Operation Drumbeat was a little-known victory for Germany. Not just in battle, but on the home front. The Northeast, which got 95 percent of its oil from the Gulf of Mexico, was starved of fuel through 1943 as a result of U-boat attacks in 1942. The fuel shortages slowed wartime production and forced gasoline rationing, one of the most unpopular restrictions of the war. At the time, many US citizens were still ignoring the calls for coastal blackouts by the government.

....

3

BUILDING A BRIDGE OF SHIPS

By 1942 there were eighteen yards across the USA building 300 Liberty ships at the same time. A spirit of competition was encouraged by the Kaiser yards' management, which quickly began to lead the nation in productivity. Portland-area shipbuilders, from the giant Kaiser yards to the smaller operations, found innovative ways to cut costs and save time, improve the product and work in cooperation with myriad federal agencies. Obstacles to production, such as training inexperienced workers and housing and feeding emigrant workers and families, had to be met and overcome. In addition to delivering ships on schedule, shipyard management had to participate in negotiations with labour unions and subcontractors.

The new year brought some important news for Portland and its neighbour Vancouver. In his log, Barber began the year 1942 with this:

11 January. 'First reports of new order for Liberty ships and new yard at Vancouver.'

12 January. 'Plans reported for new yard 1 mile above Vancouver on 186-acre site.'

15 January. 'Plans for mess hall building 60 feet by 300 feet announced at OSC. Cafeterias not satisfactory.'

17 January. '65 Liberties to be built in Vancouver on eight ways. OSC contract increased by 88 ships.'

20 January. 'FDR's third inaugural address on the radio.'

22 January. 'OSC 11th ship, *Stephen A Douglas*, launched. OSC now 18,000 employees.'

7 February. FDR establishes the War Shipping Administration, also headed by Vice Admiral Emory S Land.

15 February. 'OSC raises Navy E pennant, awarded for outstanding achievement. Only one to a maritime yard. Presented to Edgar Kaiser, also Navy E pins to Ralph Stokesberry – layout man, J J Spady – steam fitter, and L B Woods – truck crane operator. They were drawn from 22,000 employees. Their wives were selected to sponsor OSC ships.'

18 February. 'Rapid rise of Howard L Vickery from commander to rear admiral cited.'

19 February. FDR ordered the arrest and incarceration of all 110,000 US residents with Japanese ancestry living on or near the west coast, including about 80,000 'second generation' immigrants who were American-born US citizens. This contrasted with the treatment of the 12 million people with German ancestry living mainly in the mid-west. About 11,000 of them were detained. (This policy of imprisoning Japanese-Americans, euphemistically called 'internment', has returned as an issue in the twenty-first century as part of the modern movement for minority rights.)

25 February. 'Announcement that Todd and Kaiser dissolve ties. Trade stock in eastern and western yards to speed up shipbuilding program. Vancouver yard now a-building.'

7 March. 'OSC delivers SS *Philip Livingston* in 232 days.'

In March 1942, the *The Bo's'n's Whistle* had more production news to relate: the 26,000 employees at OSC had completed eight more Liberty ships over the winter as they gradually improved their skills. Now the production line really began to pick up speed! The proof that something entirely unexpected was beginning to happen beside the Willamette came with the next delivery.

10 March. 'SS *Alexander Hamilton* delivered in 171 days.'

That was 55 days faster that the *Star of Oregon* and the number of days per ship continued to drop steadily. Eleven ships left the yard in April, culminating in the 21st ship, SS *Robert G Harper* in 95 days, comfortably breaking the symbolic 100-day barrier. The next ship was named after the world-famous author Edgar Allen Poe, and took another week off the 95-day mark.

FIRST WOMEN WELDERS ARRIVE

15 April. 'First women welders sign up for OSC.'

Above: The final stages of fitting out a Liberty ship showing the hatch covers and cargo-handling derricks. This is the famous *Joseph N Teal*, built in ten days in September 1942.

19 April. First merit flag awarded to OSC. First anywhere. Tom Ray, sec. Boilermakers Union pledged cooperation in turning out ships faster. Said they can do it in 60 days now 80 days.'

27 April. 'M flag presented by Captain Edward Macauley for USMC to Clyde Nelson – electrician.'

April 1942. 'Women Welders Begin Work.'

The 20,000 mostly-male workforce now witnessed another important breakthrough when the first women welders arrived to start work. Larry identified them as Mrs Jeanne W Wilde and Mrs Mary C Carroll, who lost her son during the three-month battle of Bataan on the Philippine island of Luzon early in 1942. When asked if she could stand eight hours of hard work, she replied: 'Eight hours of hard work does not require one half as much stamina as was required of our boys in the fox holes of Bataan.'

7–8 May. Japan suffers its first defeat of the war in the Battle of the Coral Sea off New Guinea. This is the first time in history that two opposing naval forces fought using only aircraft and never sighting each other. This victory ultimately leads to the US decision to build 122 small, lightweight aircraft carriers to support the big fleet carriers. Fifty of these are built at Vancouver, Washington and another fifteen from Tacoma are towed to Portland for fitting out.

22 May. 'National Maritime Day. Three ships launched, three

Left: A typical Liberty ship launch at OSC with little fanfare. Note that the entire support system for the ship – staging, ways, props, cradle and floor was constructed entirely of wood.

keels laid, three ships delivered.' Kaiser workers were now producing a Liberty ship on average in just 46 days. This was OSC's first speed-building claim, and this stunning demonstration of its capability really put the yard in the national spotlight via the Office of War Information. With 33 ships delivered, the time to completion was now down to around 50 days, which inspired other yards to show what they could do! Ten women welders complete course in private school.

1 June. One year after the first keels were laid, the time was reduced to 46 days with the 40th ship, SS *Thomas Bailey Aldrich*.

Left: The 300th Liberty at OSC, SS *Lewis L Dyche*, was launched on 26 November 1943. Total time to delivery was 33 days. By then the company had amassed so many production awards that there was not enough space on the 'M' flag for all of the stars.

4–7 June. The Battle of Midway was a turning point in the War in the Pacific. All four large fleet carriers in the Japanese task force were sunk by US air attacks. At the same time, the Japanese invaded the sparsely populated Aleutian Islands extending west from the Alaskan coast. The new war front ran a distance of 6000 miles from Alaska to the northern coast of Australia.

27 June. 'Negro woman, Mrs Walter E Harris, wife of janitor, sponsors the SS *Jason Lee*, named after pioneer Oregon Missionary.' This may have been the first black person to christen an American ship.

16 July. 'OSC awarded first gold star for pennant.'

19 July. 'Vickery presented flag with first star, accepted by Mrs Mary Carroll, first woman welder for OSC and mother of a soldier who fought on Bataan.'

5 August. 'OSC launched its 55th Liberty, the SS *William P McArthur*, in 50 days.'

8 August. 'Rep. of British Ministry of Shipping says welded ships proving tougher than riveted ships.'

The last of the contract for 30 Ocean class ships were delivered from Richmond in July 1942. They played their part in the Battle of the North Atlantic, but 16 were sunk by torpedoes in 1942–43, and two more were put out of action. That kill rate of 30 percent was far higher than its American sister ships the Liberties suffered, which was below 10 percent. Many

Below: The OSC Horse Patrol was mainly used to prevent theft in the giant parking lot where over 5000 cars were parked for each shift. But here the officers appear to be enjoying a ride along the outfitting dock.

Early in the morning on 22 May 1942 – National Maritime Day – work continues in the pre-assembly areas under cover during the rain, while three Liberties sit ready for launching.

Above: Liberty ships being eased into the OSC outfitting dock by tugs, including a sternwheeler aft.

survived near fatal blows thanks to their watertight compartments. The remaining 40 Oceans fared as well as the Liberties post-war, and one, the SS *Ocean Merchant*, served for another 45 years, ending its career on a Chinese shipping register in 1992.

10 August. 'Assembly plant now in full operation, turns out large assemblies under roof and makes possible completion of ships in 35 days after keel laying. Building is 853 feet long, 240 feet wide, 11 bays, employs 2000 workers, more to come, cost $2,500,000. (Later enlarged.)'

16 August. A record was set In Portland, Maine when six of the Ocean class ships were launched and delivered to the British government.

20 August. 'EFK [Edgar F Kaiser] returns from Wash. DC with announcement that 6000 housing units to be built at Vanport. Kaiser says this is only beginning. Cost est. $12,500,000; 18,000 residents etc.'

30 August. *The Sunday Oregonian* appeared with an eight-page supplement, 'The Northwest's Own Magazine'. The cover story was titled 'Those Liberties are TOUGH!' by Lawrence Barber. He began with this subtitle: 'They call them "Ugly Ducklings" But They're Fast and Efficient – Just Ask the Boys Who Sail 'Em.'

> Less than eight months ago the first of them went to sea. Are these ships the lemons that are suggested by the misnomer 'Ugly Ducklings' that clings so tenaciously to the type, although they obviously are not ugly and hardly simulate down-puffed ducklings?
>
> Some of these questions were put to men who know Liberty ships by actual operation of them. Deck officers who have taken them to sea, brought them safely back to American shores, and returned to Portland for new ships, say they are good ships. Marine engineers say they are good. Crewmen say they are good.

Performance records appear particularly good when it is considered that fully-loaded Liberties carry 11,000 long tons of cargo. Cruising at 11.5 knots to 12 knots, they consume from 135 to 200 barrels of fuel a day. They are far superior to those smaller types built in world war days (1917–20), burning one third less fuel per ton of cargo.

Portland-built ships have been reported torpedoed and shelled, but they resisted destruction, remained afloat, finally were towed to ports for repairs. One crew returned to Portland for a new ship while its former vessel was repaired. Members brought back torpedo and plate fragments to show their friends here.

31 August. 'OSC delivers nine ships in one month.'

3 September. 'Third star added to M flag.'

23 September. '10-day ship' *Joseph N Teal* launched. Roosevelt and party present, but this is not released for two weeks. (See Chapter 10)

21 October. Activity returned to 'normal' in October, but that did not stop the builders from completing the SS *James B Stephens* in 40 days – another milestone in shipbuilding history.

GAINING RECOGNITION: MERIT FLAGS AND PENNANTS

George Kramer made a close study of the conditions in the Kaiser yards and the ways the management encouraged quality work. Henry Kaiser had already shown that competition could increase productivity. So the US Maritime Commission developed several award programs to mark the achievements of the yards under its review. The Navy also recognized excellence in shipbuilding and industry through a series of awards programs. Oregon's shipyards, Kaisers as well as the others, all were regularly recognized for their continual production records, contract completion, and other achievements. 'The Oregonship Corporation is the first shipyard in the United States to receive the 'M' button for outstanding production. Wear it proudly!'

A month later Oregonship became the first yard in the entire United States to receive a gold star on its Merit Flag. Rear Admiral Howard Vickery, Maritime Commission Vice-Chairman, formally presented the award at the yard, stating 'This is the yard of firsts. First to deliver a Liberty Ship on the west coast, first to win the Maritime Commission award and the only Maritime yard to receive the Navy '"E for Excellence".'

Oregonship's continual record of production, virtually unmatched nationally, brought that yard in particular almost every honour and award that was available. Having received its first flag in April 1942 and then adding gold stars for the rest of the year, the yard received a new award, the Gold Eagle flag, less than a year later. 'Already so weighted down with gold stars that it can hardly wave ... the Commission has announced that Oregon is in line of a new award to be known as the Gold Eagle flag, the first of its kind to be presented to any yard.'*

The pace continued to accelerate for the next 15 months. All succeeding ships were completed in less than 40 days until the 322nd and last Liberty in February 1944.

31 October. 'Scotch (*sic*) shipbuilder George Barrie amazed at OSC speed and increased number of women workers.' (OSC launches two ships a week in October.)

11 November. 'Richmond yard builds a 7-day ship. New ship, probably *Joseph Teal*, arrives in Australia with cargo.' (OSC launches three ships a week in November.)

7 December. 'Four ships launched in Portland yards on Pearl Harbor Day. One was the 100th Liberty launched by OSC, SS *Frank B Kellog*' (OSC launches 15 ships in December.)

31 December. 'Year-end summary reveals 100,000 workers, $6,000,000 weekly payroll, Kaiser Vancouver and Swan Island yards come into production.'

Admiral Land of USMC announces 'larger, faster Liberty ships are planned,' but does not give details. Later proved to be Victory ships.

At their peak at the end of 1943 the three Kaiser shipyards in the Van-Port area employed about 100,000 workers, including many migrants from the southern states, plus women who joined the industrial workforce in increasing numbers until they constituted about 30 percent of the shipyard staff. Show-pieces and records aside, the yard retained a virtually unchallenged record as the nation's most productive shipyard month-by-month, throughout the entire World War II period, regularly building and launching Liberty ships at the rate of sixteen to twenty each a month after the middle of 1942.

Larry Barber's OSC shipyard log continued into 1943. During that year, the 'Liberty Ship Capital of the World' hit peak performance and went on to launch almost 200 Liberties, most of them in less than a month to delivery.

7 January 1943. 'USMC announces that OSC led nation in 1942 with 113 Libs, 1,219,300 deadweight tons. Calship – 109

* Shipbuilders were not the only companies that earned production awards. Every industry that supplied the military had production goals to meet, and was rewarded for beating them. Portland Woolen Mills located near Oregonship, was awarded the prestigious 'E' award by both the US Army and Navy for making wool blankets for the armed forces. The mill also produced its own monthly newsletter that covered everything from news of the war effort to departmental musings such as 'All the single girls in the spinning room have gone into mourning since George Curtis got married last month.'

ships, Bethlehem Fairfield 77, two Richmond yards 118 ships (part for Britain).'

10 January. 'Sunday mag story on Edgar Kaiser – Portland's Man of the Year.'

15 January. 'Bill Hutchinson, survivor of Jap shelling of Lib SS *Edgar Allen Poe*, tells story.'

January. 'Ferry service finally opens; patronage very light.'

16 February. 'More stars for M flag. Now 9.'

19 Feb. 'Super buses put on.'

7 March. 'Sledge [hammer] wielders set record bending frames.'

Below: The Liberty ship SS *Theodore Sedgwick* with a sternwheel tug that was a common sight on the Columbia. Built as a combination freighter and towboat, one or two of these vessels usually attended every launch, especially if the current was strong.

13 March. 'Absenteeism combatted; enough absentees from Kaiser yards in three months to build 13½ Liberties.' (Average time to completion now 30 days.)

27 March. 'Grand Duchess Charlotte, of Luxembourg, visits OSC.'

The workers at OSC were not aware that March 1943 was the month that the U-boat offensive in the North Atlantic reached its peak, with a series of major convoy battles. Allied losses for March totalled 120 cargo ships. The escorts surprised the German U-boat arm by sinking 12 U-boats.

4 April. 'Gold Eagle flag presentation. H J Kaiser talks "presenteeism" to take sting out of absenteeism.' (Average time to completion now 27 days.)

27 April. 'Child care centers announced.'

1 May. 'OSC leads rivals in per-way record; delivered 17 ships in April for average of 1.55 ships per way; Richmond 1.04.'

On the North Atlantic, the 130th convoy of the war set off

Above: A newly completed Liberty with all its guns and military equipment in place making its first voyage downriver. Armament varied, but usually included a 4-inch or 5-inch deck gun aft, up to eight 20mm Oerlikon machine guns in gun tubs and sometimes a 3-inch/50-calibre dual-purpose gun on the bow.

from eastern Canada with 37 ships. About 25 U-boats were sent to intercept them, opposed by a 'Mid-Ocean Escort Force' of ten small British warships – the largest a destroyer – two oilers and a rescue ship. They engaged the U-boats aggressively with better weapons and methods than before, sank at least three and damaged others, while long-range RAF B-24 Liberator aircraft also sank one. The convoy reached Liverpool without loss on 26 May, while over 40 U-boats out of 120 in action were sunk in that month alone. Shocked at the losses, Admiral Dönitz ordered all remaining submarines to return to their bases in NW France.

1 June. 'Absenteeism high, Kaiser testifies at NLRB [National Labor Relations Board] hearing.'

15 June. Lady Jessy Beveridge launches SS *John F Steffen*. (Building time 27 days.) William Beveridge was a senior politician in the UK on a goodwill tour of the USA. He may have sounded like a true upper-class Brit to the Americans, but he was actually the architect of the post-war welfare state and National Health Service, and a liberal progressive throughout his career.

17 June. 'Picture published of Liberty ship SS *Anne Hutchinson*, wrecked by torpedoes, failed to sink, towed to port and salvaged.'

6 July. 'Admiral Vickery here, lauds Kaiser yards as tops.'

15 July. 'Keep Oregon Green committee promotes program at launching of SS *David Douglas*, after the discoverer of Douglas fir.' (Build time 28 days.)

18 July. 'Victory ship program delayed.'

Larry Barber's notes end here without explanation. Fortunately, the Kaiser magazine-style history of the yard *Record Breakers*

Left: Successor to the Liberty ship was the more sophisticated Victory ship. This example, built by Oregonship, is ready for delivery, with the name now painted over, as was the usual wartime practice.

published in 1945 after Germany surrendered, contains a complete record of every ship launched by OSC. It states: 'In September 1943 Oregonship management set a goal of 22 Liberty ships, but it set a pace so furious that the end of the month saw 24 launched and another 24 ships delivered. Oregon Ship launched its 300th vessel on 26 November 1943 – the SS *Lewis L Dyche*.'

'On the same day, the yard was presented the Gold Wreath award, the highest maritime honor, and the "30 Day Club" Award.' Among the last dozen ships launched was the *Grant P Marsh*. (No relation to the author.) The last Liberty was the *Peter Moran*, Liberty Number 322, delivered on 4 February after just 25 days.

To put this record into perspective, in the 960 days of OSC's operation, between the laying of its first keel for the *Star of Oregon* in May 1941 and the launching of the *Peter Moran*, they launched an ocean-going vessel every other day for a period of thirty-one months. No other yard in the United States during World War II, or since, has come close to this standard production record.

4

THE LIBERTY GIVES WAY TO THE VICTORY SHIP, 1943–1945

Early in 1942 the US War Shipping Administration, the war agency created to purchase and operate the growing fleet of emergency cargo ships, began the development of a design for a second emergency cargo ship to replace the Liberty. This modern vessel would take advantage of improvements in the supply line for engines and be drawn by the office of George G Sharp, a naval architect and former chief surveyor of the ABS. With approximately the same capacity as the Liberty at 10,674 tons deadweight, the Victory was 14ft longer at 455ft and 5ft wider at 62ft. The most visible change was in the bow, which was given a sharper angle to reduce resistance.

In contrast to the Liberty's continuous sheerline, the Victory had a raised foredeck that gave more protection from big waves and a higher elevation for the 3-inch bow gun. However, it was in the engine room that Admiral Land wanted the biggest change. With the expansion of turbine manufacturing, the navy now had all the engines it needed, and with the end of the C1 building program, Land thought there was enough extra production to supply the emergency shipyards. Once again there was debate over the change, when the yards had all become experts with the Liberty hull. The alternative was to fit the turbines in the tried and tested Liberties, and make other engineering upgrades, which would only add a few days to the time to delivery.

But this time Admiral Land was determined to move ahead with a more modern ship, and finally put an end to the production of the 'ugly duckling'. After more disagreements with the War Production Board, the Joint Chiefs of Staff stepped in to swing the decision in favour of a Westinghouse double-reduction cross-compound steam turbine supplied by two Babcock and Wilcox header-type boilers operating at 525 psi and 750° F, twice the pressure of the Liberty boilers. By this time, Oregonship was generally acknowledged as the nation's top producer, so would be the senior yard in the Victory program, with the responsibility of building the first of the class.

The first 272 Victory hulls had two-stage 6000 shp turbines, with the remaining 141 having 8500 shp turbines. The high-pressure turbine spun at 5300 rpm, which was reduced by a series of pinion gears that finally turned the 125-ton, 12ft diameter bull gear that drove the 19ft diameter propeller at 100 rpm. This gave the ship a cruising speed of 15–17 knots, significantly faster than the Liberty ships' 11 knots. Another improvement in the engine room was the change from steam auxiliaries to electric-drive for winches, pumps etc, requiring bigger generators. To prevent the hull fractures that had plagued the Liberty ships, the spacing between frames was widened by 6 inches (150 mm), to 36 inches (910 mm), making the ships less stiff. This allowed the hull to flex slightly, reducing the chance of fracture. Most of the structural modifications were made to allow greater deck loads and the cargo handling gear was improved, though the basic configuration of the booms was retained. Seven sets of cargo gear were mounted over five hatches. New 'tween decks for packaged goods were added to holds Nos 1, 2 and 3.

On 28 April 1943 the new design was officially named the 'Victory' class and designated VC2-S-AP2 (V for Victory, C2 for medium capacity cargo carrier, S for steam, and AP2 for the 6000 shaft horsepower.) Victory ships were named after a variety of things, including historic cities, educational institutions, counties and allied countries. Armament for the new ships was similar to that on Liberty ships, and included one 5-inch stern gun, one 3-inch bow anti-aircraft gun and eight 20mm machine guns at various locations on main, boat and bridge decks for protection from enemy attacks. Victory ships typically carried a crew of 62 civilian merchant sailors and 28 naval personnel to operate defensive guns and communications equipment. The crew quarters were located amidships.

Overall, the design changes were kept to an absolute minimum to reduce the disruption in production. The six west coast yards that were building Liberty ships were instructed to switch to the Victory design on the conclusion of their contracts, with OSC the lead yard. As the last Liberties built in Portland were launched, the keel blocks were re-set and other adjustments made for the Victory class. However, the first keel was not laid at Oregonship (for the SS *United Victory*) until 19 November. By the end of 1943, the yard had six Victories under way.

1944

The SS *United Victory* was launched on 12 January 1944. By February, all OSC's eleven ways were occupied by Victory ships, and the *United Victory* was delivered on 28 February after

WORLD'S FIRST VICTORY SHIP
HULL No 1001
KEEL LAID...... NOV. 19 1943
SCHEDULED LAUNCHING...... JAN 23 1944
Another "FIRST" for OREGONSHIP

102 days, compared to 226 for the first Liberty. *The Oregonian* reported: 'The SS *United Victory*, first of the nation's fleet of turbine-propelled merchant ships to succeed the slower and less graceful Liberty type, graduated with high grades and praise in its final examination during its trial run from Oregon Shipbuilding corporation to Astoria and return.'

The *Bo's'un's Whistle* dated Friday, 10 March 1944 had more to say about this auspicious event.

> After surpassing all expectations on a stiff river trial and in other rigid tests, the world's first Victory ship, the SS *United Victory*, has entered the service of the United Nations. The streamlined turbine-powered vessel was completed in 102 days from keel-laying to delivery, 15 days ahead of contract schedule. The ship underwent an exhaustive 12-hour river trial Sunday 26 February, to Astoria and return. More than 200 persons made the journey, including OSC officials, representatives of the US Maritime Commission and ABS, observers for manufacturers of ship equipment, and newspaper men.
>
> The vessel's efficient performance amazed even crew members, and no major flaws were developed. Observers praised workmanship in the ship's construction. Official speed was not disclosed, but it was evident that Edgar F

Left: Keel laying for first Victory ship in the USA, immediately after launching of the Liberty ship SS *Segundo Ruiz Belvis* on 19 November 1943.

Below: A special celebration for the launch of the first Victory, *United Victory*, with all the allied flags flying.

Kaiser, General Manager of the three Portland-Vancouver yards, made no idle boast when he declared that the new ship will be able to outdistance an enemy sub.

Al Bauer, assistant general manager of Oregon Ship was elated with the results. 'You can tell the folks out in the yard for me that they did a really first-class job on Hull No 1001,' he said. 'The quality of the work would be a credit to any shipyard in the world!' Said Captain John E Murphy who took command of the ship, 'The people who built the *United Victory* have a right to be proud of her.' And Chief Engineer Robet McGloutin commented: 'The power plant performed very smoothly. She's going to be all right.'

The next six Victory ships also took over 100 days, before the vast Oregonship machine began to pick up speed again. In April, seven keels were laid, and the twenty-eighth ship, the *Escanaba Victory*, was delivered in 61 days on 29 June. As the tide had begun to turn in the war against Japan, military planners foresaw the need for ships dedicated to carrying large numbers of soldiers and able to land them on islands under Japanese occupation. The Maritime Commission was now forced to re-design the Victory ship hull into an 'Attack Transport', an armed troopship called the *Haskell* class, with the designation VC2-S-AP5

Right: Two Victory ships in the outfitting dock. Note the dual purpose 3-inch/50-calibre gun on the bow. The sharp bow angle is the most visible difference from the Liberty ship.

Below: *United Victory* towed into outfitting dock where it spent 48 days.

SHOP No. 2

Left: *Czecholovakia Victory*, second of its class, following her launch looks shipshape – except for the name – 11 March 1944

Below: The launch of the *Marshfield Victory* on 1 April 1944. Note the timber staging between the ways. The ship enjoyed a long career and in the early 1960s, during the Cold War, she was re-named USNS *Marshfield* (T-AK-282) and was one of the four Victory ships that were converted as US Navy transports for missiles, torpedoes, fuel etc for the submarines fleet.

Below: *Gonzaga Victory* on its way to the Willamette River, 29 June 1945. It took 46 days to build and was the 434th vessel and the 82nd Victory constructed at OSC. It was launched too late to see any action.

A nighttime view of a row of Victory ships nearing completion. The yard worked around the clock.

HULL No
1023
WAY-11

30 ATTACK TRANSPORTS (AP5) NEEDED QUICKLY

Having delivered 32 Victories in 135 days, the 30,000 OSC workers found they were once again switching over to another design, this new Attack Transport (AP5), based on the Victory hull. These ships were designed to move 1500 troops and their combat equipment, and land them on hostile shores using the ships' own landing craft. From mid-May to mid-October, the entire operation at Oregonship was dedicated to producing thirty of these armed troopships. OSC launched America's first AP5, the USS *LaPorte* on 30 June, only 45 days after keel laying. It was delivered on 13 August, for a total time of 90 days – an amazing achievement for the first ship of its type.

It mounted one 5-inch/38 calibre gun on the bow, twelve Bofors 40mm guns (one quad mount, four twin mounts), and ten Oerlikon 20mm guns. This new role required a completely finished interior with bunks and all the facilities for 1500 men, with the decks laid out to stow and launch landing craft to deliver the troops and equipment right onto the beach. The twelve smaller boats were the 36ft long plywood LCVP (Landing Craft Vehicle/Personnel) or 'Higgins boat' that carried 36 fighting troops. The other landing craft were steel and much bigger: the 50ft (15m) LCM(3), capable of carrying 60 troops or 30 tons of cargo, or the 56ft (17m) LCM(6) that could carry a 30-ton tank or other vehicle. LCM stood for Landing Craft Mechanised, Marks 1-8 increasing in size from 36ft to 73.7ft.

6 June (D-Day). The daily routine was interrupted by news of D-Day as the Allies landed on the beaches of Normandy, NW France under the command of US Army General Dwight D Eisenhower. The largest amphibious landing in history involved a fleet of thousands of vessels that included many types built by the emergency shipyards, from Liberties to landing craft. The ingenious Mulberry Harbour consisted of concrete blockships and old cargo ships that were scuttled to create a two-mile breakwater. This allowed the allies to land everything they needed to wage a land war via a floating roadway without having to take one of the heavily-defended French ports.

30 June. The fastest time to complete a Victory dropped to 59 days with the SS *Hibbing Victory*. Then all the ways were devoted to the AP5. As the Army's confidence in its ability to push the Japanese back grew, a total of 117 AP5s were built in 1944 and 1945 by the four fastest yards on the west coast, three of them owned by Kaiser: Oregonship, Vancouver and Richmond. The ships all remained in the Pacific theatre of operations, landing American troops and recovering casualties at Iwo Jima and Okinawa. *Haskell* class ships were among the first Allied vessels to enter Tokyo Bay and land the first occupation troops after Japan surrendered. Most of them took part in Operation Magic Carpet, the massive sealift of US personnel back to the United States where up to 1900 soldiers per ship were carried to ports on the US west coast.

The *Record Breakers* booklet depicts the building of the attack transports as the 'Champ Flag' Race between three Kaiser yards and Calship of Wilmington, CA. The 'highly coveted' champ flag appears to have been an unofficial banner about 8ft x 3ft. Of course, since three were Kaiser yards, the odds were good that Henry would win!

August. Two Attack Transports were presented to the Navy by OSC.

September. Five ships delivered, Oregonship wins the champ flag.

19 September. The president made one of his last public statements on the US Merchant Marine.

> 'It seems to me particularly appropriate that Victory Fleet Day this year should honor the men and management of the American Merchant Marine. The operators in this war have written one of its most brilliant chapters. They have delivered the goods when and where needed in every theatre of operations and across every ocean in the biggest, the most difficult and dangerous transportation job ever undertaken. As time goes on, there will be greater public understanding of our merchant fleet's record during this war.'

October. Vancouver pulled ahead by delivering nine AP5s to OSC's eight, and the pennant went across the Columbia River to Washington. Four of the ways were returned to standard Victory ship production.

November. A goal of nine ships was set, but OSC's wooden administration building burned to the ground. This only added to the workers' determination to keep pushing production, so the goal was raised to ten ships. They went one better, delivered eleven ships. and took back the flag for good. By the end of the month, all eleven ways were back to the Victory ship, with four AP5s still at the dock for fitting out.

December. Four more ships were delivered by 14 December to complete the order – the last two both in 58 days, leaving OSC as the permanent owners of the champ flag.

Barber reported from the port of Astoria when the 30th and last *Haskell*, the USS *Lavaca* was delivered on 15 December 1944.

> Upon arrival in Astoria, the crew tied up the vessel under the direction of the executive officer, Lt Com Guy Jubitz of Portland. At age 31, he is one of the youngest Lieutenant

Left: Final preparations before the launch of the *Brainerd Victory*. Note 19ft diameter propeller and rudder with twisted trailing edge to improve steering.

Left: Launch of the SS *Brainerd Victory*, last Victory for the Maritime Commission, 23 November 1945, three months after the end of the war. Mayor Frank Johnson of Brainerd, Minnesota wrote to the Oregon Shipbuilding Company: 'The naming of a ship for Brainerd is greatly appreciated by our citizens. Boys of this community who formed a tank company fought, died and were taken prisoner on Bataan and naming of the SS *Brainerd Victory* stands as a tribute to them.'

Commanders in the navy, but he has already seen three invasions and has put troops ashore at Guadalcanal, Attu (Alaska), Tarawa and Kwajalein atoll.

'This ship contains the most perfect engine room installation possible,' declared Al Abraham, superintendent for the shipyard, who was the proud 'father' of the vessel as he led a group of inspectors and surveyors through the ship on an inspection tour. It was Abraham who sparkplugged the amazing schedule at Oregon Ship. Assigned to command is Captain W S Gabel, for 20 years a banker at New Kensington, Pa, who retained his naval reserve standing after the first world war and was recalled to service in 1941. 'I am amazed at the speed with which this ship was built in 59 days,' he declared. When he arrived in Vancouver, the paint on the decks was still soft and painters were touching up some of the gear. The general superintendent of the yard read a congratulatory telegram from Edgar Kaiser, now in Washington DC, and shipyard workers celebrated the successful end of the AP5 contract.

WORK RESUMES ON STANDARD VICTORY SHIPS

Then it was back to the standard Victory design for the remarkable crew at Oregonship. By December 1944 all eleven ways were filled with standard Victories again. The time to completion for the next 16 ships ranged from 61 days all the way up to 106 days, but settled into the 70- to 86-day range for the next 25 Victories. The workers kept up their incredible work ethic until victory was declared in the Pacific on 14 August 1945, and still delivered the SS *Binghampton Victory* in 81 days on 27 August. Seven more ships were completed before the end of 1945 at a more relaxed pace.

SS *Brainerd Victory* was the last Victory ship of over 130 hulls built at OSC and the last of the 531 built overall. Predictably, OSC had turned out the greatest number of Victories, and had the distinction of building the first and the last of the class. Because they did not see action until 1944, the Victories avoided any loss from U-boats, and survived the D-Day landings. However, three were sunk by Japanese kamikaze attack in April 1945.

The Victory ships continued to play an important part in the Pacific after Japan surrendered, ferrying troops home, then using their higher speed to carry desperately needed food and supplies back to the ravaged cities and islands liberated by US forces. More Lend-Lease cargoes were delivered to Siberia to support the population and re-build the Soviet transportation system. In Europe the Marshall Plan needed a large fleet of all available cargo ships to supply Europe until societies and economies began to regain momentum.

When the war with Japan ended, the American defence industries were already winding down their production, and by the end of 1945 the 18 emergency shipyards had fallen silent after four years of non-stop motion and noise. The three Kaiser yards in the NW and the four in California passed into history. According to Barber, the final total was 322 Liberties, and 136 Victories – 34 of them finished as attack transports. The total output was therefore 458 vessels.

THE VICTORY SHIP IN PEACETIME

The Maritime Commission intended the Victory ship to continue the modernization US merchant fleet that it had begun in the pre-war years. It was designed specifically to allow for easy modification into a general cargo carrier, or for other specific tasks. About 170 Victories were sold to commercial operators – 72 in the USA, and around 100 to owners in Great Britain, the Netherlands, and Argentina. They proved to be suitable for many different cargoes and routes, and even as passenger ships.

But unfortunately for the Commission, the Victory failed to excite the international shipping companies that emerged in the post-war world. Instead, the ship owners and operators immediately recognized the value and utility of the over 2000 Liberty ships that were put up for sale. In the chaotic situation in many ports, their outmoded steam engines were far easier and cheaper to operate and maintain than the turbines of the Victories. Despite the best attempts of the Maritime Commission to weigh the scales in the Victory's favour, it was the slow but steady Liberty ships that continued to add to their wartime reputation into the 1980s.

That left the US government with over 200 surplus Victory ships. Many were put into mothballs in the National Defense Reserve Fleet, and some of them were recalled during the Korean and Vietnam conflicts. When the US began developing missiles in the Cold War, eight Victory ships were reclassified and refitted as instrumentation, telemetry, and recovery ships in 1960 for the National Aeronautics and Space Administration (NASA). They also carried cargoes to Asia during the Vietnam War before returning to the National Defense Reserve Fleet to be mothballed for the final time. All the remaining ships in the reserve were scrapped in the early 2000s.

Three Victories have been preserved as historic vessels: the SS *Red Oak Victory* is berthed in Richmond, across the bay from San Francisco, and is part of the Rosie the Riveter/World War II Home Front National Historical Park. The SS *Lane Victory* is based in San Pedro, south of Los Angeles, and is preserved by the United States Merchant Marine Veterans of World War II. The SS *American Victory*, built in 55 days by Calship, is on display in Tampa, Florida. Time has taken its toll on all the US-based museum ships, and none of them were able to leave the dock under their own power in 2020. They all require expen-

Right: Victory ship in the final stages of fitting-out and preparing to depart from OSC.

16
NO.4

Left: The construction of standard Victory ships at OSC was interrupted by an urgent order for the Attack Transport version. This is USS *Glynn* (APA-239), the last of these completed by Oregonship, in October 1945 after the end of the war.

sive repairs to their boilers and the Victory's steam turbines in order to pass stringent Coast Guard surveys for steam-powered vessels carrying passengers.

While Oregonship had closed in the fall of 1945, ending the history of one of the most productive shipyards in maritime history, there were still two unfinished Victory hulls that were available for peace-time conversion. The Kaisers were approached by the Alcoa Steamship Co (formerly the Aluminium Company of America) of New York about completing the pair as passenger and cargo carriers. Their novel plan was to combine luxury Caribbean cruises with bauxite shipping from mines in what is now Suriname and Guyana to aluminium mills in the United States.

In 1946 Kaiser re-hired some of their managers and foremen to supervise the completion of the *Alcoa Cavalier* and *Alcoa Clipper*. In 1947 they established a scheduled service between New Orleans and South America with stops at several islands. The ships were modern and provided excellent service for 96 first class passengers. But the mounting costs of US-flag operations, forced the company to abandon their passenger service in 1960. They were returned to the Maritime Commission and broken up in New Orleans in 1968.

The Kaiser archive contains another interesting piece of the company's shipping history in the late 1940s. Another Victory, the SS *Silverbow Victory*, was converted to a cement carrier by Kaiser for their Permanente Steamship Co and renamed *Permanente Silverbow* in 1947. It carried bulk cement to Hawaii until Kaiser built a cement plant on Oahu in the mid-1950s.

In 1950 the Kaiser Gypsum Company had chartered a Liberty ship from a Greek-American owner who attempted to employ a foreign crew. The Sailors' Union of the Pacific picketed the Panamanian-flagged SS *Pho Pho* at the port of Redwood City in Northern California. Henry Kaiser decided to support the union, bought the ship, and it became the first American ship to be crewed entirely by union members. Kaiser renamed the ship after the union president – the SS *Harry Lundeberg* – and became a public supporter of labour, stipulating union wages on all of his jobs.

5

KAISER VANCOUVER: 'THE SHORT ORDER YARD'

After Pearl Harbor, the national shipbuilding program took on a new urgency. In January 1942, less than a month later, the Kaiser company had already begun breaking ground for its second yard in the region, across the Columbia River from Portland in Vancouver, Washington. The site was on a 200-acre plot of farmland set between the river and the transcontinental railroad line, which followed the Columbia River from the SE corner of the state and met the main north–south line a mile to the west. The two-lane bridge that crossed the river here carried most of the north–south road traffic on the west coast. This made Vancouver an important crossroad, but it had only attracted a small part of the region's industry and was still a relatively small town with a population of only 18,000. This was a complete contrast to Portland, which had overtaken Vancouver by 1860, and never looked back.

The Columbia drained a vast area reaching all the way to the Rocky Mountains, so was subject to a large annual rise in level when the snowfields melted in the spring. On the east side of the city centre, the waterfront was completely undeveloped and regularly subject to minor flooding, so extensive ground preparation was needed to raise the shoreline for the new yard, an average of ten feet with fill. It began with floating dredges pumping two million cubic yards of sand and sediment from the bottom of the river to raise it safely above the flood level.

Within a month, there were 2000 men driving 40,000 wooden piles and laying the foundations for the ten ways and an outfitting dock half a mile long. When it was complete, they had laid a branch line from the railway station downtown connecting to sidings inside the yard with a total of twelve miles of new track. (This would soon prove to be one of the factors in its success.) There were 28 crane ways to unload the steel plate from railcars and drop it in stacks behind the plate shops.

Above: *The Bo's'n's Whistle* of 8 April 1943 celebrates the launch of Vancouver's first escort carrier, at the time known as *Alazon Bay* but later rechristened *Casablanca*. The yard's nickname, 'short order yard' is borrowed from the modern American lunch counters that served food that was quickly prepared and eaten.

A second advantage of the layout was the excavation of the so-called 'Big Tube' or tunnel, which extended for 1496ft at the head of the ways. It was seven feet in diameter and was lined with 10-gauge pipe. Oxygen, air, water, steam, and other piped supply lines were suspended on one wall, while all electric and telephone lines were positioned on the other. Transformer stations and manholes were located at six points along the length. This removed all the power poles and above-ground lines that hindered easy movement of cranes, parts, and the organization of lay-down areas. Edgar Kaiser and his family moved into a house on the heights a few miles north of the yard, which enabled him to give the yard as much of his attention as possible.

This night scene shows the full extent of Kaiser Vancouver's layout and production-line method, which ran 24 hours a day for four years.

MARINE MACHINISTS

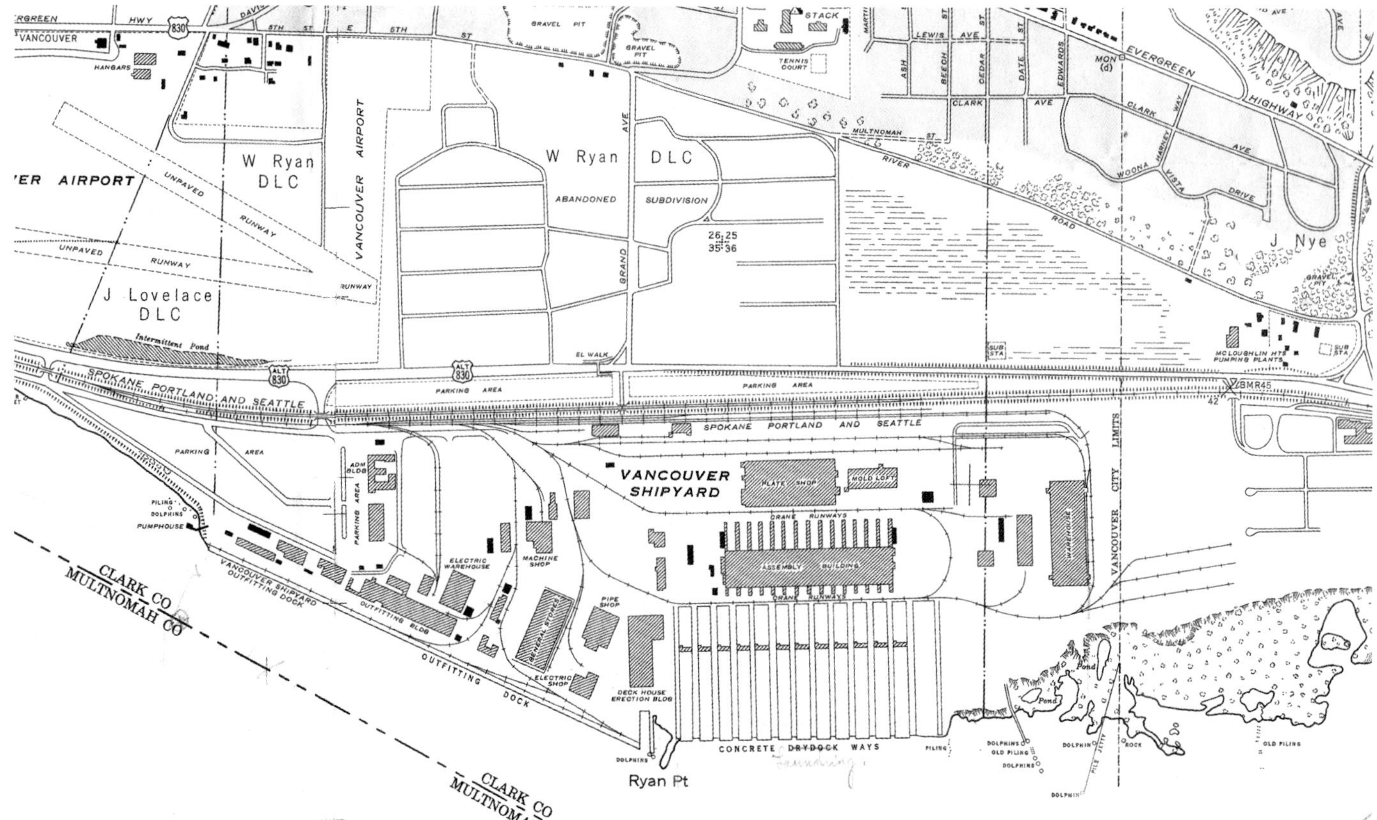

Above: Kaiser Vancouver map shows the adjacent main railway line and the highway running along the north shore of the Columbia, and the long expanse of shoreline suitable for the third Kaiser shipyard.

MORE LIBERTY SHIPS

The keel of the first vessel, the Liberty ship SS *George Vancouver,* was laid without any ceremony or fanfare on 15 March, when 'Kaiser Vancouver' was still mostly bare land. The ship was built as the yard grew around it, and benefited greatly from the experience of OSC. It was launched just 80 days later on 4 July and was delivered after 98 days. Each of the ten original ways built just one Liberty ship, and then began the first of many changes in design and type as a new contract was signed to build 30 LSTs (Landing Ship Tank) in the winter of 1942–43.

A GOOD IDEA THAT WENT ASTRAY

In Vancouver, the engineers were able to try some radical ideas to accelerate prefabrication and production that had not been possible at OSC. They were not always successful, though the failures were usually not publicized, but there was no attempt to cover up one minor but very visible disaster. During the excavation stage and filling of the waterfront, the crews had dug a cut into the shore big enough to accommodate a Liberty ship, and fitted tracks for 150-ton whirley cranes on both sides. The aim was to hoist a complete superstructure onto a Liberty or other ship in one move, instead of lifting several smaller sections on board and then welding them back together. In October 1942 the Liberty ship *Samuel Colt* was transferred from Oregonship to Vancouver for fitting out – and to test the twin crane system for the first time.

The complete 210-ton three-storey superstructure was carefully lifted off the ground at the head of the slip and the cranes rolled along their rails to the centre of the ship. As the crane operators began to lower the house, two steel cross beams spreading the cables bent under the strain, and the deckhouse dropped 20ft onto the deck. Two men were riding on the assembly: the lookout was slightly injured but the rigging foreman walked away from the wreck.

The deckhouse was then lifted from its fallen position and reseated squarely on its foundations. Then the ship was towed back to Oregonship where the bent bulkheads, etc were straightened, and the fitting out completed.

The experiment was never repeated, but this episode shows the Kaisers' willingness to take risks with new techniques.

LANDING SHIP TANK – LST

When the British prime minister Winston Churchill requested that the United States design and build a new class of ship that was large enough to traverse an ocean fully loaded with armoured vehicles and personnel, and also have the ability to unload quickly and efficiently on to an unimproved beach, he was speaking from a politically painful experience. His long career in British politics had included a short spell as First Lord of the Admiralty early in the Great War. He had always considered himself an expert in military strategy and promoted the invasion of Turkey by sea as a way to tip the scales and end the carnage of trench warfare on the western front.

The first step was to be a naval bombardment followed by a landing on the Gallipoli Peninsula and a quick attack to secure a bridgehead. The reality in 1915 proved to be a debacle, sunk either by the incompetence and hesitancy of the commanders, or by the failure of Churchill's planning to account for a determined and well-equipped Turkish army. The British and ANZAC (Australian and New Zealand Army Corps) forces lost 46,000 men, the government was thrown into crisis, and Churchill was fired and was said to have been 'haunted by this disaster for the next two decades'.

Churchill became prime minister on 10 May 1940, eight months after the outbreak of World War II. Two months later he presided over the evacuation of the British Expeditionary Force from Dunkirk, which he called 'a colossal military disaster'. That was the background to his understanding that Europe could never he regained and the war ended without the ability to land a complete army on a beach under attack from well-defended enemy positions. This thinking was directed to the European coast and the war against Germany, and in November 1941 a small delegation from the Admiralty arrived in the United States to share their ideas with the US Navy's Bureau of Ships.

Pearl Harbor was attacked less than a month later, and the Americans immediately understood that the new approach to the 'landing craft/ship' would apply equally well to the war against Japan. Within a few days, John C Niedermair of the Bureau of Ships had drawn up a slab-sided hull with a unique feature: a pair of vertically-hinged bow doors behind which was a large vertical door that could be lowered to form a sturdy ramp to disembark the vehicles. It had to be capable of handling the strain of twenty tanks disembarking on a beach with the likelihood of enemy attack ever-present.

The Landing Ship Tank (LST) was an entirely new concept in naval architecture, designed around the demand that it could safely ground itself on a beach – an action that defied the most basic rule of seamanship. It was 328ft long, 50ft wide and was designed with a flat-bottomed hull to keep the draft forward as shallow as possible. Unloaded, these boxy vessels drew only 2.4ft forward and 7.5ft aft where the twin propellers increased the depth of hull. A full load of 2400 tons increased the draft by 6ft, making it impossible for infantry to wade ashore. The blunt bow limited the speed to 10 knots, making the LST the real 'ugly duckling' of the US Navy, but the crews went one better and decided that LST stood for 'Large Slow Target'.

This change from the Liberty to the LST meant a complete

Above: In 1942, seven months after the first keel was laid, Kaiser Vancouver built a 382ft x 64ft Landing Ship Tank (LST) in an amazing 2 days 23.5 hours. This was a fully-planned event, shown by the start time at one minute after midnight on Saturday 14 November. By the evening of Monday the 16th, the official launching program was on stand-by until the ship was declared complete at 11:30 pm. The USS *LST-475* was immediately christened and launched by Mrs Edgar F Kaiser before midnight with a large placard already showing the time for construction. Unfortunately, this record did not gain much recognition in the rush to build over 1000 LSTs in emergency shipyards all over the USA.

turnover on the ground in Vancouver and a whole new set of challenges: new plans had to be copied and studied, hundreds of wooden patterns needed to be marked out for all the different steel shapes to ensure every hull was identical. Then the new production schedule would have to be created and passed around to all the departments, while all the teams were briefed on the part they would play in building the first LST.

This reorganization would occupy months in peacetime, but had to be accomplished in days, then constantly updated as the theory was put into practice and improvements incorporated. That was the key to the Kaiser shipyards' ability to mass produce thousands of components that went into a ship and enabled teams to pre-fabricate entire blocks in the assembly halls. Flat-bottom boats have a notoriously bad motion in a seaway, so the LST could be ballasted down with tons of water to improve the motion and seaworthiness, borrowing some ideas from submarine engineering. This required ballast tanks throughout the hull each with its own pumps, valves and controls.

The LST could carry 20 Sherman tanks in the hold, and a full load of trucks and jeeps on the main deck that could be lowered via a portable elevator platform. This gave the Allies a technical and strategic advantage that was critical in enabling D-Day to succeed, according to General Dwight Eisenhauer, the Supreme Allied Commander in Europe, and for the many amphibious assaults in the SW Pacific.

However, this ability to carry vehicles posed a very basic question: how to avoid poisoning the air in the tank deck when all the tank engines were running prior to landing? To ensure the correct number and size of fans were specified, the naval architects insisted that a full-scale test was needed. In April 1942 a mock-up of the tank deck was built at Fort Knox, Kentucky, home of the US Army Armor Center. (This historic building has been preserved.) Several options for ventilation were tested and the final design was proven at this facility.

Propulsion was by two 900 hp (670 kW) Electro-Motive Diesel 12-567A engines, a V-12 originally developed for locomotives in 1938, which gave a maximum speed of 12 knots loaded, and a range of 24,000 nautical miles at 9 knots. When close to shore, the ballast tanks would be pumped dry to reduce the draft for running ashore in shallow water. For amphibious operations, they carried six Higgins plywood landing craft in davits that were lowered into the sea and loaded with 36 troops.

LESS THAN THREE DAYS TO LAUNCH A 328-FOOT LST

To keep up the Kaiser Company's reputation for record breaking, one crew in Vancouver decided to shoot for a stunning record for completing an LST – three days! The keel was laid at 12:01 am on Saturday 14 November 1942; then it was another case of extensive prefabrication and the assembly and welding of the biggest sections that could be handled on the ways. Some 1500 tons of steel was installed before *LST-475* was ready for launching by Edgar F Kaiser's wife, Mrs Susan Mead Kaiser, only 2 days, 23 hours later.

This record-breaking feat should not be regarded as a stunt because it served to demonstrate the accomplishments of planned organization and preassembly methods. Edgar Kaiser warmly complimented the shipyard crews for their achievement, and declared that the Vancouver yard would have been turning out Liberty ships at the rate of twenty a month if the contract had not been redrawn and the yard changed to build other types of vessels. *LST-475* earned six battle stars for her service in the Pacific.

At the beginning of 1943 Kaiser & Company's Vancouver Washington yard engaged in a unique program of shipbuilding. On the ways in various stages of were seven Liberty ships and five escort aircraft carriers while the outfitting dock engaged in work on tank landing ships launched the previous year. The schedule allowed four months from keel laying to commissioning; that schedule was reduced to two months by the end of the war. By March 1943, Kaiser Van had delivered the 30 LSTs in the contract, turning out the first after 180 days and the thirtieth after 135 days.

LSTs were a high priority during the war, and about 670 were built far inland, most in small barge yards in rather unlikely locales like Seneca, Illinois and Evansville and Jeffersonville, Indiana on the inland waterways. Known as the 'Cornfield Navy', their shallow draft allowed them to float down small rivers, but on some minor waterways, low bridges had to be removed or modified. The LST was adapted and converted to numerous special uses from hospital ship to floating workshop; it is often shown carrying two 175ft x 14ft ramps, lashed to its topsides. All these options led to it being called 'the most versatile ship in World War II'.

Eighteen shipyards produced more than 1000 LSTs overall, which were a key element in the war against Germany and Japan. They participated in amphibious landings in Sicily, Italy, Normandy, southern France, the Philippines, and the capture of Iwo Jima and Okinawa. Even though the crews sometime doubted their seaworthiness, only 26 were lost to enemy action.

WORKFORCE GROWS TO 39,000

As the pace picked up in the shipyard, more workers and their families arrived, quickly doubling the population of Vancouver to 40,000. Housing all these workers was another challenge that the Kaiser organization had to overcome. The Vancouver Housing Authority (VHA) was established in 1942 to accommodate the new employees in the aluminium and shipyard industries. The VHA received financing from the federal government to acquire 1600 acres of farmland and started six new communities in and around the city. The VHA built 1000 permanent homes and 11,396 temporary units capable of housing 50,000 people. When the war was over the temporary units were sold to buyers who agreed to dismantle and remove them. The land was then re-developed into some of Vancouver's best-planned neighbourhoods.

With thousands more women moving into the area, Kaiser began to advertise for women for welding and other occupations which had previously been considered male professions. By 1944, more than 10,000 women were working at the Vancouver shipyards. Many of them held journeymen-level positions which had once only been available to men and paid the same – $1.20 an hour. For the first time in local history, women found themselves working beside men as equals, doing the same jobs and getting the same pay.

THE ESCORT CARRIER (CVE)

Unlike most emergency shipyards, Kaiser Vancouver was never allowed to specialize in a particular type of vessel, building five different classes in less than four years. However, its finest achievement was undoubtedly the third order, for another new class of vessel – the escort carrier (CVE) – of which five were already laid down.

The concept of a small economical carrier platform had been debated for some time in the US Navy, and in March 1939 Captain John S McCain (father of the late US senator and navy pilot in the Vietnam War) had written to the Secretary of the Navy advocating the building of at least eight 'pocket-size' carriers of cruiser speed. By 1940, the British were testing small carrier conversion in their fight against the German U-boats that were terrorizing shipping in the Atlantic, but were unable to produce sufficient numbers to have a significant impact. A British mission to the USA requested more small carriers for the Royal Navy, as aircraft transports and submarine hunters. This move paralleled the British order for 60 Ocean class cargo ships for the UK's Ministry of War Transport.

There were several designs and prototypes of escort carrier (CVE) under consideration in the US Navy. All were about 500ft long – slightly more than half the length of US Navy fleet carriers, and less than a third of the tonnage. Their capacity of 24–28 aircraft was about a quarter to a third that of the full-size carriers. In April 1941 Ingalls Shipbuilding in Mississippi began construction of the first *Bogue* class CVEs based on the standard C3 cargo ship hull, but both the carriers and the cargo ships got off to a slow start as the emergency shipyards were still recruiting workers. The keel of the first carrier was laid in April 1941, in Mississippi, but it was not delivered until November 1942. The Todd Corporation's Seattle-Tacoma Shipbuilding became involved in October 1941, and began production of escort carriers on its eight ways. But it took over a year to deliver its first *Bogue* class carrier, and the next twelve in 1942–43 all took a year or more.

To speed up delivery, fifteen were launched and towed to Portland unfinished for fitting out by Commercial Iron Works (CIW) and Willamette Iron and Steel Company (WISCO) and delivered directly to the Royal Navy. Todd was given a second order for 24 *Bogue* class with improved weaponry and they delivered the last 12 in less than a year. Overall, 35 of these ships went to the Royal Navy in the North Atlantic and were renamed the *Attacker* and *Ruler* classes. They all had one notable feature the Vancouver-built carriers would lack: they were propelled by modern diesels or steam turbines. They took part in convoy escort operations in the Atlantic and even participated in the attacks on the German battleship *Tirpitz*. Early in 1945, several were ordered to join the British Pacific Fleet supporting the US invasion of Okinawa.

KAISER'S CARRIERS: THE CASABLANCA CLASS

When Henry Kaiser first proposed building escort carriers at his Vancouver yard on 2 June 1942, the US Navy leaders voted him down 16 to 0, because the design was not seen as capable of withstanding heavy attack, and was considered a diversion of a yard from vital cargo ship production. According to the Kaiser Permanente archives, 'a chance encounter with a contact who happened to have close connections to President Roosevelt's staff led to a meeting the next morning with FDR insisting to several admirals that these carriers must be given priority.'

Above: Naval Architect George Sharp designed the Victory ship and the 50 Kaiser carriers, the only escort carriers not based on standard cargo ship hulls. Despite this, they were not noticeably better performers than the 80 other CVEs.

A fleet aircraft carrier could take two to three years from keel laying to launch and was so valuable to the navy's strategy that they required an entire fleet to protect them, while the CVEs were cheap and quick to build and were indeed considered 'expendable'. Kaiser had promised the president that he could deliver 50 small aircraft carriers in less than two years – about the time it took the US Navy to design a full-size fleet carrier. This ultimately won the admirals over – or perhaps they thought Kaiser had finally promised more than he could possibly deliver with these complex fighting ships. He was awarded a contract for 50 ships at a price of $350 million, or $7 million each, and was even given a new hull design from the keel up, instead of the standard cargo hulls that other yards converted into carriers.

The naval architects were George Sharp & Co of New York, who also designed the C2 and the Victory ship. This 'Kaiser class' was to be built exclusively in Vancouver, and when completed would double the number of escort carriers launched to over 100. It was 512.3ft overall, 65.2ft beam of hull, flight deck width 89ft, maximum deck width 108ft. The deck gear included two hydraulic catapults, two elevators, nine arresting wires and three barrier nets. Armament was one 5-inch 38 calibre dual-purpose gun on the stern, four twin 40mm Bofors anti-aircraft guns and twelve single Oerlikon 20mm. This was later increased to thirty 20mm guns and eight twin 40mm guns.

It had a larger and more useful hangar deck than previous conversions and a larger flight deck, 476ft long, gaining a few feet on previous escorts, with a draft of 22–23ft. Because of their short flight decks, the escort carriers were limited to smaller aircraft. The typical complement consisted of 16 Grumman Wildcat fighters (F4F) and 12 Grumman Avenger torpedo bombers (TBM). (In the Royal Navy, the Wildcat was originally known as the Martlet.) This program began in the spring of 1943 and the first vessel – and the class – was originally named *Ameer*, became *Alazon Bay*, and was changed again to *Casablanca* to commemorate the recent Allied landings in North Africa.

This change of direction still seems stunning: after less than a year in operation, the workers in Vancouver were now switching from the basic LST to the highly complex CVE, a huge challenge for management and employees at Vancouver. The carrier was the most complicated and deadly fighting ship ever devised, yet there was no time allocated to testing or prototypes: these ships had to be ready for action when they left the Columbia River. The idea that they could produce 50 of these sophisticated ships in just 20 months must have seemed absolutely impossible. It would need a miracle to accomplish, but the entire Kaiser Van-Port operation seemed to take these challenges in its stride.

The Kaiser system enabled any employee to suggest improvements in the process and every idea was considered. (The best were rewarded with war bonds and featured in *The Bo's'un's Whistle*.) One of the biggest successes was described in *The Log*, the west coast's monthly nautical publication. Lee Donaldson, a hull control supervisor in Vancouver, invented a photographic template system to reduce wastage in cutting small steel parts from large plates. This was approved and he was able to erect a high platform where he could systematically photograph every wooden template needed for each ship. Office staff then cut the shapes out and traced them onto cardboard at a small scale. This allowed the staff to visually arrange the shapes until they had arrived at the best way to get the most parts from every steel plate, saving large amount of time and material. (It took another 50 years before shipyards adopted computerized 'nesting' software to perform the same task.)

The first of the class was laid down on 3 November 1942 as MarCom hull 1092, later renamed *Casablanca* on 3 April 1943. (Casablanca was the week-long US Navy battle with the Vichy French forces off the coast of Morocco in November 1942, immediately preceding the Allied landings in North Africa.) However, it was too late to change the name from USS *Alazon Bay* (CVE-55) before the launch on 5 April by First Lady Eleanor Roosevelt. This occasion attracted by far the largest crowd in the history of Vancouver, estimated at 75,000. The youngest female employee in the yard, Jean Larsen, was chosen as 'flower girl' for the ceremony.

The governors of Oregon and Washington, and Henry Kaiser also attended the ceremony and addressed the huge crowd. A large photo spread was published the next day in *The Oregonian*. *The Bo's'n's Whistle* reported:

> A HUGE crowd of tin-hatted workers and their families took enough time off from building other carriers to watch their first product safely launched. Cheers of workers and managers alike swelled visibly when she paid tribute to their efforts. 'Building ships is an absolute necessity – building ships, making them ready to carry the things which are needed by our men, by our allies throughout the world is one of the essentials of winning the war. You are doing it! You are doing it magnificently and I congratulate you today and I wish for your good health and good luck in the future.'
>
> Then they felt a glow of satisfaction in their boss's words: 'You who have labored on this hull have the gratitude, not only of America, but of all mankind who live in the hope of liberty.' It was also a proud day for Governor Langlie of Washington. 'Our nation is engaged in the greatest wartime production of any kind in the world, of any nation in the world,' he declared. 'We who participate in it are thankful that on the Pacific Coast we have this organization that is playing a part in the production medium.'

Only two weeks later, on 18 April 1943, the yard was ready to launch the second carrier, the USS *Liscome Bay* (CVE-56). There was no ceremony this time, and the yard soon had other issues to contend when the mighty Columbia River tried its best to bring production in the entire Van-Port area to a halt. The next day when Barber's weekly round-up of shipyard news appeared, it was headlined: 'Shipyards Fear Flood May Sabotage War Jobs if 25ft Rise Reached.' Fortunately, the 'Flood of 1943' that broke highwater records upstream, failed to breach the banks and dykes on the lower river, or production would have been slowed or stopped at all the area's shipyards.

Right: The *Casablanca* class was powered with twin five-cylinder Uniflow steam engines giving a top speed of 19 knots. One is shown here in the process of being installed.

8

Left: The prefabricated forward section of the carrier's flight deck is lifted into place by two whirley cranes.

The *Casablanca* was commissioned on 8 July 1943, eight months or 240 days after keel laying. This was comparable to the first Liberty ship in Portland, and also just the beginning of a record-breaking run. Another VIP event was organized for the launching of the sixth carrier, USS *Natoma Bay* (CVE-62), which later played an important role in several campaigns against Japan. On 20 July 1943 the United Kingdom's ambassador, the Earl of Halifax attended the ceremony with his wife Countess Halifax as the sponsor. Halifax was quite likely the highest-ranking British leader to visit the region that was so important to his nation's survival.

The Kaiser carriers had a crew of around 110 officers and 750 men, plus the 50–60 aircrew and their mechanics, who all required a bunk, mess, washrooms etc, plus workshops for the two dozen planes. Two aircraft elevators hoisted the planes to the flight deck where the catapult would launch them. These were the only US Navy fighting ships that Kaiser built, and yet the company was unable to secure modern diesels or steam turbines in the size and number they needed. The alternative they chose was a reciprocating steam engine made by the Nordberg Manufacturing Company in Milwaukee, Wisconsin under the Skinner Unaflow patent.

This was a unique design configuration and was the most efficient steam engine ever mass-produced. When it was introduced in 1926, it was recognized for solving the fundamental

Below: This carrier launch was recorded by three movie cameras on the tall launching platform and one on the flight deck, with a good crowd of workers on the bow ready to enjoy the ride down the ways.

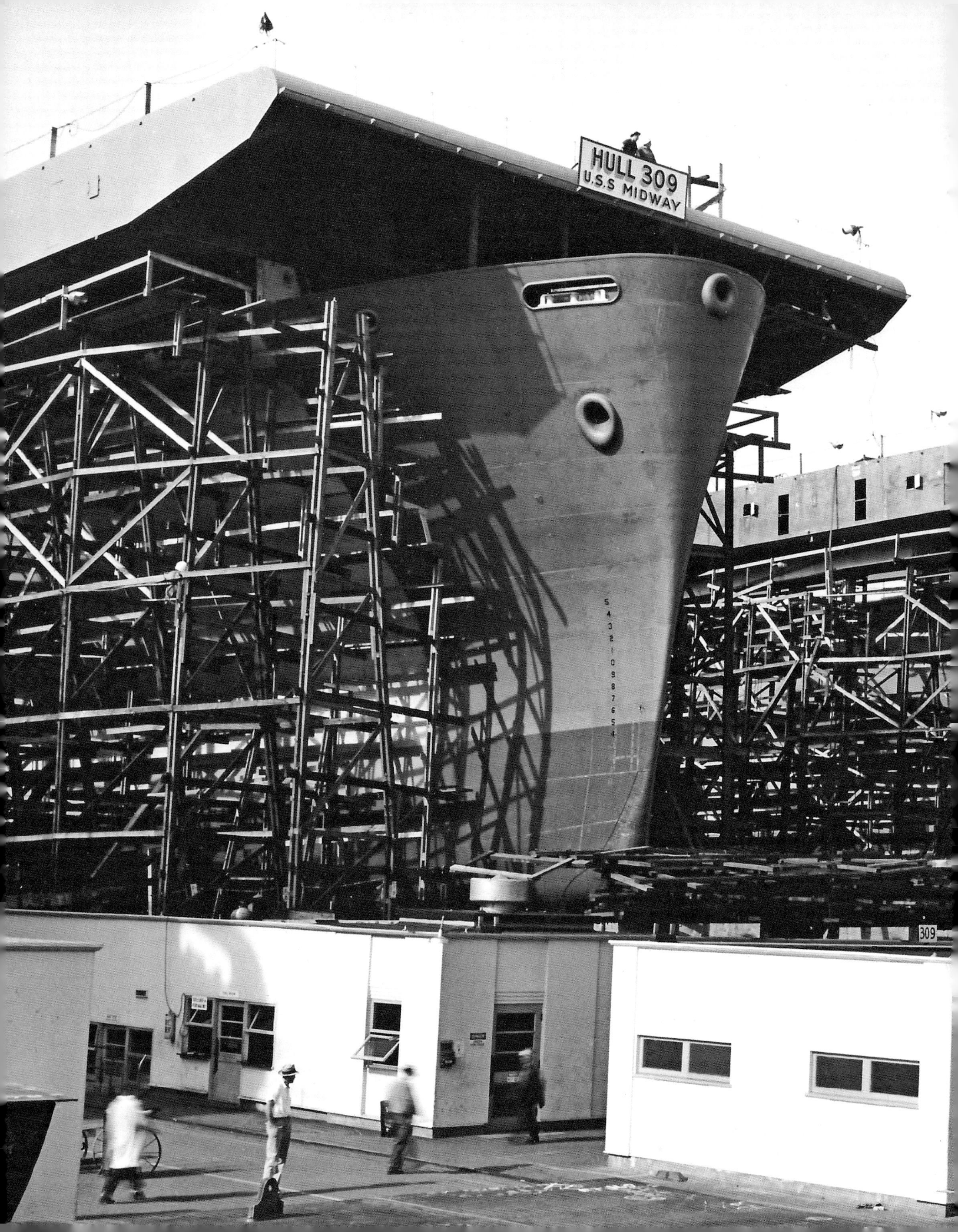
HULL 309
U.S.S MIDWAY
309

Three *Casablanca* class carriers with hull numbers 307 USS *Manila Bay*, 308 HMS *Begum* and 309 USS *Midway* are taking shape. All three were to suffer name changes: *Manila Bay* had been *Bucareli Bay* when ordered; *Begum* was taken over from the Royal Navy and renamed *Natoma Bay*; and *Midway* became *St Lo* when the name was needed for a new fleet carrier.

Above: Eleanor Roosevelt launches the escort carrier USS *Casablanca*, the first of its class, on 5 April 1943. She also toured the new Kaiser Permanente Foundation hospital nearby and discussed the need for child care for women workers with Edgar Kaiser.

Right: The launch program for the first *Casablanca* class CVE on 5 April 1943. At that point the ship was still known as *Alazon Bay*.

heating/cooling inefficiency of standard steam engines by allowing steam to pass through the cylinder in one direction, utilizing intake valves in the head, and exhaust ports in the cylinder walls, like the successful GM two-stroke diesel. It was popular as a commercial stationary engine for powering mills or as a generator.

A pair of five-cylinder Unaflows were installed in the escorts with a 27in bore and a 30in stroke. They were supplied by two boilers per engine running at 275 psi (1970 kPa). The engines' combined output was 9000 shp (6700 kW) for a trial speed of 20 knots, which still required them to turn into the wind to provide enough lift for the planes to safely take off. The engine had a direct reverse that was very easy to engage and was fully enclosed like a diesel. Range was 10,240 nautical miles (18,960 km; 11,780 miles) at 15 knots with a fuel capacity of 2279 tons.

Approximately 2,500,000 man-hours were required to produce the first carriers, which was roughly the equivalent in man-hours of eight Liberty ships. In the autumn, the 39,000 men and women of the yard pledged themselves to produce the equivalent of an additional 5,000,000 man-hours in two months' time. Sister ships followed at a rate of three a month into November with overall times of around nine months. The extra effort resulted in nineteen carriers delivered by the end of 1943, thus giving the Navy three more vessels than they had expected. By the 25th carrier, that time had been halved to four months, around 120 days. The later ships came in at just over 100 days. The last was the USS *Munda* (CVE-104) in July 1944.

Because of the amount of work needed to ready a carrier for service, all the *Casablanca* class ships spent time at the Port of Astoria where the Astoria Marine Construction Company was responsible for final fitting out and commissioning. They employed as many as 1000 workers while another 400 were engaged in building wooden minesweepers in their own yard.

Right: USS *Manila Bay* halfway down the ways during its launch on 10 July 1943. The ship saw extensive action against Japan and was awarded eight battle stars.

HULL 307
U.S.S. MANILA BAY

The escort carriers still needed thousands of hours of work before they were ready for departure. Note that they left the Columbia without aircraft or pilots, and steamed to one of the three major naval air stations on the west coast – Puget Sound, Alameda and San Diego – where the planes, pilots, and crews were embarked and commenced flight training prior to entering the conflict zones.

The entire class was originally earmarked for Lend-Lease to Britain until the first sea and flight trials took place. The *Casablanca* performed far above expectations and all the contracts were changed to retain them as US Navy vessels, the British allocation being replaced by the *Bogue* class from

Below: It was a festive day in Vancouver when over 70,000 citizens attended the launch of the first carrier.

Right, top: A CVE and two sternwheel steam tugs, which were preferred by the river pilots for handling all the big ships in the strong river currents.

Right, bottom: Shaver Transportation's 160ft wooden sternwheel steam tug *Henderson*, built 1906, moves a newly-launched carrier to the outfitting dock. In 1952, it appeared in a steamboat race in the film *Bend of the River*, starring Jimmy Stewart and Rock Hudson.

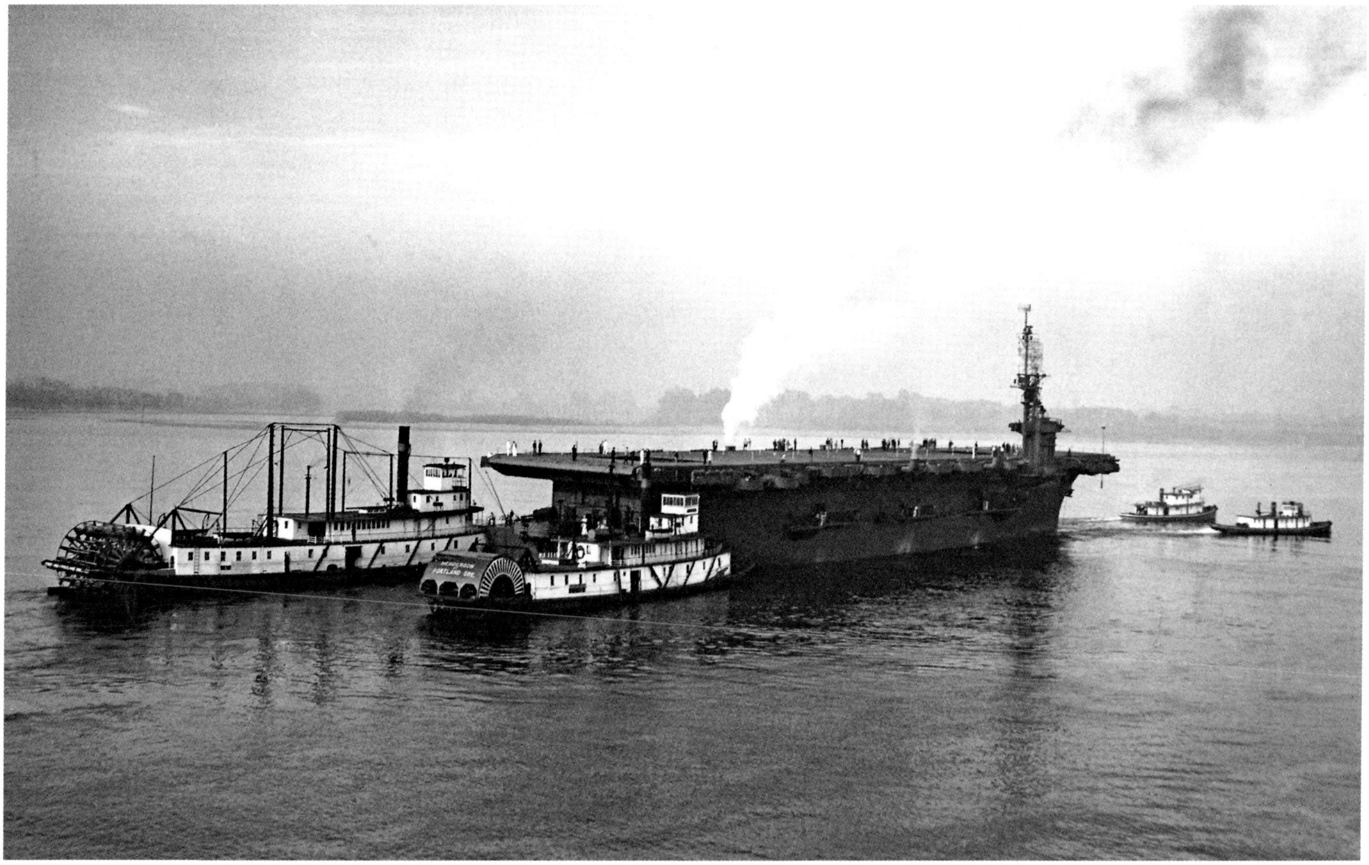

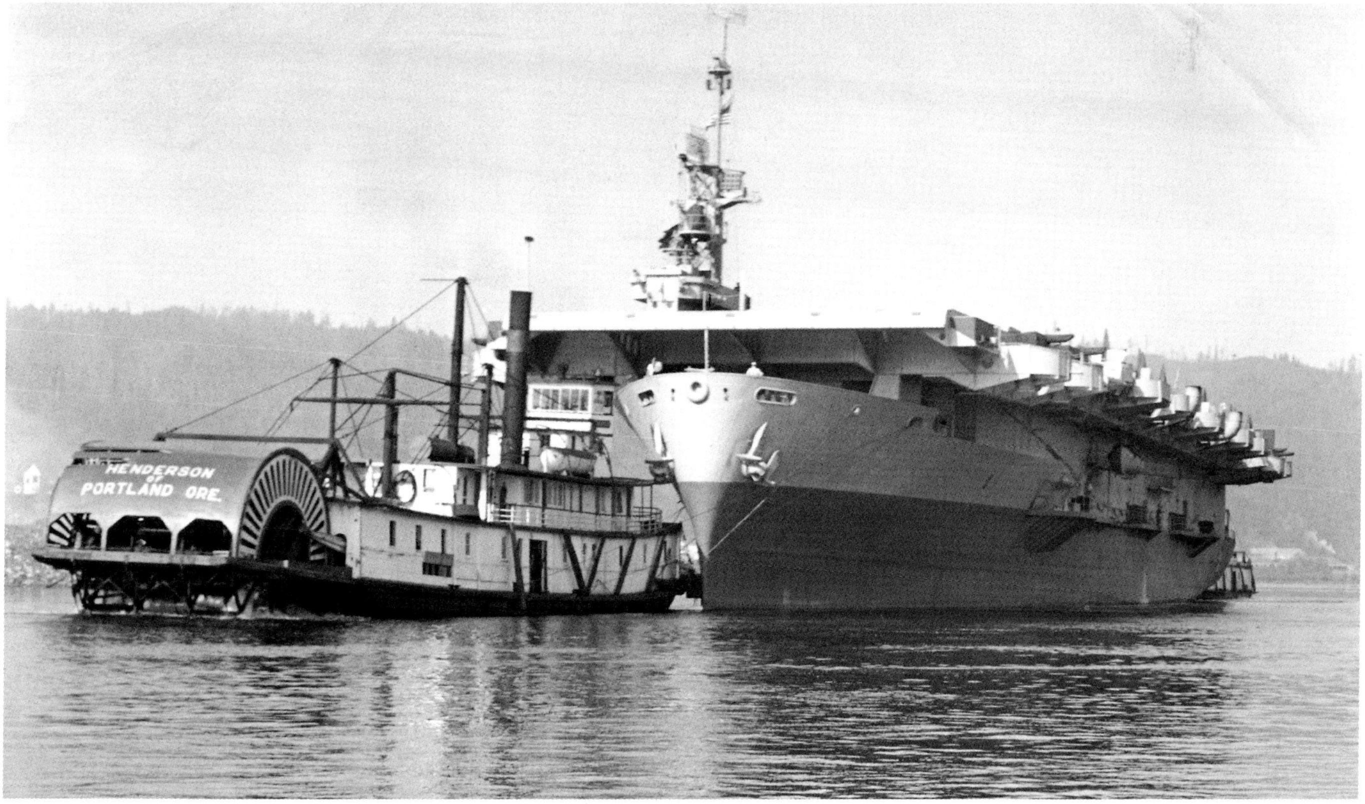
HENDERSON
OF
PORTLAND ORE.

Above: Photographer Jerry Scanlan found a ride on a tug or a launch to get close to a CVE during a trial run, and was rewarded with this superb shot.

Tacoma. All the escort carriers of World War II were lightly armed and armoured, and relatively slow at less than 20 knots maximum, compared to the fleet carriers. They were intended to do just what their name says: escort convoys of cargo ships. This was especially important in the middle of the North Atlantic where the Allied ships were out of range of their land-based anti-submarine aircraft.

Since the *Casablanca* class was designed specifically as carriers, it was hoped they would out-perform the *Bogue* class C3 hull, also designed by Sharp. But unfortunately, the Kaiser carriers were later found to exhibit severe rolling when they were beam-on to large waves, which made them unsuitable for North Atlantic operations in winter. Most of them were assigned to the war in the warm waters of the Pacific. (Larry Barber saved a few snapshots taken by a seaman that show his ship heeling at an alarming angle, so steep every man on deck must have been hanging on for his life.) The USA built 122 CVEs during the war: five were lost to enemy action, with three sunk by kamikazes. The remainder were all scrapped, but the *Casablanca* class remains the most numerous class of aircraft carrier ever built.

THE HASKELL CLASS ATTACK TRANSPORT (APA)

But there was still more work to do in Vancouver before the end of hostilities in the Pacific. The yard returned to cargo ship building with 31 of the new Victory hulls – the second emergency cargo class. But this was not the basic five-hold design: to close out the momentous year of 1944, both Portland and Vancouver were given orders for a more complex version called the *Haskell* class Attack Transport variant (VC2-S-AP5), as

Above: In the spring of 1944, Kaiser Vancouver transferred its production to Attack Transports of the *Haskell* class. Although based on a Victory hull, these ships were much more complex in their fittings, as seen in this view of USS *Renville* (APA-227), completed in November 1944, after only 67 days from keel-laying.

Below: USS *Olmsted* (APA-188) was one of the first Attack Transports built by Kaiser Vancouver. Construction took 147 days.

detailed in Chapter 4. The first ten took 140–150 days, the last ships were finished in less than half that time, the record being a remarkable 60 days.

TROOPSHIPS C4-S-A3

The schedule for 1945 brought an order for another 20 ships using the 523ft x 72ft C4 hull that had been designed in the late 1930s. This was the largest cargo ship built by the Maritime Commission during World War II. The design was originally developed for the American-Hawaiian Lines in 1941. The first twelve were C4-S-A3 troopships, also known as the *Marine Adder* class. The ship's complement was 356 officers and enlisted men, troop capacity was around 3675. Speed was 17 knots.

The last troopship memorialized Ernie Pyle, the most famous American War Correspondent who covered all the action in the European theatre until Germany fell, then went to the Pacific where he was killed by a Japanese sniper. Former First Lady Eleanor Roosevelt, who frequently quoted Pyle's war dispatches in her newspaper column, paid tribute to him the day after his death, writing: 'I shall never forget how much I enjoyed meeting him last year, and how much I admired this frail and modest man who could endure hardships because he loved his job and our men.' Fittingly, the SS *Ernie Pyle* was used after the war to carry Jewish displaced persons and other refugees from Europe to the USA in 1946–52.

The order was completed with eight hulls finished as the C4-S-A4 cargo carrier, ending in May 1946 with the *Scott E Land*. The yard continued to be active, focused on decommissioning US Navy vessels at the outfitting dock. In all, it produced 10 Liberty ships, 30 LSTs, 50 aircraft carriers, 12 C4 troopships, 31 AP5 troop transports, and 8 C4 cargo vessels. The yard also built two 14,000-ton dry docks: one was towed to California, the other only went as far as Swan Island, where it became the centrepiece of the civilian ship repair facility that was still thriving in 2020.

Left: An aerial view of Kaiser's Vancouver yard at the end of the war with a line six 520ft C4 cargo ships filling the 1100-yard/1000-metre outfitting dock. The last remaining ship on the ways at the east end of the yard is therefore the *Scott E Land* in the spring of 1946. The large assembly building above the twelve ways is still in use in 2020. *(US Navy photo.)*

Overleaf: The Vancouver yard was called the 'finest in America' during the war, but closed permanently after the C4 cargo ship *Scott E Land* was delivered in May, 1946.

E. N°17

6

KAISER SWAN ISLAND: 'TANKER CHAMPIONS OF THE WORLD'

Tankers were vital to the Allied war effort, and the standard T2 was the tanker equivalent of the Liberty. In less than four years, from February 1942 to November 1945, four shipyards delivered 533 of these 16,600-ton tankers, construction being divided as follows:

Sun Shipbuilding, south of Philadelphia on the Delaware River – 206 ships;
Kaiser Swan Island, Portland – 147 ships;
ADDSCO (Alabama Dry Dock & Shipbuilding Company) on the Gulf Coast – 102 ships
Marinship – built by the W A Bechtel Co at the north end of San Francisco Bay in Sausalito – 78 ships

Below: Swan Island yard layout – the last stage of the Kaiser production line assembled all the pre-fabricated parts ready for assembly into another T2 tanker.

Kaiser Swan Island was the third and last of the Kaiser Van-Port emergency shipyards, located two miles upstream from Oregonship and close enough to the city centre to make it the most visible and accessible of the Kaiser yards. It only built one type of ship, and became very proficient at it. The proof was that it flew the 'M' flag for two and a half years and the coveted 'Tanker Champion' flag flew over the Swan Island yard for twelve out of the fifteen months to the end of 1944.

Swan Island had a very curious history in the early 1900s, before becoming the site of 'Tanker champions of the World'. Into the early 1920s, Swan Island was just a wetland in the middle of the Willamette River, a mile downstream of central Portland and eight miles above the confluence with the Columbia. Curiously, the deep-water channel to the city docks had meandered to the east side of the island sometime in the past, although the direct route was on the west side. When the Port of Portland began planning a major program of dredging

Above: Swan Island floating bridge was the 'short cut' off the island to the huge parking lot, site of daily traffic jams at rush hours.

and wharf building after World War I, they convinced the US Army Corps of Engineers to re-route the shipping channel back to the west side of the island, and dump the dredge spoils on the east side to block the old channel and connect the island to the east bank. Although it was no longer an island, the name remained as a reminder of its history.

By 1927 the shipping channel was straighter and deeper, exports of wheat and lumber had increased, and a road was being laid across the land bridge to the peninsula that had tripled in size to 900 acres. It was now about a mile long by a third of mile wide – big enough to become the site of Portland's first airport. On 14 September the airstrip was completed in time for a celebrity opening event. The first pilot to land was none other than Charles Lindbergh – hailed as the 'most famous person in the world' at the time – flying his equally famous plane, the *Spirit of St Louis*.

His short stay in Portland allowed for time to visit the famous old battleship USS *Oregon*, then employed as a museum ship. Lindbergh arrived from Seattle and continued south to San Francisco, stopping in all 48 states and visiting 92 cities to promote air travel. By 1935 air travel had boomed, and the runway was considered too short to land the latest and most popular airliner, the DC-3, so the city and port chose a site on the south shore of the Columbia River for its new airport. Construction of the airport during 1936–1940 steadily employed over 1000 men, and was recognized as Portland's most important public works project during the New Deal era.

When the Maritime Commission began planning for a third wave of emergency shipyards in 1941, it saw Swan Island as the ideal spot for a third Kaiser yard. The compact site with water on three sides was well-suited to shipbuilding and fitting out. There was enough room for the pre-fabrication and assembly work to proceed through the yard towards the ways, while the newly-launched ships could be moored in the Swan Island Basin on the east side for fitting out just a few yards from the machine shops. The completed ships could dock on the west side for commissioning, head straight out into the river for sea trials, and still moor close to the workshops on their return. (This was not the case at OSC, where only four or five ships could be moored.)

The contract to convert the Swan Island municipal airport was signed on 4 March 1942, only two months after work had started at Kaiser Vancouver. By 16 March the first ground had been broken and workmen began to drive some wooden 22,000 piles for the outfitting dock. It was planned with ten 550ft shipways that would have completely filled the north end of the

Right: Swan Island aerial: space for eight building ways and one dry dock on the downriver end, and eight ships outfitting alongside in the lagoon, dormitory housing upper left, parking lot lower left. The lay-down area extends over a mile seemingly with 'a place for everything'.

2811

Left: This coffer dam weighed 78 tons and included the fore pump room with all its piping.

island, but this was cut back to eight, which turned out to be more than enough for the Kaisers to set more records.

The yard centred on the huge plate and assembly buildings with a 593-ton electrically-driven press break; and a 96in. gauge shear, the largest in the West. Of the eleven bays, three were equipped with 25-ton bridge cranes devoted to erecting Isherwood-type corrugated bulkheads weighing 30 tons. The rest of the bays had different cranes for lifting various bulkhead and deck sections, necessary for the largest ships ever built in the Portland area. Shell plates were pre-fabricated in complete 36ft by 40ft sections.

Hull assembly began by laying the keel and the adjacent bottom plating. Starting amidships the first of 21 bulkheads was set in position and the erection is carried out in both directions toward the ends. Two longitudinal bulkheads divided the tank spaces into three compartments, then the longitudinal stringers that support the shell and decks were set in place. The ends of the vessel were finished last, and often the tank spaces were complete and tested, capable of floating the vessel before the ends were fully plated. The policy of continuous improvement quickly led to the total prefabrication of the poop deck assembly, which could be completed in five days welded in the inverted position. Weighing in at 56 tons, it could be lifted by two whirley cranes. The poop deck crew quarters were well under construction when the vessel was launched.

'WE BUILD TANKERS'

The 21-minute film *We Build Tankers* is a remarkable work by Leonard Delano. Although unfinished, it carefully documents a 'typical day' at Swan Island in 1944, showing two tankers being launched – the SS *Fort Matanzas* on 11 July, and the SS *Grand Teton* on 1 August. (One fact that is rarely mentioned is that the ship's name was immediately painted out as soon as it was berthed – for security reasons.) Among the scenes that give a real inside look at the assembly-line system are shots of the whirley cranes with eights sets of tracks running from the assembly halls to the eight ways, and the small steam locomotives hauling wagons loaded with boxes of gear along the dock past a line of moored ships.

It also shows a 20ft-wide flatbed trailer carrying a large prefabricated section and a straddle carrier, which was a local invention originally developed for carrying small logs and stacked lumber. It was manufactured by a local business that became the Hyster Company, and grew into a successful international corporation in the 1960s. The cameraman focuses on women workers in several shots of pattern making and lofting, including a group of six women carrying a long wooden pattern through the yard. Large pre-fabricated parts are shown being carried and placed by whirleys, with one hoist displaying a stern section from Columbia Steel Casting, complete with rudder stock and propeller shaft bearing.

In 1943 the average Swan tanker was built in 115.5 days, but in 1944 that time was cut to 63 days, a theme worthy of a proper documentary. One fact that is rarely mentioned is that the ship's name was immediately painted out as soon as it was berthed – for security reasons. The film looks like it began as a serious attempt to preserve the achievement of the Kaiser organization, but sadly was never given a sound track. Like the magazine-style souvenir book from OSC *Record Breakers*, it also failed to reach a wider audience.

Here's a description of the way it was done from the *Bo's'n's Whistle* of December,1943.

> Swan Islanders have clipped another week per vessel off their high-speed tanker program by prefabricating the forward cofferdam on a jig, fitting the piping and the pump house, then installing each completed section as a unit on the keel. The huge 82-ton forepeak section is built as nearly complete as possible at some distance from the ways. It is then lifted easily by two whirley cranes and dropped neatly on the keel in the ways. The new method saves 784 man-hours on each unit compared to the old method which consisted of erecting 13 separate sections plus eight tons of piping, all of which had to be fitted together piece by piece on the hull.

All these ships were designated T2-SE-A1, a design developed from a tanker introduced in 1940 by the Sun Shipbuilding Company of Chester, Pennsylvania for the Standard Oil Company. They were 523ft long, 68ft beam, measuring 10,448 gross register tons (GRT) and 16,613 DWT. The nine tanks held almost six million gallons [141,000 barrels] of oil, diesel or petrol. The boilers were supplied by the Combustion Engineering Company. The steam turbine-electric transmission system delivered 6000 shaft horsepower, with a maximum thrust of 7240 horsepower (5400 kW), which produced a top speed of 15 knots with a cruising range at 12 knots of up to 12,500 miles.

The first keel at Swan Island, for the *SS Schenectady*, was not laid until 1 July because of a delay in procuring the two big 'hammerhead' cranes and other materials, but that was still only four months after the land was cleared. The first oiler was on the ways for 115 days and dockside for 83 days – a total of six months – and was delivered on 31 December 1942. The name *Schenectady* came from the town in NW New York state that was the home of the great General Electric Corporation. GE had grown from a merger with the Edison Electric Light Company in the 1880s and by the 1930s it was one of the largest companies in the USA with plants producing steam turbines and electric motors that would be used in the tanker's

There is no sign of the day shift at Swan Island on 21 January 1943 with a record snowfall of 14.5 inches halting traffic throughout the region. (This record still stands.)

D NO 4
WAY END NO 3

Above: Launch of the *Swan Island*, named after its place of build, on 16 August 1944. After the war the ship was operated by Shell until scrapped in 1961.

steam turbine-electric propulsion system. This had been used extensively by the US Navy in the early 1900s and World War I, but had fallen out of favour with the admirals in the 1920s as too complex. By the 1930s most ocean-going ships in the US Merchant Marine and the US Navy were powered by steam turbines spinning at 3000–5000 rpm. This required a very reliable reduction gear to lower the output to the propeller at about 100 rpm. By 1942, US industry was finally meeting the navy's high demand for steam turbines, but there were still delays in manufacturing the large reduction gears, so MarCom bypassed the problem by making the T2s electric drive.

THE SS SCHENECTADY SURVIVES A WRECK BY 'BRITTLE FRACTURE'

There appear to be no details on record about the launch ceremony, perhaps because the yard wanted to make sure they had the system worked out first. This was just as well, because the day after it had completed successful sea trials, the first tanker from Swan Island experienced a major disaster at its berth. The combination of freezing cold air and relatively warm river water caused a reaction in the *Schenectady*'s welded-steel hull. 'Without warning and with a report which was heard for at least a mile, the deck and sides of the vessel fractured just aft of the bridge superstructure. The fracture extended almost instantaneously to the turn of the bilge port and starboard. Only the bottom plating held. The vessel jack-knifed and the center portion rose up so that no water entered. The bow and stern settled into the silt of the river bottom,' said *The Oregonian*.

US Coast Guard engineers who studied the incident erroneously concluded that faulty welds were the culprit, then Rear Admiral Howard L Vickery arrived to lead the formal investigation. While this was proceeding, the ship was ballasted down and towed to a dry dock, where it was repaired with a series of plates secured inside the tank over the cracks – literally 'patched up'. The *Schenectady* then departed and successfully delivered cargoes all over the Pacific until Japan was defeated. The ship was sold to an Italian company in 1948 and served in the Mediterranean until it was finally scrapped at Genoa in 1962. The 20 years of service from a seriously wounded ship like this certainly proved the durability of Kaiser's welded ships, despite their shortcomings.

The same problem of 'brittle fracture' arose in other emergency welded ships: three of the Liberties also broke in half without warning, and several changes in design and assembly resolved the issue. But it was only in this century that advanced instruments and experiments proved it was actually a metallurgy problem. The pouring, rolling, and shaping processes used to make the steel sometimes resulted in a change in the chemistry, while the heat of welding reduced the annealed zone. This gave it a tendency to grow brittle in cold temperatures.

This near-disaster did nothing to stop the inexorable

Below: Swan Island's 'Tanker Champ' flag presentation. The yard delivered 43 tankers in 1943, incidentally winning the Tanker Champion Flag on 23 October of that year for achieving the highest productivity of any tanker yard and making the crew the 'Tanker Champions of the World'.

progress of the yard. In fact, the crew who were building the second tanker were more determined than ever to cheer up the yard, so they came up with the first of many morale boosters on Swan Island. One of the workers dreamed up the odd idea of persuading his workmates to stop shaving until their ship was launched. An article in *The Bo's'n's Whistle* on 5 November 1942, was wittily titled 'Toil and sweat, steel and whiskers'.

A follow-up two weeks later on the progress of the SS *Quebec* was headlined 'Whiskers measure tanker progress'; it went on:

> Some shipyards get the boys to make bigger and better records with pep talks. But at Swan Island they are having pioneer days – no launch, no shave! You ought to see it: with thousands of Rip Van Winkles on their island, toiling into the night surrounded by whiskers. Brunettes with red beards, blondes with black beards, goatees, Van Dykes, sheriff's mustaches, and stubble.
>
> The ban on shaving is ruthlessly enforced; in two different kangaroo-court sessions, fines were levied for failure to comply. At a trial on November 9, Edgar Kaiser was fined a total of $37.10 for failure to comply with the ordinance. His heavy fine included $10 for filing a motion in bad faith, 10c for contempt of court, $20 for failure to grow a beard, and $7 court costs. [He had worn a fake beard.]

The campaign's end on December 10 was headlined 'Swan Island Shaves! At Swan Island they literally work up a lather over a tanker launching.'

The next seven ships each required over seven months to deliver as the workforce grew to 30,000, most of whom had no experience in shipyard trades. By the tenth ship, the employees had learned how the Kaiser's system worked and the complex web of pipes and valves that controlled the cargo loading and unloading. Now the yard was really up and running: production figures ramped up with the SS *Hadley;* it was completed in 175 days. Through the summer of 1942, the second series of ten ships went into the water at an increasing rate until the twentieth ship had cut the time to delivery down to just 90 days. It should be stressed that a tanker is a far more complex ship than the simple cargo-carrying Liberty, and this was reflected in the longer building times.

Swan Island jumped swiftly into top gear in 1943 and delivered 43 tankers, incidentally winning the Tanker Champion Flag on 23 October of that year for achieving the highest productivity per way of any American yard building tankers. Portland's famous wet weather returned in October, but the crews continued to find ways to speed up the work. By the end of the year, the yard had reached peak performance with a stunning total of seven ships delivered in December, the last two, the *Grande Ronde* and the *Coquille*, in just 63 days each. That was not all: in the same month they also launched seven more hulls. For the first half of 1944, they completed almost 30 ships in 70–85 days, and in the second half of the year completed well over 30 ships in 65–72 days. By the end of the year, the final tally was 64 T2s delivered, plus outfitting six fleet oilers towed in from Puget Sound. To end the year, they set an all-time record by launching seven and delivering another seven tankers in December.

The workers may not have had much time to enjoy the scenery around Swan Island, but overlooking the ways was the scenic Waud's Bluff where a Roman Catholic priest had opened Columbia University in 1901. In the 1930s the school's name was changed to the University of Portland, and today it has over 4000 students and is considered one of the best small universities on the west coast. It also provided an excellent viewpoint of the yard, and today overlooks the marine activities of the modern shipyard. Another excellent photo opportunity was provided by the thousands of workers who parked their vehicles on the large lot on the east shore of the basin then walked into the shipyard across the floating footbridge.

This bridge was opened whenever tankers needed to enter or leave the fitting-out dock in the basin. Beyond the huge parking area was another Kaiser triumph: a military or industrial-style housing development for single male workers that was described as either like a barracks or rows of dormitories. It looks bleak in aerial photos, but eliminated the traffic jams that other workers faced on their daily commute – the residents could walk to work in a few minutes, night or day. Swan Island's 'Bachelor City', housed more than 5000 workers and included mess halls, a separate recreation centre, an auditorium, gymnasium, movie theatre as well as an infirmary, a barber shop and a small commissary. The mess hall had two dining rooms each seating 504 men.

Each of the ships built in the Van-Port shipyards was assigned a female sponsor who christened the ship by breaking the traditional bottle of champagne on the bow. This title was bestowed on women shipyard workers in all occupations, and to family members of those with greater responsibilities. Swan Island had an advantage when it came to organizing launch ceremonies because many of the tankers were named after places in Oregon and others after national parks and monuments. This helped to add a theme to the event. On 5 January 1944, the first tanker of the year, the SS *Nehalem*, was named after a coastal river. To acknowledge the 8000 women who were working on Swan Island, the launch was staffed entirely by women.

A launch was a time of celebration, but it also caused some anxiety. (The process of safely releasing a new ship off the building way is still an engineering challenge today.) The launching sequence was carefully choreographed and dozens of female shipyard employees had specific jobs to do. Miss Venus Dean was a shipwright's helper who was assigned to the under-

Left: A Kaiser photographer was given a ride by a crane to catch this unusual view of the launch, attended by a big crowd, even though there is no name on the bow to identify the ship.

side of the ship to supervise the placement of the wedges, which are hammered into place under the ship to lift it up above the ways, and the removal of the dog-shores – struts that hold the ship in place before launch. A temporary phone line was installed for her to communicate directly with the launch party, so they would know when to break the champagne bottle. The local bands that played the tanker out onto the Willamette River were also all-women. The only man allowed near the ship was the master shipwright, Robert Sweizer, who 'almost stole the show in his costume complete with curls and long lace dress,' according to the *Whistle*.

Two weeks later it was the turn of the SS *Pendleton*, the 49th tanker to launch. This town in the NE corner of the state is famous for the Pendleton Round-Up, one of the largest and most prestigious rodeos in the world, held almost continuously since 1910. So the launch ceremony on 21 January 1944 became a tribute to the 40,000 Native Americans engaged in war production around the country. This was considered to be the most colourful launch ever staged in the Van-Port yards. The sponsor of the *Pendleton* was Princess Melissa Parr, a member of the Cayuse tribe and direct descendant of the famous Chief Joseph.

Right: *Fort Wood* goes down the ways on a foggy day in September 1944. The tanker was lengthened into a 13,966 gross ton bulk carrier in the 1960s and renamed *Southern Eagle*. It was finally scrapped at Split, Yugoslavia in 1979.

A two-page spread in *The Bo's'n's Whistle* described the launching this way:

> Indians in striking regalia staged (*sic*) war dances, sang and beat their drums on the launching platform. Indian workers of the yard were honored guests at the launching and the luncheon which followed. The yard took on a real Western flavor during the day, with Indian tepees drawing crowds of interested spectators. Rear Admiral Howard L Vickery of the Maritime Commission made the principal address at the launching ceremonies.

An audio recording in the Kaiser Permanente heritage archives recorded his speech:

> Gathered here on the platform below, as special guests today, are Indians from various tribes of the Northwest. A good many of them work here in the yards and play an important part in the production of our tankers ...We feel that this occasion, in honor of American Indians, is proper not only in view of their vast contribution on the battle front and the production front, but also in view of the fact that the American Indian was actually the first ship builder in the Northwest.
>
> Too often the American Indian is not sufficiently thought of when we speak of the various nationalities and races living harmoniously in America, yet they have shown that great attribute – forgiveness. Reports of courage and skill of the American Indians in our armed forces is well known to us all. Their bravery has set an example to the most daring. In this area, there are more than one thousand Indians contributing their skill and effort in the building of ships. Here, again, their performance ranks among the finest ...The Indians, our first Americans, are still leading Americans.

MRS EDNA BARBER LAUNCHES THE SS FORT WOOD

Swan Island kept the pace up in 1944, delivering an incredible 70 tankers. For the 93rd launch it was decided that the staff of *The Oregonian* should be guests of honour and the Barber family was naturally chosen to represent the paper. This was one launch that Larry could not cover himself, but he had clipped and copied the paper's short story in the 17 September 1944 issue.

> In a ceremony honoring the staff of the newspaper, the SS *Fort Wood* was launched at Swan Island shipyard on Saturday with Mrs Lawrence Barber, wife of *The Oregonian*'s marine editor, as sponsor, and the marine editor as principal speaker. Barber shortened his talk because of a light rain falling on the spectators, and stressed the need for continued effort as the end of one phase of the war seemingly approaches.
>
> 'As the war draws toward a climax,' he declared, 'all of us have jobs to do – we must stay on the job and hew to the line.' Many employees of *The Oregonian* attended the launch, and master of ceremonies Tommy Hoxie, Swan Island public relations director, paid high tribute to the American press in general and praised the services of *The Oregonian* in the Portland territory. Hoxie also introduced two champion welders from Brunswick, Georgia (one male, one female) here to compete with Swan Island welders.

Above: Larry Barber was on the other side of the camera when his wife Edna christened the SS *Fort Wood* on 16 September 1944. They were representing the press corps at the ceremony, and Larry shortened his speech because 'a light rain was falling on the spectators'.

A separate story explains that Fort Wood was erected on an island in New York harbour in 1841 and was chosen as the site for the Statue of Liberty in 1885.

The 100th ship was launched on 22 November, and was the

Right: Launch of 99th tanker, *Mesa Verde*, 24 October 1944. It was later operated by British and French owners and scrapped at La Seyne sur Mer in 1961

MESA VERD
99

W. L. R. EMMET
100
WAY

only tanker named after a person – W L R Emmet (1859–1941), known as 'the father of turbo-electric propulsion'. Swan Island went on to build over one hundred ships in the final 18 months with an average time of about 70 days, launching at least one ship a week. They built a total of 147 tankers in three years out of a national total of 533 T2s. But even this did not have sufficient appeal to the newspapers, whose need for a steady stream of good production news could be filled a couple of miles downstream, where Oregonship was producing double that number of the iconic Liberty and Victory ships.

Overall, this emergency tanker was a handsome modern ship compared to the boxy vessel that the US government had repeatedly told the nation was 'an ugly duckling'. It had a superior propulsion system that gave it nearly 50 percent more speed, and was fully engineered and equipped to load and unload the petroleum fuel that was of such vital importance to the war effort. The civilian crews who manned these ships and ferried this dangerous cargo across the Atlantic and Pacific Oceans to the Allies' far-flung forces faced the extra risk from enemy submarines that their cargo could turn into a fireball in seconds.

Left: launch on 28 October 1944 of 100th T2, *W L R Emmert*, named after the pioneer of steam turbine-electric propulsion, the type of machinery that drove the T2s. The GE logo above the name honoured the General Electric Company, the leading US manufacturer of steam turbines, generators and electric motors.

TWO YARDS ARE COMPANY, THREE'S A CROWD!

Having written several pages in praise of the amazing tanker builders, I have to add a post script and a caveat: very little of this chapter came from Larry Barber's writing. Indeed, it came

Below: A T2 tanker leaving the dock at Swan Island for trials.

Above: A T2 tanker under way and showing a good turn of speed during trials on the lower Columbia River.

as a shock to me to find that all the fine work done on tankers by the Kaiser organization barely rated a brief mention in *The Oregonian*'s wartime reports. Larry Barber left a hundred fine photos of Liberty ships, but only a handful of tankers, mostly focusing on the SS *Mesa Verde*, the 99th launch. The only tanker story he saved was about the SS *Fort Wood*, and featured his wife, Edna and son Eugene!

This is not to question in any way Barber's devotion to his coverage of the wartime shipyards. In fact, when *The Oregonian* ran a remembrance of his life in 1995 after he died at 93, a reporter wrote: 'He wanted to be on hand for the launching of the Portland-area Liberty ships, all 332 of them. If he ever missed a launch, those who worked with him could not remember it.' Concentrating on Liberty ships is hardly surprising considering that Oregonship was launching three or four of them a week, while the president was exhorting shipyard workers to 'build more and more ships!'

There were over 1600 launch ceremonies performed in the seven local shipyards during World War II, and only one quarter of them were Liberty ships. But when Larry returned to this subject for *The Oregonian* several times in the post-war years, the title always included the iconic Liberty ship. On the 25th anniversary of Pearl Harbor in 1966, he wrote a full-page story that devoted less than two column inches to Swan Island. In the 1970s he returned to the story twice more and his titles clearly showed how he recalled the era: 'Liberty ships fading away' (1978); 'Liberty ship capital just a memory now' (1979). The bias continues to this day: the official state record online, 'The Oregon Encyclopedia', makes this bizarre statement: 'Between 1942 and 1945, the Kaiser shipyards produced 147 T2 tankers at Swan Island, making it the Liberty and Victory ship capital of the United States.'

Despite this lack of attention or appreciation, the tankers certainly had the last word, surviving far longer than the rest of the emergency ships. Most of them continued working for

Right: The *Victory Loan* launch on 6 October 1945, after the end of the war, was a gala event, with eight high school bands playing for a crowd of 5000. One of the last T2s built at Swan Island, the ship had a remarkably long career and was rebuilt to 13,899 gross tons in the 1960s and renamed *Texaco Melbourne;* it remained in service until 1985.

VICTORY LOAN
VICTORY LOAN
KAISER SWAN ISLAND
VICTORY LOAN
Swan Island
WELCOME
WAR BOND WORK
WAY END
HULL

about twenty years, and many that were still in good shape in the 1960s were lengthened with an additional mid-body section to about 580ft, and went on to pass the forty-year mark, when most other wartime cargo ships had completely disappeared. A handful of tankers made it to fifty years, and one stayed in service into the twenty-first century. This was a remarkable testament to a ship only intended to last until the war was won.

TURBO-ELECTRIC PROPULSION

The T2 was propelled by a system consisting of two standard Babcock & Wilcox oil-fired boilers burning 'Bunker C' heavy fuel oil. (Pre-war boiler production at B&W averaged two to three boilers a week; at the end of the shipbuilding program, they produced about 30 boilers a week. In total, 4100 of the 5400 major vessels constructed for the war effort were equipped with B&W boilers.) A continuous supply of steam was supplied to heating coils located in each of the fuel tanks. The fuel supply to the burners had to be heated to 180° F to reduce its viscosity.

The GE steam turbine model was a ten-stage single-casing design, directly shafted to a 5400 kW 2300 VAC 3 phase, 62 Hz main generator that operated over a speed range of about 900 to 3700 rpm. The generator supplied power to a synchronous motor with a continuous rating of 6000 shp at 90 rpm that was directly connected to the propeller shaft. The generator had two poles, while the motor had eighty. This gave a speed ratio of 40:1 between the main turbine and propeller shaft. So the overall effect of the electric propulsion system was to act just like a reverse-reduction gear for the main turbine. For comparison, the T2 could generate enough power to supply light, power and heat to a city of 25,000.

A synchronous motor is not self-starting. During the starting period, the turbine was at idle speed. When the motor was ready to be synchronized, as indicated by flickering on the ammeter, DC field excitation was applied to the rotor and the generator excitation was reduced to normal. Only when the motor was 'in step' with the generator, could you increase the turbine speed. Variations in propeller speed were controlled by varying the speed of the main turbine generator by means of the governor control lever at the engineer's control cubicle.

Most of the auxiliary equipment in the machinery spaces was

Below: The World War II assembly building was still in use in the Swan Island shipyard in 2020.

Above: T2 electric shaft motor had a continuous rating of 6000 shaft horsepower (4500 kW) at 90 rpm, giving a top speed of 16 knots.

electric, like the three 200 hp cargo pumps and two 50 hp stripping pumps. Major deck machinery was steam-driven to facilitate speed control. Since the main power system operated at variable voltage and frequency, the main generator could not be used to supply auxiliary power, except when the ship was in port. The steering gear was electro-hydraulic with two motor driven pumps. Bridge control was by means of a hydraulic telemotor.

....

Part Two

The Kaiser Yards in Close-up

7

HENRY J KAISER – THE FATHER OF MODERN SHIPBUILDING

Henry J Kaiser was born in 1882 in the village of Sprout Brook in the Mohawk Valley, a rural area of northern NY state usually referred to as 'up-state New York.' His family had immigrated from Germany and his father was a shoemaker who moved the growing family to the town of Whitesboro, four miles from the city of Utica. Henry dropped out of school at the of age thirteen after his mother died, and by the time he was sixteen, he had begun a career in photography. He married his wife Bess in 1907, and they moved west to Spokane, where he decided the new world of road building offered better prospects. He worked as a salesman of construction material, tools, and machines, and came into contact with the managers of civil engineering and road construction projects. When his employer went bankrupt in 1914 building a 2½-mile road in British Columbia, he decided to take over the job after a local bank offered him a loan of $25,000. He succeeded and began bidding on contracts as the 'Henry J Kaiser Company, Ltd'.

He was known for working long hours, often spending the entire day supervising his men, and quickly earned the reputation for finishing jobs ahead of time and on budget. Soon the company began winning contracts for million-dollar projects and the focal point of its operations shifted permanently to Oakland, California. Kaiser achieved considerable financial success and Bess gave birth to two sons: Edgar Fosburgh (1908–1981) and Henry John, Jr (1917–1961).

Kaiser expanded the scope of his business by vertical integration, operating his own gravel and sand pits and building concrete-mixing plants. One significant step came in 1927 when he won a contract to build roads in Camagüey Province, Cuba. His team laid down over 300 miles of roads and more than 500 bridges through some very swampy country. Kaiser was now becoming well-known in the USA and became friends with Warren A Bechtel, also a descendant of German immigrants, who would go on to lead the largest construction company in the United States. He made an important connection with the pioneer heavy-equipment manufacturer, R G LeTourneau, who invented and produced many types of earth-moving machines that replaced horse-drawn equipment and totally revolutionized the industry. (In 1958, he introduced the electric axle-drive concept that has become the basis of modern hybrid electric-vehicle design.)

Above: Henry Kaiser (left) and his son Edgar, who was responsible for all three Kaiser Van-Port shipyards. Behind them is Albert Bauer, manager of OSC.

Kaiser also contributed to the evolution of heavy vehicles when truck manufacturers refused to make dump trucks for him powered by diesels. He bought the trucks anyway and swapped out the gasoline engines. This resulted in an increase in power and huge savings in fuel. This experience would prove invaluable when the 1920s road-building boom subsided. Kaiser began to look for new sectors to keep his small army of construction workers employed; in 1928 he approached Warren Bechtel and suggested that their two companies join forces to bid on a huge dam proposal for the US Department of Reclamation on the Colorado River south of Las Vegas in southern Nevada.

Eventually, Kaiser and Bechtel realized the project was too large even for them and the bidding team expanded into a

Previous pages: Swan Island piping shop with a total of 14 women and 33 men hard at work during the graveyard shift. Hanging tubes and funnels are to extract fumes. The graveyard shift was the best paid, but the hard work and antisocial hours are apparent in this image. (See p 192)

Above: Boulder Dam dump truck: the Six Companies pioneered the use of modern transport methods to move vast quantities of sand, rock and cement by rail, conveyor belt and truck to reach the dam site.

collective of some of the largest construction firms in the western United States that became known as the 'Six Companies'. Kaiser was made chairman of the consortium in recognition of his unique ability to get people to work together. Observers have noted that this was the time when he began to emerge as a national figure because of his flair for public speaking – and self-promotion. With Kaiser representing the group, the Six Companies won the contract to build the new dam.

The Hoover Dam (known as the Boulder Dam during construction) was one of the largest projects in the world and many engineering problems had to be solved before it was completed in 1935 in the middle of the Great Depression. The Six Companies remained active and was responsible for projects like the San Francisco-Oakland Bay Bridge and some complex highway tunnels that changed the landscape and lives of millions of people in the western states. This success resulted in national acclaim for the Six Companies – and Kaiser in particular – as he began to develop a personal relationship with President Franklin D Roosevelt.

In 1932, while campaigning for the presidency, Roosevelt called attention to the 'vast possibilities of power development on the Columbia River'. He envisioned two big dams, the largest in Northeast Washington state, the second at the western end of the Columbia Gorge. They would fit into his plan for a 'New Deal' under the Public Works Administration by creating jobs, farms and the development of new business opportunities. The Six Companies joined another conglomerate to start the construction of the Grand Coulee dam in 1935. It was one of the largest structures ever built by mankind – a mass of concrete standing 550ft high and almost a mile long. It contains 12 million cubic yards of concrete, took eight years to build, and employed thousands of men during the Great

Above: Henty Kaiser and *The Oregonian* publisher Palmer Hoyt discuss how to publicize his 'sky ships' scheme.

Depression. When completed in 1942, Grand Coulee was the largest power station in the United States, at maximum flow generating 6809 MW. This provided the enormous electrical power necessary to manufacture aluminium in the region, essential for wartime production of planes and ships, and powered the production of plutonium at the nearby Hanford Site, where the first atomic bombs were produced.

The Six Companies also began work on the Bonneville dam, 40 miles upstream from Vancouver, Washington. It too provided many technical challenges before it was opened in 1938. These two Columbia River dams brought Henry Kaiser – and his son and top manager Edgar – back to the Pacific Northwest and rewarded him with an Increased reputation as a 'can-do' leader, new skills, and perhaps most importantly, the international contacts that gave him access to national leaders.

The national interest in the Grand Coulee was so great that the media turned Kaiser into one of the senior circle of top busi-

Below: Boulder Dam First Aid Post: this huge project in the Nevada desert provided the first lesson for Henry Kaiser of the need to protect the workforce from heat-related conditions and industrial accidents, which enabled him to provide full health insurance for his men on the Grand Coulee Dam.

Above: Henry Kaiser and a Liberty ship model at the Oregon Ship Corporation offices.

nessmen in the public mindset. In one *Fortune* magazine article, Kaiser was referred to as an 'Atlas of Industry'. In 1941 the BPA (Bonneville Power Administration) hired folk singer Woody Guthrie to compose songs to help inform the public about the benefits from Bonneville and other Columbia River hydroelectric facilities, but Pearl Harbor intervened and they were lost to the world for a decade.

In 1935, as work was progressing on the Hoover Dam, Henry and Edgar decided to take on a smaller more artistic project: a summer retreat on Lake Tahoe. Henry was drawn to this location as a place where he could pursue his interest in boating, especially powerboat racing, that he had developed when he worked at Lake Placid, New York. He found a 15-acre lake-front parcel in Tahoe Pines with a spectacular setting. With a stream traversing the property, it was quite marshy, especially in the spring when the snow melted, and considered 'un-buildable'. As usual, Henry saw only opportunity and of course, it was done in typical Kaiser style in a mere 30 days, employing a crew of 300 around the clock with few of the architect's plans complete. The lavish estate included a boat dock and private yacht club. They called it Fleur du Lac ('Flower of the Lake').

Henry Jr was also active in the business; he was administrative manager of one of the shipyards at Richmond, California and the Kaiser Steel plant at Fontana, California early in the war. He later took over direction and reorganization of the Brewster Aeronautical Corporation at Bristol, Pennsylvania at the request of the US Navy. His goal was to speed up the production lines for its Corsair fighter planes. In 1944, he learned he was suffering from multiple sclerosis, but continued with his workload through the war and into the 1950s.

In 1944 Kaiser's conglomerate employed 250,000 workers: they extracted coal and ore, produced cement, steel, and magnesium, and built roads, dams, ports, cargo ships, airplanes, and munitions. After the war, Kaiser's empire grew. He moved into steel, aluminium and concrete production, real estate and health care. In 1946 he teamed with auto executive Joseph Frazer to assemble Kaiser and Frazer cars. Production was centred at Willow Run, Michigan, the largest building in the world, constructed by the US government for Henry Ford to build B-24 Liberator bombers. Kaiser quit building cars in 1955, and the following year they switched to making a commercial version of the World War II Jeep, originally built

Below: Henry Kaiser giving a speech at a launch.

Above: Edgar Kaiser and the wife of Oscar S Cox, Assistant Solicitor General of the USA, at the launch of SS *Bladensburg*, the 26th tanker.

by the ailing Willys-Overland company. The Jeep models turned a healthy profit and the Kaiser Jeep Corporation was sold to AMC in 1970.

In 1961 Henry Jr died aged 44, despite his father's best efforts to find a cure. Edgar began spending most of his time on his Orcas Island home in the San Juan Islands, and Fleur du Lac fell into disuse. It was sold but the next owner had difficulty making it pay – until 1973, when it was chosen by Francis Ford Coppola as a location for the second Godfather film. It won six Oscars and the lakefront scenes are remembered by millions of the fans of the Godfather series as the residence of the Corleone clan. But the connection with the Kaisers was rarely if ever mentioned in any reviews.

Henry Kaiser delivered nearly 1500 vessels in the war effort and has been called the 'father of modern shipbuilding'. He was the most influential businessman in the western states during the emergency period 1940–45. His organization directed over a hundred companies that supplied materials to all branches of the US military machine. The concrete he manufactured at the Permanente plant built docks, runways and bases in the Pacific theatre – and now looks down on Silicon Valley. The Kaiser steel mill in Ontario in southern California delivered steel to all his shipyards and to many other users. And as many writers have

Above: Henry Kaiser and Admiral Vickery of MarCom seated, with Edgar Kaiser and Carl Flesher, Pacific coast regional director MarCom, standing.

noted, the electricity generated by the dams he built fuelled the war industries on the Columbia River and in the Bay Area.

However, despite his numerous achievements, Henry felt the Kaiser 'Permanente' health foundation he established was the most lasting. On his 85th birthday, he told reporters: 'Of all the things I've done, I expect only to be remembered for my hospitals. They're the things that are filling the people's greatest need – good health.' Affordable health care was a new idea in 1941 where people would prepay for health services at Kaiser's hospitals and clinics rather than go to higher cost fee-for-service providers, but providing it for all Americans remains as elusive as it was in the Depression. Henry J Kaiser died in 1967, aged 85, in Honolulu, Hawaii.

Kaiser's greatest achievement was memorialized by the naming of the USNS *Henry J Kaiser* (T-AO-187), the first of an 18-ship class of 677ft fleet replenishment oilers, all delivered between 1986 and 1995. They carry 180,000 barrels of diesel and jet fuel, and replaced ageing vessels dating back to World War II and the 1950s.

8

THE 'OBSOLETE' STEAM ENGINE THAT POWERED THE LIBERTY FLEET

The question of how to power the ships of the Liberty Fleet occupied the finest minds at the Maritime Commission for many months, as they tried to continue the line of superior modern ships they had been developing in the late 1930s. This was in direct contrast to the Ocean class ship that the British

Below: The Iron Fireman brochure featured the completely assembled Liberty engine before shipping. This one was installed in the *Joseph N Teal*, the famous '10-Day ship'. According to the brochure, 'These 2500 hp engines are 23 feet high, 22 feet long, 16 feet 8 inches wide and weigh 270,000 lbs.'

The marine engines which Iron Fireman Industrial Division is producing, one of which is shown above, are 23 ft. high, 22 ft. long, 16 ft. 8 in. wide, weigh 270,000 lbs. and develop 2500 h.p. Engine No. 12 was used on the 10-day Kaiser-built Liberty ship "The Joseph N. Teal," which was launched in Portland recently.

mission was seeking to commission, and for a very obvious reason: Britain was at war, with bombs falling daily on London and the industrial centres, and the Royal Navy had requisitioned every steam turbine the country could produce for the foreseeable future.

There was really no debate over the decision to choose a traditional triple-expansion reciprocating (piston-driven) steam engine, based on a design from the North Eastern Marine Engineering Co of Wallsend-on-Tyne in north-eastern England. This company was established in 1865 and was one of Britain's leading manufacturers of marine engines. Their 2500 hp (1900 kW) engine was 21ft (6.4m) long, 19ft (5.8m) tall and weighed 135 tons. It was designed to directly drive the propeller at 76 rpm and should propel a Liberty ship at about 11 knots. One of the last great ships to use this 'obsolete' technology was none other than the RMS *Titanic* in 1911, but it continued to be installed in common coasters and tramp ships into the 1930s.

By the time President Roosevelt had made the decision to order 200 emergency cargo ships, every steam turbine produced in the USA was reserved for the US Navy and the Maritime Commission found itself in exactly the same quandary as the British. The controversial choice to follow the British example was quickly proven to be correct. Compared to the complex steam turbine with its multiple rows of precisely angled fan-blades and high-speed reduction gear, the traditional steam engine was much cheaper and far easier to build in the vast numbers required for the Liberty ship program.

The plans were re-drawn to include the change from a coal-burner to an oil-burning boiler, reviewed, approved and sent to the General Machinery Corporation of Hamilton, Ohio. This was where the first patterns were made, castings poured and machined, and the cylinders and their associated valve chests bolted together forming a complete block. This could easily be dis-assembled for overhauls or repair. The prototype was given a test run in the shop and, immediately after, the systems were checked and the engine stripped down so all the moving parts could be examined carefully to ensure the tolerances were still correct.

Only then could the plans be reproduced and sent to the

Above: Cranes lift the 40-ton engine block No 12 at OSC for the *Joseph N Teal*. 'The 2500 hp 135-ton steam engine was separated into three parts for handling – base, condenser and the 40-ton cylinder block shown here were lifted into the hull in a brief and record-breaking hour.'

Right: A closer view of the engine being hoisted into the *Joseph N Teal*.

foundries and machine shops that had been selected as official engine builders. These steps were vitally important because the EC2 was about to become the first design of merchant ship in the world to have a standard engine-room and machinery design with complete inter-changeability of all parts. This was a revolutionary feature for a large ship and later made for great savings in time needed for repairs. Ships could assist each other with spare parts, or usable parts could be removed from vessels damaged beyond repair. It was also a remarkable reversal for the Maritime Commission and the established shipyard owners who had viewed the British choice of a 'no-frills' ship with a traditional steam engine with complete disdain only a few months before.

These triple expansion 2500 h.p. engines weigh 135 tons.

IRON FIREMAN
MANUFACTURING COMPANY

T. H. BANFIELD, *President*
E. C. SAMMONS, *Vice President*
FRANK S. HECOX, *Secretary-Treasurer*

ADMINISTRATIVE OFFICES

4784 S. E. 17th Avenue
Portland, Oregon

Plants at
PORTLAND, CLEVELAND, TORONTO

Branches and offices at Chicago, St. Louis, New York, Brooklyn, Boston, Milwaukee, Montreal

☆

INDUSTRIAL DIVISION

1870 S. W. Front Avenue
Portland, Oregon

JACK L. JENNINGS, *Production Manager*
H. W. BATES, *Director of Purchasing*
FRANK S. WHITE, *Superintendent of Production*
WALTER W. JAHNKE, *General Shop Foreman*
CHARLES G. THOMAS, *Assembly Foreman*

First Anniversary

IRON FIREMAN

PLANT NO. 3

PORTLAND, OREGON
February 14, 1943

End of First Year . . .
67 Engines Old

Willamette Iron & Steel, and Iron Fireman Manufacturing were able to start producing these engines with only a few weeks preparation. The speed with which the Portland foundries were quickly able to tool up and begin manufacturing this machinery proved that this was a completely functional product for an emergency ship, if somewhat anachronistic. Their first impression of the engine was the openness of its structure that made most of its moving parts easy to see and access.

The steam enters at a pressure of 220 pounds per square inch with a maximum (superheat) steam temperature of 450° F and 26 inches of vacuum. The term 'triple expansion' refers to the fact that steam is fed in turn to the three cylinders, one after the

Left: The Iron Fireman brochure promoting the company's production of steam engines in Portland and aircraft parts in the large Cleveland, Ohio plant.

Below: According to their publicity, 'The Iron Fireman plant covers approximately 200ft x 600ft. This plant produced 10 Liberty engines a month, most are delivered to the famous Kaiser Oregon Shipbuilding Corporation. A large expansion is now under construction.'

other. The beauty of this system is that although there is a drop in steam pressure in each cylinder, they all have the same stroke of 48 inches and a progressive increase in the diameter of the cylinders produces the same power from each, which balances the loading on the crankshaft.

The three cylinders were:

1) High Pressure (24 inches diameter, 220 psi)
2) Intermediate Pressure (37 inches diameter, 75 psi)
3) Low Pressure (70 inches diameter, 15 psi)

Lubrication of the engine was performed manually and by gravity feed, with engineers and oilers having to lean over into the massive, moving parts to oil the critical points using the 'hands-on' technique. One issue was that the only men who had experience with steam engines were near or past retirement age, and they would all be needed to train a new generation. But the engine's workings could be learned quickly and many Liberties sailed with 'black gang' crews of oilers and firemen as young as 16 years of age – with one or two veterans in their 70s.

The Liberty ship's twin oil-fired boilers were based on a Babcock & Wilcox water-tube design with a cross drum, 4852 square feet of heating surface, and superheaters. This type had been used extensively in ships built by the US Government during and after World War I. They were suitable for the Liberty ship design because of their simplicity, reliability, durability and ease of fabrication by other industrial boiler makers like the Puget Sound Machinery Depot in Washington, who produced most of the boilers for the Van-Port Kaiser yards.

The propeller shaft was 13½ inches in diameter and ran some 150ft from the engine to the propeller, which was 18ft wide. The shaft was separated from the cargo hold by a watertight shaft tunnel, big enough for a man to walk through and inspect the nine bearings supporting the shaft, which had to be checked twice a week.

Below: Iron Fireman was one of several foundries in Portland casting steel for the war effort. The Liberty ship engine required numerous 'pours' of molten steel to produce the cylinders, legs and base.

IRON FIREMAN

The Iron Fireman company was the first to start pouring steel. Its original plant occupied an old building in SW Portland on Front Street, built in 1853 as the Oregon Territory Prison. In 1866 it was converted to a factory making paper-mill machinery. In the 1920s, Iron Fireman made mechanical stokers for coal furnaces here before moving into a bigger space across the Willamette in 1942. Fortunately, Larry Barber saved the brochure and photos celebrating the 'First Anniversary of Plant No 3' on 14 February 1943, having delivered 67 engines. It lists a calendar of achievements in 1942 that reveals how it had re-tooled to produce the most important component of the Liberty Fleet. The first complete engine went straight into one of Kaiser's Liberty ships.

1942

14 February. Received order from Maritime Commission for 45 triple-expansion marine engines.

20 February. Signed lease for vacant plant.

16 March. Started moving in machinery.

Above: Small horizontal boring machine finishing casting for steam engine base at Iron Fireman.

1 May 1. Production started.

18 June. Delivered first engine – 6 weeks ahead of schedule.

30 June. Production for June – 2 engines.

21 July. Admiral Howard L Vickery of the USMC visited the plant and expressed amazement that a plant starting from scratch could be producing ahead of schedule.

31 July. Production for July – 4 engines.

14 August. Purchased plant.

31 August. Production for August – 5 engines. (Engine # 12, delivered at the end of August, was installed in the *Joseph N Teal* – the famous 'Ten Day Ship'.)

30 September. Production for September – 6 engines.

5 October. Received contract from USMC for 84 additional engines.

31 October. Production for October – 8 engines.

30 November. Production for November – 10 engines.

22 December. Received contract from USMC for additional 52 engines.

31 December. Production for December – 12 engines.

1943. We expect to produce 200 engines in 1943.

31 January. Production for month – 14 engines.

(The first 105 engines were priced at $120,000 each.)

On 15 September 1942, the Defense Plant Corporation had authorized a 50 percent increase in capacity. A 24,000 sq ft wooden addition was erected and more machinery installed, making this the third largest builder of the engines with a total of 345 delivered. Iron Fireman also built parts for Oregon War Industries and Willamette Iron & Steel. They won the Maritime 'M' award given to only about 3 percent of the manufacturers supporting the World War II maritime effort. At the peak, the workforce numbered 1200 – 400 per shift.

23 June 1943. Order for 207 engines at 22–24 per month costing $96,628 each.

2 February 1944. The entire plant burned to the ground. 'The fire blazed most of the night. The next day, the smouldering ruins revealed the stark skeletons of four completed engines. 21 engines were in various stages of completion. It was one of the most costly and spectacular fires in the city's history,' said *The Oregonian*. The factory had completed 358 engines, and a dozen more stood in the midst of the wreckage after the fire was extinguished.

Since Oregonship was converting to turbine-engined Victory ships, that was the end of the major war effort for Iron Fireman. The 77 engines remaining from their contract were assigned to Hendy Iron Works in California. The Portland foundries produced a total of 567 engines, 292 for local use. After the war, Iron Fireman developed oil-fired burners at their Cleveland facility, and consolidated the business in that location.

US FOUNDRIES BUILT 2744 IDENTICAL 135-TON ENGINES

Eighteen American companies on the east and west coast built identical engines, plus two in Canada supplying Canadian shipyards. Iron Fireman was the third most productive on this list, and WISCO built over 200. The leader was the Joshua Hendy Iron Works in Sunnyvale, California, founded in 1859 during the California Gold Rush. The company became famous for its mining equipment, but slumped during the Depression and found a new market by contracting for the building of giant gates and valves for the Hoover, Boulder and Grand Coulee dams. It was close to shutting down in 1940 when it was rescued with financial support from the Six Companies.

Below: Iron Fireman: boring the low-pressure cylinder of the triple-expansion engine. This is the largest cylinder with a bore (diameter) of 70in and stroke of 48in.

The Hendy Iron Works was one of the first companies to win an order from the Maritime Commission – for twelve steam engines. By 1943 it had reduced the time required to manufacture a marine steam engine from 4500 hours to 1800 hours. The number of workers employed by the company also grew dramatically, reaching a peak of 11,500. By the end of the war, Hendy had supplied the engines for 754 of America's 2751 Liberty ships, over one quarter of the total. They also produced diesels, steam turbines and reduction gears, showing a remarkable ability to meet the needs of California's busy shipyards.

AUXILIARY MACHINERY

On the Liberty ships, steam powered every system using numerous small piston-driven steam engines. Electrical power was furnished by three steam-powered 400 rpm, 167 amps, 120 volts, 25 kW generators. Electrical requirements were moderate during wartime service since the ship was blacked out at night. The only demands were for navigation and radio equipment, two fresh water pumps, the degaussing system (to protect against magnetic mines), room fans and interior lighting.

The refrigeration compressor kept the meat and fish rooms at 15° F, dairy room at 30° F, vegetable room at 40° F. Fresh water for boilers and drinking was provided by a high pressure vertical submerged type, salt water evaporator capable of desalinating 25 tons of sea water per day, at a cost of one barrel of fuel per ton of water. One distiller had a capacity of 6000 gallons per day.

The steering gear was of the two-cylinder type, with a steam engine controlled by telemotor from the wheelhouse and an extension from the steering wheel to the upper bridge. On the

Below: Iron Fireman: machining the 36,000 lbs crankshaft on a large lathe.

west coast, over 1000 steering engines were manufactured by the Webster-Brinckley company of Seattle. This gear was capable of moving the rudder from hard-over to hard-over (70 degrees) in 30 seconds when the vessel was going full ahead.

SPEED AND PERFORMANCE

The Liberty Fleet is generally described – and criticized – as being 'underpowered' with only 2500 hp resulting in a service speed of 11 knots and a maximum of 13 knots. Critics pointed out that this made them easy targets for enemy submarines and aircraft. Certainly, the crews had no defence against a U-boat and would have welcomed more speed when they were trying to outrun a submarine. But this criticism does not stand up well to examination. Consider that many passenger liners and naval vessels were torpedoed while travelling at a far higher speed than 12 knots. And what difference would a couple of knots make when under attack by an aircraft? The speed of a convoy was dictated by the slowest vessel in the fleet, which was likely to be an older ship from the 1920s, not a Liberty. And if the convoy encountered a wolf pack of six or more submarines, it was the actions of the escort ships, more than the speed of the convoy, that would protect the cargo ships.

In the 1930s 2500 hp was still the standard size for a low-power cargo ship of around 400ft in length, regardless of the engine type. A larger steam engine of 3000 hp or more would have been harder to build and heavier to transport to the yards. It would also have taken up more hold space and burned more fuel at 12–15 knots. The Liberty hull has a beam/length ratio of 7.3 and is slender by today's standards. The prismatic coefficient is about 0.75 and the speed–length ratio at 11.5 knots was about 0.55. This meant it was very efficient at that speed. At 11 knots, fuel burn on a Liberty was 170 barrels per day for a range of 20,000 miles. A temporary higher speed of 12.5 knots was possible with a slightly higher steam pressure, increase in fuel consumption to 240 barrels per day, and a drop in range to about 14,000 miles.

In 1940 when Britain's survival depended on this turn-of-the-century engineering marvel, neither the British or the Americans seemed to think the engine deserved a name, a number or any combination of the two. Except for a small builder's nameplate, it remained anonymous throughout its life. Yet many hundreds of these ships and their obsolete engines remained in civilian service until the 1960s with a remarkably good record for reliability.

....

9

PRE-FABRICATION AND MASS PRODUCTION IN THE KAISER SHIPYARDS

'No shipyard in the world ever built a big freighter as quickly as the Oregon Shipbuilding Corp of Portland, Oregon, owned by Henry J Kaiser, who by now has hardly any shipbuilding records to break except those that he himself has set.'

LIFE Magazine, 12 October 1942

Todd and Kaiser intended to revolutionize shipbuilding by adopting pre-fabrication to streamline the traditional process that required cutting each part individually and assembling them one by one on the slipway. Instead, they would mass-produce parts for a half dozen ships at a time, weld them into sections, then weld these sections together on the slip rather than rivet them. Previously, shipyards had been thought of in terms of acres; Kaiser's yards covered square miles so that the mountains of materials could be stored and handled efficiently.

His yards were laid out like giant factories with the steel plate and parts flowing smoothly from railcars through the shops to the vessel under construction. It was here that all the dynamics of material flow, the rhythm of operations, and the management of masses of workers that the company had learned in a quarter century of civil engineering came into play. Like the dams, roads, and the other Kaiser projects, the ships were illuminated at night by great banks of floodlights – running on hydro-electric power from the Bonneville dam – so the action never stopped.

Each Liberty ship consumed about 3425 tons of hull steel, of which 2725 tons was plate, plus 700 tons of shaped steel and 50,000 castings. At the peak of shipbuilding in 1943, Oregonship used more than a hundred receiving agents to handle as many railcars each day. A team of steel checkers organized 600,000 different plates and shapes in their 'library of steel', from two-ton plates for tanker hulls to thousands of smaller shapes. The amount of steel in storage ranged from 50,000 to 115,000 tons, all marked and stacked to be available whenever needed. Something like 250,000 separate parts went into the finished ship, and every part had to be inventoried by hand.

Then it was picked up by mobile cranes that ran in tracks across the yard and deposited outside the plate shop that needed it. There was a separate shop for each of the eleven ways and it was here that the plate was transformed into a part of the ship by cutting to shape, bending or flanging if necessary, punching and drilling. The goal was to have most of these parts welded into a sub-assembly. Every finished part had to have a code number painted on it to indicate what it was and where it went.

The major yards received raw materials by rail and loads of pre-assembled components from local metal shops by truck. Small parts that were easy to pack and transport like nuts and bolts, switches and a thousand other items were supplied by large and small manufacturing facilities all across America. These deliveries went to many distinct departments all over the yards: the pipe shop where great lengths of piping and hundreds of valves were prepared for each ship, and the electrical shop where enough wire, lights, switches and fuse boxes to equip a village had to be boxed up and ready when the electricians moved onboard at the outfitting dock. There was as much as five miles of wiring and seven miles of piping in each ship.

In the machine shops, the activity needed to produce any part of the hull was broken down into a series of simple tasks on a short production line where steel plate was marked, cut, holes drilled, angles bent, and stiffeners welded on. It emerged from the line as a standard item ready to move into the assembly hall. For an example, consider a large beam that was cut to length to support the main deck. Its code might look like this: 'D-DKL-GIRD WEB PLT FRS 12–17 HULL 2268 STAR'. This identified it as the fourth (D) deck girder (DKL-GIRD) running between the twelfth and seventeenth (12–17) web plate frames (WEB PLT FRS) on the starboard side of hull 2268. Transferring those codes from the wooden template to the finished part was a task that required a sharp mind – and a steady hand with a paint brush. This important work was often done by teams of women working under older shipyard professionals who may have been happily retired before Pearl Harbor. Hundreds of full-size templates were stored in the mold loft, some of them as wide as the ship. They had to be pulled out and laid on the raw plate to ensure every part was identical.

Most of the sub-assembly work could be done under the

extended roof of the prefab shop, which was welcome in the rainy weather that Portland experienced for much of the year. This enabled large sections of the ship like deckhouses, double-bottom sections, bulkheads and bow and stern units to be assembled as efficiently as possible. The complete section was then pushed down the roller way and moved outside where the overhead crane lifted it onto a 20ft-wide multi-wheel trailer to be stockpiled at the head of the ways.

The exception was the massive forepeak that was simply too big to build indoors. Oregonship fabricated them on a special skid that combined a tall A-shaped jig with scaffolding to form the bow section upside down. Mobile cranes were used to hoist the curved plates into place to form the stem, cutwater and cable locker with hawseholes port and starboard for the two anchor chains. The finished product stood 40ft in height and weighed 50 tons, and looked quite alien until it was turned over and lifted onto the front of the keel.

Effective transportation within the yard was vital to avoid bottlenecks and traffic jams when sections weighing up to 85 tons were being transported directly to the head of the ways. Contemporary film makers always included shots of the double-wide flat-bed vehicles hauling a large section across the yard. (Today we call them 'modules' and think they are a very modern invention of the computer age.) When the section was needed, one or two Whirley cranes lifted it up and into the hull. Only then was it necessary for the welding teams to climb up onto the ship to join the section to the hull.

An early experiment was attempted in Vancouver to lift a complete deckhouse onto the deck of a Liberty ship in a special berth with an overhead crane, but the spreader bar could not take the strain and dropped the house onto the deck. Luckily, there were no serious injuries on that occasion,

Below: By the look of the spectators, this is a demonstration of an automated oxy-acetylene cutting-table, one of the earliest advances in automation that the Kaiser yards quickly adopted and adapted.

Left: A wide-angle view of Swan Island's eight ways. The centre building is marked 'Way End No 4'. Completed assemblies are moved down each roadway to the ship by trailer or crane, when needed. The large number, and variety of cranes is apparent.

Left and below: Two men operate a Unionmelt machine that is welding a series of plates together on the assembly hall floor. The reel automatically feeds the wire into the seam while the funnel feeds flux onto the wire.

Above: A welder drives a wedge to align two plates before welding commences.

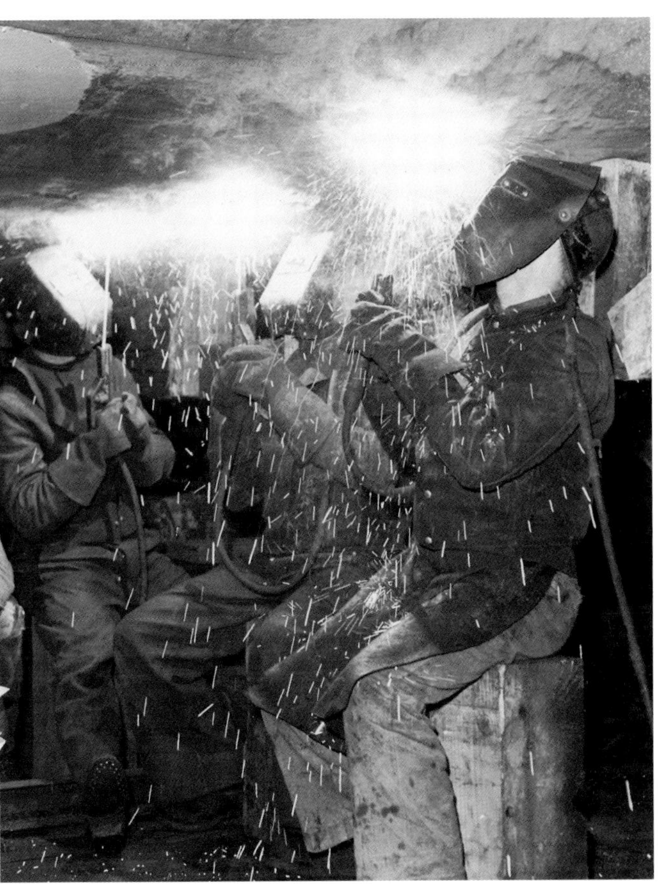

Above: Three welders working on one bottom plate. Overhead welding was only performed by experienced craftsmen or women.

Right: Two welders working on one bottom seam. Because overhead welding was the most difficult, it often attracted the attention of the photographer.

though these did occur more often than the public imagined, and lives were lost in the rush to meet quotas that left no time for safety inspections. After that failure, the yards resumed the original procedure of cutting the finished house into four or five blocks and lifting them one at a time, then welding them back together.

The local press gave Kaiser all the credit for applying mass production techniques, as do most modern historians, but this technology was being used at all the emergency yards, especially in the biggest yard in the nation, Bethlehem-Fairfield in Baltimore, Maryland, which employed 46,700 workers at its peak, including 6000 African-Americans. Running full bore and prefabricating anything their cranes could lift, the Kaiser yards all shrank construction time from the 240 days at the start of the war to 60 days a year later, then dropped still further to an unimaginable average of 30 days in 1943. By then as many as three Liberties a day were being launched. With the benefit of its own steel works nearby, the Baltimore yard rivalled the Kaiser plants with its own proud record of 384 Liberty ships, 94 Victories and 30 LSTs – also celebrated locally as a 'world record'. In 1946 government records showed that the seven Kaiser yards had delivered 1490 vessels: 821 Liberties, 219 Victories, 147 tankers, 87 combat transports, 50 escort carriers, 45 troop transports, 45 LSTs, and 12 frigates. Total cost was about $5 billion and the net profit was about $40 million or 1 percent. They built Liberty ships in ⅔ the time and at ¾ the cost of all other shipyards, thus saving the government more than $266 million.

STANDING TALL – SHIPYARD CRANES

A forest of cranes stood over the shipyards and were an essential part of the arsenal of democracy. Many types of cranes filled

Left: Transporting Liberty ship inner bottom sections to the 'pre-erection assembly area'.

different niches within the yard: gantry cranes ran through the biggest workshops and could lift sections up to 100 tons. A special hammerhead crane used two 'arms' to sort and feed raw steel in the plate shop. Railway cranes were used in the steel storage yard, while mobile cranes on tracks or wheels could be dispatched wherever they were needed. The most visible and photogenic were the whirley cranes.

Before he entered the shipbuilding business, Henry Kaiser's last project had been on the Grand Coulee Dam in NE Washington. During the six years it was under construction, a new type of crane was developed to get the job done quicker. It was called a 'whirley crane', a fast, readily moveable vehicle capable of handling large steel supports, big batches of concrete, and large dam conduits. The whirley was invented in the early 1920s by Clyde Wiley, president of the Clyde Iron Works, established in Duluth, Minnesota, in 1889. He designed it so that the boom and 'A' frame would turn in a 360-degree circle – hence the name. The cranes at the dam site had a 200-horsepower electric motor for the hoist cable and another 50 hp motor for swinging the boom, and could lift as much as 60 tons. The control cabin was 90 feet in the air, and skilled operating engineers communicated with riggers on the ground by telephone.

Below: Preparations for a Liberty ship launch on OSC's Way No 8 with mobile crane parked next to VIPs' cars.

HYSTER STRADDLE CARRIER

There were many other small ways the Kaiser yards became so efficient, like the many different vehicles that were used to lift

Liberty ships nearing completion and pre-fabricated inner bottom sections ready for the external plating. Four of these pre-erection areas built the bottoms for ships on the adjacent ways.

and carry small loads around the sprawling yards. The whirley cranes towered above the shipyards and were an appealing subject for journalists and photographers, but down on the ground, hundreds of minor lifts were required every day – specially to move steel plates into workshops. This was accomplished by the Hyster straddle carrier, a superbly functional vehicle that was invented in the northwest for the lumber business.

It seems to have escaped the eye of the historians, but makes a short appearance in a couple of shipyard films, including *We Build Tankers* about Swan Island. Here you will see a Hyster straddle carrier going about its daily work operated by a driver perched high in the air over its four spindly legs. The Hyster company began in Portland in the 1920s developing compact load-carrying vehicles to meet the needs of Pacific Northwest industries, especially lumber mills and yards. Their first heavy-duty forklift was built in 1935 with a lifting capacity up to 6000 lbs. Then the straddle carrier arrived on the scene with the ability to pick up and carry a standard stack of lumber between the four tall legs. This was immediately recognized as a valuable tool for the shipyards and was quickly adapted to move steel plates, long tubes and bars.

The Hysters did have a weak spot. Perched high above the ground, the drivers could barely see pedestrians, many of whom underestimated the vehicles' speed and were occasionally struck. The workers quickly identified this problem, and ingeniously solved the issue by equipping every Hyster with warning

Right: Activity stops in the yard while everyone watches as two cranes perform the delicate high-wire act of hoisting the bridge onto the superstructure.

Below: Three banks of welding machines at OSC, each supplying six welders, set in place around a hatch by a crane as work on the main deck beams proceeds.

6
WELDERS
OFFICE

bells and repositioning the driver's seat for better visibility. These vehicles were so well integrated into the Kaiser yards that the storage system where steel was held in vertical rows became known as a 'Hyster rack'.

By 1940 Hyster had developed another type of mobile lifter with a 10ft horizontal boom that was raised by a hydraulic ram that could lift almost any heavy item a foot or two off the ground. First known as the Cranemobile, it was renamed the Karry Krane and given a capacity of 4000 lbs at its tip and 10,000 lbs with the lifting point closest to the chassis. It was originally intended for use on the docks, but was also found to be a valuable vehicle in the shipyards. Kaiser loaded one on every escort carrier to move planes that were damaged, and almost 1000 were used during the war years from the home front to the bomb-damaged ports of Europe.

BRIGHTER THAN THE SUN – THE WELDER'S ART

As useful as pre-assembly was in cutting production time, the real key to speeding up shipbuilding was welding. It was calculated that there was over 100 miles of welding in a Liberty ship, and welders averaged 4–8 feet per hour, depending on the difficulty of the work and the worker's experience. Welding accounted for one third of the total time needed to build a Liberty ship, which was reduced to a total of around 500,000 man-hours in 1943. Compared to riveting, one worker could do the work of two or three. The first all-welded ship, the *Exchequer,* launched in 1940, came not from an old-line yard like Sun Ship, but the new Ingalls shipyard in Pascagoula, Mississippi.

Below: Oregonship burner cutting small parts from heavy steel plate. He is casually dressed, wearing only one glove, with no eye protection or apron.

Properly welded joints and seams were as strong or stronger than the surrounding steel, and automatic seam-welding machines added even greater speed to the process. The anonymous welder in a dark mask illuminated by the brilliant arc became the symbol of the shipyards and the physical connection between all the activities in the yard. A skilled welder can make a good solid seam almost anywhere, horizontal, vertical, overhead, angled. The novice welder had neither the skill nor experience to match an old hand. Welding seams on flat deck plates with gravity helping the flow was simple enough but overhead welding was much more difficult. The solution was to position seams so that the welder could work in a 'down-hand' position: that is, with gravity, not against it. That meant positioning the work in the shop to suit the worker. Large parts were rolled over with the overhead crane, so that most of the welding could be done by novices.

WELDING FAILURES

Welding was fast, but it had its drawbacks: uneven heating could result in weak joints or stress fractures. Where this occurred, it could be handled by reinforcing the affected areas with doublers, gussets, or riveted patches, as was done with the first T2 tanker. But the problem went deeper than that. When the SS *John P Gaines* broke in half and sank on 24 November 1943 with the loss of 10 lives, the Maritime Commission hurriedly set up a laboratory to investigate the causes.

This team of researchers were among the first to apply new methods and theories to materials science, which enabled them to identify low temperature, steel composition, and overheating of the weld as factors causing what they termed 'brittle fracture'. By the end of the war, three ships had been lost and hundreds repaired, but the Liberty fleet went on to serve for many more years, and ship technology improved markedly after the war.

RISKY BUSINESS

Other war industries competed for labour that was not as physically taxing or dangerous – and paid similar wages. So there was a slow but steady drift of workers from one defence industry to another and often shipbuilding lost more people than it gained. Working in production in the shipyards was not for the faint-hearted. Men and women suffered from the cold and

Above: A crew poses for Barber's camera. They look like shipwrights, responsible for building and maintaining all the wooden structures needed in the shipyard, from the staging around the hull to the wedges that released it onto the slipway. Note that most of them look too old for the military draft.

dampness in the winter in shipyards in cold climates; respiratory illnesses, especially pneumonia, were very common – and this was before penicillin was available.

Between the bombing of Pearl Harbor in December 1941 and the D-Day Invasion of Europe in June 1944, there were more industrial casualties on the Home Front than on the War Front. This high number of deaths would lead to improved workplace safety and regulations, as well as better access to affordable health care. Injuries were common in all the nation's shipyards, which were among the most dangerous occupations – more risky than the manufacture of tanks, aircraft or explosives!

There were dangers at every turn, and many injuries for Kaiser's clinics to treat. The pressure to produce was unrelenting with the continual reminder that more soldiers would die unless every worker did their part. Black novelist Chester Himes described a California shipyard this way: 'Everywhere was the hustle and bustle of moving, busy workers, trucks, plate lifts, yard cranes, electric mules, the blue flashes of arc welders brighter than the noonday sun. And the noise, always loud, unabating, ear-splitting.'

In his 1951 book *Ships for Victory* Frederic Lane stated there were 655 reported private shipyard fatalities in the nation during 1943 and 1944; falls caused almost 40 percent, vehicles or loads striking workers caused about 25 percent. In 1943 the US Maritime Commission launched a safety program that ultimately reduced the injury rate in the shipyards. For every 100 shipyard employees, there were 7.3 injuries in 1943, 5.5 in 1944, and 4.9 in 1945; in Richmond from 1942 to 1944, 248,000 patients were seen in Permanente Hospitals. A total of 13,261 fractures were treated; most common were fractures of the hands, of the feet, and of the ribs.

Welders, the 'royalty' of the shipyard, were proud of their status but faced complaints that they were overpaid. However, they were also exposed to hazards like the toxic fumes of vaporized metals. This was long before there was any public awareness of the health risks of industrial processes, so the issue of air pollution was low on the list of priorities in the yards. Most cases of 'metal fume fever' occurred when working on galvanized metals that give off zinc oxide gas.

Ventilation became a major issue for Maritime Commission health inspectors, who recommended the use of powerful fans and long canvas ducts to vent confined spaces where welding or painting was occurring, but they often failed to win the battle, despite its importance for the wellbeing of the workers. A common ailment in newly-trained welders who gripped the torch too tightly was commonly known as 'trigger fingers', which struck the third and fourth digits of the major hand.

THE OUTFITTING DOCK

In several of their official publications, the Kaiser company stressed the importance of the outfitting dock as the 'pivot point' of the whole yard.

> It is upon this division that the US Maritime Commission pins its hopes for the delivery of ships to meet the demands of the war. This is the 'home stretch' where every effort is made for a fast finish. The split-second schedule is even

Below: Launching a ship represents a considerable engineering challenge as well as a public spectacle and requires careful work by an experienced team. In World War II shipyards like this one, a special crew of craftsmen was organized and trained as slipway and launch specialists. They moved from shipway to shipway, preparing each hull well in advance for its eventual launch, starting with the keel blocks, temporary cribbing, and hull props. They returned when the launch ceremony neared to slather large amounts of grease along the ways, then drive heavy wooden wedges called 'poppets' under the hull, placed to leave space to assemble the timbers of the launch cradles.

During the launch ceremony, a signal was sent down via telephone to the crew under the ship – as seen here – the poppets were knocked away, one by one, until the ship finally began moving of its own weight to the river. A number of cables were connected to the ship stern with heavy 'drag' chains attached, to slow the hull as it accelerated down the ways. In Portland, the small tugs were diesel-powered but the large ones were steam-powered sternwheelers – a holdover from the pioneer days.

more important at this stage of construction than when the ship was on the ways. Any letdown, any slowing up, and or any bottleneck that occurs in outfitting is a direct hindrance to the war effort.

As soon as the vessel pulls up at the dock, riggers set about removing launching equipment. Whirley cranes load on welding machines, bundles of hoses, ventilating blowers, pipes and tools of all descriptions. At the first two berths, welding is completed on the superstructure and magazines so that water tests can be made. One craft cannot do its work until another is through. If any craft should become delayed,

Below: The busy outfitting dock at OSC with several Liberty ships moored.

Above: Carpenter connects speaking tube in the engine room to the bridge.

Below: Four plasterers leveling the poured floor in the ship's accommodation area during fitting-out.

it would disrupt the whole schedule. For example, there is certain welding that must be done before piping and wiring can be installed.

The ship moves from berth to berth as work progresses. There is a multitude of different types of work to be done by different classes of skilled workers. Laying the flooring takes two full days using a special red coating that spreads like cement. This work is done by National Tile & Marble Co. Painters begin work on decks, holds, and superstructures. Insulation and sheet metal work is done in the engine room, ammunition room and bilges. Gravel ballast is poured into the bilges of holds 2,3,4 and 5. An important job is pouring the plastic armor. This is a tar-like substance used around gun turrets and part of the superstructure. Oregon Ship credited a dozen local contractors who supplied important skills or products to the outfitting dock from engine room insulation to galley equipment.

Another big job is installation of eleven cargo booms. One is a 50-ton capacity boom, one a 15-ton, and the remaining nine are 5 tons. This is done by riggers who also attach ropes, cables, and tackle blocks. There were also hundreds of other tasks like installation of partitions, doors and fixtures by the joiners; finish carpentry in the officers' quarters; electrical work on the ship's bridge, asbestos insulation installation around pipes and wires; sheet-metal installation in the galleys and heads; the erection of cargo booms and fitted them with the cable, winches, and pulleys.

Various tests are also made. Such as the generator trials, yard test trials, and official dock trials. When Liberty ships were being outfitted, there were five berths on the outfitting dock, four alongside, and one on the end. When the longer Victories and AP-5s came in, this was cut down to four berths.

If the naval architects did not consider the function of every part, then the thousands of workers who handled them in the eighteen shipyards were happy to perform that task. And they invented literally thousands of ideas to reduce the production time.

THE EXPEDITER

Along with the recurring problems of insufficient manpower, training, facilities and transportation, there was always a shortage of materials. In response, the role of the 'expediter' was created. He was a 'salesman in reverse', a go-getter who found and bought hard-to-get parts and materials from coast to coast. Not allowed by railroad regulations to ride in the freight train caboose, he jumped on passenger trains, went on ahead, and waited in the freight yard for the boxcars with their big Kaiser stickers to roll in. Then he bothered everybody in sight until the train was on its way again, hopped another passenger train, and did the same thing at the next terminal. In short, he made life difficult for everybody who said 'It can't be done!' and has remained a symbol of the Kaiser spirit.

Perhaps the greatest triumph for the unseen, unsung expediters was in January 1945 when a string of sixteen flatcars loaded with main gears and turbines from the GE Plant in Schenectady, NY rolled into Oregon Ship after a hectic 7-day transcontinental freight run. This averted a serious delay in construction of four Victory ships on the ways. The three OSC expediters in Washington, DC described it as the most challenging of the war effort. They secured authorization for a special train from the U.S Maritime Commission regional office in Oakland, California and the Interstate Commerce Commission. The train departed on 15 January at 12:30 am on the New York Central Railway, flying the special blue train flag.

The expediters won an extension of the ICC special permit for the Union Pacific line as the train steamed west. It reached Porter, Indiana in just under 24 hours, and was turned over to the Chicago & Northwestern line to Council Bluffs, Iowa where the ICC special permit was extended. The train arrived at Cheyenne, Wyoming on 1 pm, Friday 19 January at near-passenger train speed. The crew next encountered blinding snow storms crossing the Continental Divide, but reached Pocatello, Idaho, at 9 am on Saturday. It finally pulled into the Oregon Ship yard on Monday night, 22 January, where the cargo was immediately unloaded and transported to the four ships. 'Orchids are certainly due to the fellows in Washington,' said Lee Damon, OSC Traffic department chief, and Charles Reynolds, OSC chief expediter.

HOUSE CLEANING IN THE SHIPYARD

Keeping the shipyard clean was one simple way of reducing injuries and there was an entire department dedicated to this with 1000 women and 414 men working full time at Oregonship, according to *The Bo's'n's Whistle*, the magazine of the Kaiser shipyards, in May 1943. Regardless of experience or job desired, all women began as sweepers. One group of 120 sweepers was kept at work on the 96,000 sq ft sub-assembly hall in front of the ways. On the ways, 450 workers were kept busy sweeping, picking up and salvaging steel scrap.

On the ships at the outfitting dock, 137 men and 144 women cleaned up in the holds, engine room and on deck. A crew of 24 men on each shift manned dump-trucks to haul away material collected by the cleaners. Every two hours, a truck full of salvaged material pulled away from the ways. Cleaners also picked up left-over welding rods, tools, hoses and electric cables and returned them to the tool room. Overall, a total of 3776 men and women kept the three Kaiser yards clean, wearing out about 1500 brooms a month!

....

10

THE TEN-DAY SHIP

On 28 September 1938 Franklin Delano Roosevelt made his second visit to the Pacific Northwest as US President for the ceremonial opening of the Bonneville Dam, the first hydro-electric barrage on the Columbia River that opened navigation upstream. The next five years saw a remarkable change in the region 100 miles inland from the Pacific Ocean. The twin cities of Portland, Oregon and Vancouver, Washington had leaped almost overnight from the hard-scrabble decade of the Great Depression and into one of the country's most productive ship-building centres.

On 23 September 1942 FDR returned to a city transformed by the war into a shipbuilding centre that was leading a revolution in ship construction methods. His arrival in Portland by special train was precisely scheduled to coincide with the launching of the Liberty ship SS *Joseph N Teal*, which was completed in the incredible time of ten days. The ship was launched by his daughter Anna as the sponsor, with the president watching from his open limousine.

The photograph of this ceremony and the report of FDR's speech are still used today to symbolize the impressive feats of the Kaiser yards and the entire emergency shipbuilding program. There are many second-hand accounts of this event that typically look like this: 'The Kaiser shipyard in Portland established a speed record for construction of a Liberty ship when the *Joseph N Teal* was completed in ten days. President Franklin D Roosevelt secretly attended the ship's christening by his daughter Anna Boettiger.'

This may be adequate in the age of the 'sound bite' but begs several important questions about this epic achievement, which was one of the most successful morale boosters of the entire war – and a severe blow to Axis propaganda. Using the fragile copies of *The Oregonian* that covered this event, which Larry Barber filed away, I have endeavoured to shed some light on the planning and organization behind this public-relations coup.

First of all, this was clearly not a last-minute decision: the Kaiser organization must have communicated with the White House well in advance to get approval for the idea of building a Liberty ship in record time. The best time in Portland was 26 days to launch in August, 1942, so they could have chosen 20 days and would still have made a statement about their ability. But Edgar and Henry Kaiser wanted more than a statement: they wanted to show the world what American ingenuity and fighting spirit could really do on the home front. They chose ten days, and they threw down the added challenge of completing the ship on the morning of the day that the presidential train would arrive.

Second, we must consider that knowledge of the presidential tour of defence plants was to be kept top secret. Of the approximately 14,000 people at work at Oregonship, only a handful knew that FDR would attend the launch. Strict secrecy had to be maintained, so only a handful of senior managers were informed of the presidential visit. Even then, no news of the tour was permitted in the media until the president had returned safely to the White House. (The only clue in Portland was the ramp that had been constructed in front of the record-breaking ship for the president's car.)

In this timetable, I have tried to combine the president's daily itinerary with Larry Barber's progress reports from OSC to show how challenging this task was.

13 September. Portland Day 1 – The keel blocks are already in place at Oregonship Slipway No 6 at 12:01 am. The whistle is blown and the crane lays the keel of the 80th Liberty ship, Hull No 581, *Joseph N Teal* in 15ft sections that are carefully aligned and welded together. The bottom plating comes next to create the outer skin, followed by the 60-ton double-bottom assemblies that are lowered by a pair of whirley cranes onto the bottom shell. The entire keel, shell, and double-bottom is welded into a single continuous structure, 400 feet long with a honeycomb of four-foot square boxes supporting the outer shell. It involves 6663 linear feet of welding.

14 September. Portland Day 2 – Transverse bulkheads, centre-line bulkheads, first section second deck, shell and frames begun, totalling 14,055 feet of linear welding.

Right: Day 5, 17 September – 'Second Deck completed. Machinery casing bulkheads, pumps-generators in place, main engine installation begins.' (It looks like summer is ending in Portland. Note the numerous portable shelters to protect the welding teams from the rain.)

15 September. Portland Day 3 – Shaft tunnel, second deck section; 23,091 feet of linear welding.

16 September. Portland Day 4 – Two boilers, generators, tool-room flats, additional second deck pumps; 35,403 feet of linear welding.

17 September. Portland Day 5 – Pipefitters begin laying and connecting 15,000 feet of piping. Installation of the 72-ton forepeak and stem, the 13-ton stern casting and 27-ton fantail, and more bulkheads. Second deck completed, machinery casing bulkheads, pumps, generators, main engine begun; 47,902 feet of linear welding.

Presidential train departs Washington DC.

18 September. Portland Day 6 – Hatch coamings begun, first section upper deck, main condensers; 62,749 feet of linear welding.

Below: Day 6, 18 September – 'Hatch coamings begun, first section upper deck, main condensers, 62,749ft linear welding.' (Note that the hatch coamings were fully assembled and painted before installation, and another welding station is being lowered to main deck by crane.)

Right: Day 8, 20 September – 'Mid superstructure, main engine installed, boilers bricked, mast houses, completion upper deck, hatch coamings. 92,273ft linear welding.' The 90-ton deckhouse was lifted in sections by two whirley cranes and re-assembled on the deck.

H580

FDR in Michigan state at Chrysler automobile plant producing Sherman tanks and the giant Ford plant building B-24 Liberator bombers.

19 September. Portland Day 7 – Completion upper deck, completion hatch coamings, 76,993 feet of linear welding.

FDR in Milwaukie, Wisconsin at Allis Chalmers, builders of M4 High Speed Tractors.

FDR's train begins heading west across the great plains.

20 September. Portland Day 8 – Main engine installed, boilers bricked, mast houses, mid superstructure; 92,273 feet of linear welding.

FDR's train reaches Rocky Mountains.

21 September. Portland Day 9 – Mid superstructure completed,

Above: Women's welding crew. Barber: 'Women burners who worked on the *Teal*'s house took time out for lunch, but the noon hour was their only relaxation as they helped to set the ten-day construction record.' This is one of the very rare occasions when Barber paid attention to the women in the shipyard.

Right: Day 9, 21 September – The superstructure is completed and the stack erected. The circular barbettes to protect the gun platforms have been installed on the foredeck and midships, work is proceeding on the lookout shields, rails and stanchions. In 48 hours, the ship must be ready to launch.

10
DAYS

Left: Day 11, 23 September – Ship 87 percent complete, launch crowd gathers before noon. (Barber took this shot before President Roosevelt made his surprise arrival.)

Below: Day 11, 23 September – FDR's daughter Anna Boettiger launches the *Joseph N Teal* with a traditional bottle of champagne. There were no matrons of honour present. Howard Nesbitt, pipefitter, presented a bouquet of savings stamps to her. She was the eldest and only girl of six children, who had a career as a journalist and publisher. By 1944, she had replaced her mother Eleanor in the White House and took over many of the duties of the First Lady. Her independent mother was then able to devote her time to charities and social programs involved in the war effort.

Overleaf, left: Day 11, 23 September – FDR and Henry Kaiser watch the christening from a platform specially built to allow him to remain seated in his car.

Overleaf, right: Day 11, 23 September – Launch: Oregonship's 75th Liberty ship, slides down the ways ten days after the keel was laid. (Barber gave the precise elapsed time as 10 days and 54 minutes.) This was the feat that put Henry Kaiser's first Portland yard in the headlines throughout the free world.

10
DAYS
WAY
5

10
DAYS

stack erected, barbettes fore and midships, lookout shields, rails and stanchions – 107,477 feet of linear welding.

FDR tours a naval training station near Sandpoint, Idaho. His daughter Anna Roosevelt Boettiger and her two children board the train.

FDR's train crosses North Cascades mountains.

22 September. Portland Day 10 – Deck winches, first mast erected, vertical ladders throughout holds, bulwark, mast completed, portable crow's nest, shroud lines, lifeboat davits, propeller and rudder, after deckhouse and barbettes, hull painted; 110,250 feet of linear welding.

The presidential party reached Puget Sound, Washington and took a ferry across the Tacoma Narrows, where the bridge built in 1940 had famously collapsed later that year. They drove to the Puget Sound Navy Yard in Bremerton, on the west side of Puget Sound, then rode a ferry 18 miles back to Seattle, followed by a short drive to the Boeing Aircraft plant in South Seattle.

FDR spent the night at the home of his daughter and her husband John Boettiger on the northwest tip of Mercer Island, while guard boats patrolled the local waters.

23 September. Portland Day 11 – Work continues on deck, firebox bricks going in.

Early morning, train travels south to Vancouver, Washington for stop at ALCOA aluminium plant. Around 11 am, train crosses Columbia River and enters Portland, Oregon. All rail traffic stops as presidential train is directed into Oregonship yard at approximately 11.30 am. Presidential limousine drives him up onto viewing stand.

11:54 am: *Joseph N Teal* launched. 12 noon: vessel moored in outfitting dock at 87 per cent complete. Joiner work, plastic armour, painting, guns.

24–25 September. Portland Days 12 &13 – Boom installation, anchors and chains, lifeboat and life rafts, plumbing, furnishing interior, electrical system, radio, communication and navigation systems. (Ship 100 per cent complete)

26 September. Portland Day 14. 8.58 am: *Joseph N Teal* left

Left: Day 11, 23 September – In outfitting dock. Six minutes after the launch, the *Joseph N Teal* was safely moored in the OSC outfitting dock. It was here that hundreds of skilled workers installed all the systems and interior fittings needed to complete the ship in just three days. These included 'Boom Installation, Anchors and Chains, Lifeboat and Liferafts, Plumbing, Furnishing Interior, Electrical System, Radio, Communication and Navigation Systems. (100 per cent complete.)'

JOSEPH N. TEAL

Left: Day 14, 26 September – Barber: 'Looking down at the painters from the flying bridge and wearing jackets are Captain Evensen, and R C Robinson, general manager of Hammond Shipping Co Ltd, San Francisco, which took over operation of the ship after its trial.'

Above: Day 14, 26 September – Barber: 'While engineers and inspectors checked the ship's mechanical systems, the painting crew applied finish coats all over the ship's interior and exterior during the trial run.' The tall angled object on the right is a life raft launcher.

dock on trial run. 3.55 pm: returned from trial run with new records for speed and crash-stop test. 11.30 pm: delivered, left Oregon Shipbuilding Corporation dock in service of operators.

Naturally, Larry Barber was on the job covering the Ten-Day Ship story when the ten-car presidential train was pulled through a gate and into Oregonship by a small diesel locomotive. A small convoy of open cars assembles beside the train, which is surrounded by a force of plainclothes men and soldiers with bayonets fixed and wearing combat helmets. I assume this is the first sign Barber or any of the 14,000 workers on the day shift have of the visit, but word passes quickly around the yard.

The convoy travels slowly around the crowded yard with the president waving to cheering workers from the convertible limousine as security men jog alongside. Three cars ascend the ramp where the presidential car parks in the centre of the viewing platform. Seated next to FDR is Henry J Kaiser with Oregon Governor Charles A Sprague in the rear seat. They witness the short ceremony before his daughter, Anna Roosevelt Boettiger, christens the SS *Joseph N Teal* in front of thousands of excited workers.

High above her hangs a large sign saying '10 Days' to proclaim their achievement. After she has broken a bottle of champagne on its bow with a mighty swing, the ship slides smoothly into the Willamette River, with steam in the boiler and the whistle blowing. The whole launch ceremony is over in less than ten minutes, and is reported on the cover of *The Oregonian* the next morning.

However, there is no mention of the president's visit – or his impromptu speech – in accordance with the censor's instructions to newspapers, radio stations etc that there could be no reporting the tour until it was completed. So the launch was reported again, on 2 October, this time on page two, where Barber finally told the whole story. This is what he wrote about what really happened after the launch:

> The attention of the crowd turned back to the presidential car high up on the platform. 'How about a speech,' shouted a husky male voice. 'Speech, speech' echoed his mates, and the crowd cheered, clapped and whistled. A hasty conference took place at the president's car, and the microphone was passed to the president. Visibly affected by the stirring scene, the he began slowly, carefully weighing his words.
>
> 'I have been very much inspired by what I have seen and I wish that every man, woman and child in the United States could have been here today to see that launching and realize what it means in the winning of this war. You know I am not supposed to be here today (laughter – the crowd really went wild), so you are the possessors of a secret which even the newspapers of the United states don't know, and I hope you will keep the secret because I am under military and naval orders, and like the ship that we have just seen go overboard, my motions and movements are supposed to be secret. I do not know whether they are or not.* You are doing a wonderful piece of work for your country and for our civilization, and with the help of God we are going to, see this thing through together.' [Luckily, FDR's last personal secretary, Grace Tully, was present and managed to record the speech for posterity.]
>
> Now, the cars slowly descended the ramp and proceeded to the outer end of the outfitting dock where the Liberty SS *William S Rosecrans*, launched 12 days before, had steam up and was ready to depart downriver and into the Pacific Ocean to enter service. Tugs brought the *Joseph Teal* around to the dock right on time, just as the crew of the *Rosecrans* was about to cast off their mooring lines. The two ships exchange whistle blasts as if they did this every day, and Anna Boettiger walked across the dock to admire the ship she had just launched.
>
> The convoy now returned to the train, where Henry and Edgar Kaiser and Al Bauer, Edgar's second in command, sat in the car in the warm sun for 15 minutes engaging in earnest conversation with FDR. One hour and ten minutes after he arrived, the president departed, having seen and experienced the yard that can do the most work in the least amount of time.

Above: Day 14, 26 September – Barber: 'Painter Osmund Haugset stencils the record on a boiler condenser and other flat surfaces in the engine room.'

Above: Day 14, 26 September – Barber: 'Shown in the *Teal*'s engine room: George A Patterson, senior machinery inspector of MarCom handles the throttle and watches gauges, while Chief Engineer A G Graham telephones the bridge. The ship established new records for crash stop, measured mile and engine performance.'

That could equally be said of this marathon two-week tour,

* Unaware of the censor's order, a small Seattle weekly for Boeing union members printed a 24 September article on his visit, but the Secret Service was able intercept and destroy most of the 30,000 copies.

Above: Day 14, 26 September – The 60 painters take their official lunch break during the trial, which started at 3.55 pm and finished at 11.30 pm. Barber: 'Smoke was poured only for the benefit of the photographers, Captain Frank Gillard, OSC's port captain, explained.'

when the president covered 8754 miles and dropped in on eleven private war industry plants that were helping win the war at home, plus eight army, seven navy and two marine bases that were doing the *real* fighting. The *Joseph N Teal* was 87 percent complete at launching – a higher figure than Kaiser normally achieved. At least one report claimed Henry Kaiser said 'We could have launched it in eight days, but we waited two days so the president could attend the launch.'

The total construction time to delivery including the sea trial was officially 13 days, 23½ hours. The previous dozen ships had taken 40–45 days to delivery. After the ceremony, the time for the next dozen dropped to under 40 days. These two figures show clearly that production at the yard was not noticeably affected by the extra effort needed for the Ten-Day Ship.

This achievement inspired the Sunday edition of the *San Francisco Chronicle* magazine to publish a substantial profile of Kaiser that rhapsodized over the recent 'miracle' at Oregonship – and undoubtedly convinced Clay Bedford, general manager at Richmond, to respond with an even greater feat: the assembly of the SS *Robert E Peary* in under five days. This pushed the technology of pre-fabrication to new heights at the Permanente No 2 yard. Following its famous launch, it appears that the *Joseph N Teal** disappeared into the huge Liberty fleet without making any further headlines. The ship survived the war and was scrapped in 1965.

* Joseph Nathan Teal (1858–1929) was a prominent attorney and civic leader in Portland, known as an advocate of waterway development in the Pacific Northwest. He served as the US Shipping Commissioner in 1920–21.

11

INSIDE THE KAISER YARDS

HOW KAISER MEN SKETCHED 'BOTTLE-NECK BUSTERS ON TABLE CLOTHS'

Larry Barber's reporting on the shipyards was intended for the average reader, and he usually tried to avoid too much technical information. The stories focused on the 'who, what and when' of important events like keel layings, launches, and sea trials. One aspect of the Kaiser shipbuilding system was noticeably absent from his coverage: the top level of the organization that managed this vast machine with all its departments and deadlines. The one occasion when he managed to get a closer look at Oregonship's senior executives and superintendents as a group was on 20 November 1942, just before the company celebrated the launching of their 100th Liberty ship.

Below: Kaiser shipyards policy was to provide meals for all the workers who wanted them, typically by contracting with a local caterer. Like everything else in the yard, the lunch room was well run and provided appetizing food in shifts. According to Barber, the management used their lunch breaks to thrash out production problems.

In just 18 months, the yard had reduced the time to deliver a Liberty from 226 days to 36 days, and was now launching a ship every 2–3 days. *The Sunday Oregonian* planned to dedicate its front page to this achievement, so Larry was looking for a new angle that would appeal to the readers. He found the story in a most surprising interview that took place in the executive's private dining room – not with a senior manager, but with a waitress. He does not reveal whether he had been invited into the room, or was just looking for a manager to interview, but what he learned gave him a unique inside view of the way the yard functioned at the top level.

Here is his account of one of the company's 'top secrets' that has not seen the light of day for nearly 80 years. 'In a way, Zola Hummel is a fortunate person. For a year, she has watched the world's finest shipbuilders work – on table cloths.' Next, he carefully noted her description of how the managers communicate: 'They draw hundreds of pictures every day while they eat, but they have never drawn any doodles that anybody else could understand.' The headline of the Sunday paper read: 'Oregon Poises Its 100th Liberty,' with this sub-title: 'Here's How Doodling Helped. At Their Roundtable Luncheons, Kaiser Men Sketch Bottle-Neck Busters on Table Cloths'.

> 'At the daily Kaiser roundtable have been born many of the new ideas, methods and tools that have made this outfit the toast of the merchant shipbuilding world,' he wrote. 'Eighteen superintendents and a dozen or more executives sit down to eat close enough to the man they need to meet to sort out a problem. Quite often they lick those issues before they leave the room,' he explained. He traced this noon-time ritual back to the Grand Coulee dam and credited Edgar Kaiser with getting it started, and reckoned this was really 'the heart and nerve centre of Oregon Ship'.

Encouraging informal communication between department heads in the relaxed atmosphere of the lunch room is a concept that still sounds relevant today in the age of Twitter. After meeting Miss Hummel, Larry managed to spend a few minutes with Oregonship's General Superintendent Russ Hoffman, a college football star and engineer, who joined Edgar Kaiser in 1931 to lay a welded pipeline to carry gas from Texas to Arizona. He worked on all three dams and came to Portland after his team finished their time at the Grand Coulee.

He was promoted to General Superintendent at Oregonship when the original man was shifted to the Vancouver yard to bring them up to speed. Hoffman explained in more hands-on terms how the dam builders turned to shipbuilding this way: 'The hard core of the early labor force were seasoned workers and foremen from Grand Coulee Dam who were split between Richmond and Portland. They rapidly mastered the new shipbuilding skills the Kaisers needed, since many of them had worked on the drum gates at Coulee Dam. There were 11 of those steel gates, 135 long and 28 feet high and put together much like ships,' he told Barber.

When Larry asked for the outstanding development that made this plant what it is, Hoffman did not hesitate, replying: 'The assembly plant that Edgar Kaiser persuaded the Maritime Commission to pay for. Now the bulk of the assembly is done under that roof, which covers five acres, by a large corps of specialists who each have a particular job they do.' He also credited close cooperation between all crafts as the key to keeping the shipyard humming.

Barber went on to give short biographies of most of the men in the room, who appeared in his photographs. Some of them were old enough to have experienced the emergency shipbuilding program in 1917–18. He also noted that there were three Scottish superintendents in the room. They were Ed Michelson (shipwrights and facilities); George 'Scotty' Wright (steel erection) who built ships on the Clyde in 1914–18; and Jack McGregor (riveters and chippers) who built ships in Portland in 1917–18.

SUGGESTION CLEARING OFFICE

The concept of the 'Suggestion Clearing Office' sounds almost as modern as the Kaiser's modular building system – an early form of 'crowd-sourcing' solutions – and appears to have been a fully-functioning arm of the Kaiser shipyards. Employees were invited to submit ideas for changes in the design or production of any of the thousands of parts that were fabricated in the yard or the way they were installed. War bonds were offered as prizes for the best submissions. The Suggestion Office was set up to keep track of the flood of ideas that came in.

The official report for 1943 from the Vancouver yard records that 4896 suggestions were processed. Of this total, 603 were accepted: 330 were production-oriented, 273 were non-production (about ⅛ of the total). These are listed by month with October seeing a huge jump thanks to the escort carrier production drive titled '18 or more by '44'. Integration of these suggestions into the building process was said to have resulted in the saving of 888,560 man-hours on an accumulative (annual) basis. At an average wage rate of $1.40 per hour, they saved about $1,250,000 per year.

Three examples were given: one tip showed a net saving of $5000 in flat bar per hull and about 4000ft of welding; another saved 167 tons of lead by salvaging the scraps. Larry mentioned the successful ideas whenever there was an announcement of a prize-giving from the War Production Drive officials. He saved the photos of one worker holding a large gusset (angle) that was originally stiffened by a welded rib. The worker suggested the stiffener could be created by using a press break to form it in a few seconds, eliminating the need for cutting the rib, clamping and welding it. Suggestions ranged from minor ideas like a

Left: A team of ten welders prefabricating box sections in the plate shop. Oregonship's General Superintendent Russ Hoffman regarded the covered assembly plant as the key to the yard's efficiency.

better handle on a tool or an improved jig to elaborate pre-fab concepts like a 'mock-up of the engine room, which made it possible to lay out and fit the entire engine room floor plating' before actually installing it aboard ship, and saved 4000 hours of labour. Suggestions on material flow could be easily adopted by department managers, who were constantly trying to improve their team's output.

With the constant decrease of man-hours on each carrier hull, the Suggestion Clearing House reckoned that the total man-hours saved per year would be enough to build an entire extra ship. By 1945, the yards had passed more than three thousand suggestions to the Maritime Commission, which in turn compiled them in digests and distributed them throughout the merchant shipbuilding industry. Ninety percent received awards, and in total the suggestions saved $45 million and 31 million manhours.

LARRY BARBER PROFILES 'VICTORY WORKERS'

There were many stories to be found among the tens of thousands of workers who kept the arsenal of democracy running 24 hours a day, seven days a week. The only problem was knowing where to start. Luckily, Larry only had to pick up the latest issue of *The Bo's'n's Whistle* to read about workers with an unusual background. In spring 1942 he began a series of profiles titled 'Victory Workers', described as '... a series of articles about interesting people who changed their occupations to work in Portland's defense industries', published sporadically throughout the year. They all make for fascinating reading, documenting the wide range of individuals and their varied

Below: The pipe assembly superintendent Chester Spiering revolutionized the cut-and-fit method of pipe assembly at Oregonship by re-creating a Liberty engine room with a mock-up in a 260ft by 80ft loft. This full-scale model functioned in all three dimensions with jigs and stands that accurately reproduced the situation on the ship. The five separate pipe systems were denoted by colours that were marked on the pipes, flanges, valves and the jigs. This reduced welding time by as much as 85 percent, and was a shining example of the Kaiser philosophy of worker participation and 'continuous improvement'.

backgrounds that the war drew to Portland. There were former circus and vaudeville performers, college athletes, preachers, retired World War I officers, artists; these are just a few:

> Les Steers became an engineer's supervisor at OSC after attending Oregon State University where he set a world high-jump record of 2.11m (6ft 1in) on 7 June 1941.
>
> Everett Lawrence represented the USA in the pole vault and high jump at the Berlin Olympic Games, 1936. He was discharged from the army after being wounded and is now an electrician at Swan Island.
>
> Roy N Shannon, the former Treasurer of the State of Montana, found work as a swing shift guard at Oregonship.
>
> Louis Zanon, a steamfitter, had been known as Bull Dog Louie, when he was touring with the Barnum and Bailey Circus as a fire-eater.
>
> Patricia Simmons, described as a 'brown-eyed brunette', worked as a statistical clerk at Oregonship, having represented Jefferson High School as a Portland Rose Festival princess in 1939.
>
> Charles Lautrop, a graduate of the Royal Danish University and former director of the Portland Philharmonic Orchestra, found himself in charge of a pipe shop at Oregonship. 'I like this work … it is reassuring to be hearing the symphony of riveting hammers and American workmen doing their jobs.'
>
> The Rev H Edward Pierce, a Congregationalist Minister with 14 years' experience in the pulpit, who found work as a machinist at the Marine Electric Company.
>
> Portland-raised Ah Wing Lee, who gained fame as a lightweight boxer in the early 1930s, found work at Commercial Iron Works as a draftsman.
>
> Willian Brubaker served on the battleship USS *Oregon* in the early 1900s, retired from the US Navy in 1910, and became a barnstorming aviator in 1919, then took up aerial photography and mapping. He is a machinist at Oregonship.
>
> Colonel Clarence Hotchkiss enlisted in the army in 1898 and fought in the Spanish-American War. He was sent to France in 1917 and served on the front line. He retired in 1939 and is now a material expediter at Swan Island.

In addition to attracting workers from throughout the United States, the Kaiser yards also included an international component. 'America's bridge of ships is being built by workmen from practically all of the United Nations and numerous other countries,' said *The Bo's'n's Whistle* in February 1943. Workers from Nova Scotia, France, Belgium, Poland, Austria, Russia, China and the Philippines, among others, were all employed in various shipyard jobs, most with tales of having left their country just prior to occupation. Mrs Viky Bush, a welder at Oregonship, was visiting the United States in 1938 when Hitler invaded Austria. Her husband escaped to Belgium and the family was re-united in New York before moving to Oregon to work in the yards.

HENRY KAISER PRAISES 'PRESENTEEISM'

Portland shipyard workers worked seven-day weeks before each day off. In order to allow the shipyards to be open constantly, labourers belonged to different groups – A, B, C, D, E, F or G – and all members of a group would get the same day off. Despite the high pay, many benefits, and patriotic atmosphere, nearly one of every ten workers was typically absent from work, whether for true health reasons or something more frivolous. Pleas from the President, from celebrities and war heroes all attempted to encourage defence workers to stay on the job unless they were unable.

At the Vancouver yard with twelve ways, the company developed the notion of 'Way Thirteen', on which the lost man hours 'built' a ship for the Axis and erected huge billboards to track those hours. All of the Kaiser yards had similar programs, tracking lost hours and appealing to workers' patriotism to keep working. Early 1943 appears to have been the peak of concern about absenteeism and resulted in a nationwide effort to bring attention to the problem and improve worker attendance. As with everything else, the yards compared records of attendance and tracked 'records' to spur workers to improve. WISCO summarily fired 150 workers for excessive absenteeism, inviting them to return only if they agreed to remain steadily on the job. Some foremen replaced absent workers' time cards with a colourful 'AWOL' card in an effort to identify slackers and discourage them.

When some conservatives accused the nation's blue-collar workers of excessive absenteeism, Henry Kaiser replied: 'Talk about this is greatly overdone, our shipyards have a 93 percent rate of presenteeism.' The word he invented never went out of fashion and is often used in the twenty-first century. In a speech to a crowd of workers early in 1943, Kaiser spoke of the success at Oregonship, telling his workers

> Let's Talk about 'Presenteeism'. Rampant in the land is the idea that workers in shipyards and other war plants are slackers at heart, lazy in body, committing with a closed mind the unpardonable crime of deliberate absenteeism in a time of national crisis. Nothing is farther from the truth. No

Above: Edgar Kaiser addressed all three shifts at Swan Island on 15 September 1945 to inform the employees that their jobs were safe well into the future, because the United Nations (the Allies) required another 70 tankers to ensure a reliable fuel supply after the occupation of Japan. He also informed them that 3000 of their workmates had quit in August, and the absentee rate was now at an unacceptable 11 per cent, so they all had to pull together to continue the yard's reputation as 'the tanker capital of the world'. This was a far cry from his father's public emphasis on 'Presenteeism'.

> conception is more unjust to those who toil long, sacrifice the comforts of home and family, and who endure silently the curse of the few ... my hat is off to the 93 percent faithful men and women in those shipyards that are in the Portland and San Francisco areas.

Another issue was called 'job-hopping', when skilled workers took advantage of the shortage of labour by moving from one yard or defence industry to another in search of better wages or conditions. This disrupted productivity and was roundly criticized as being counter to the war effort. 'The more you move from place to place, the more you are slowing the construction of our ships which are needed most urgently to support our forces in combat ...', warned Commander James G McPheron at the launching of the USS *Catskill* at WISCO in May1942. This eventually resulted in an agreement between most yards to simply not hire away workers employed in a 'critical' industry, which included mining, logging, farming and fishing.

KAISER MEDICAL SERVICE TREATED SHIPYARD INJURIES

Injuries were common in all the nation's shipyards: in fact, working in a shipyard was one of the most dangerous jobs in the wartime industries, riskier even than the the production of munitions or explosives. In his 1951 book *Ships for Victory*, Frederic Lane states: 'Of the 655 reported private shipyard fatalities in the nation during 1943 and 1944, falls caused almost 40 percent, vehicles or loads striking workers caused about 25 percent.' In 1943, the US Maritime Commission launched a safety program that ultimately reduced the injury rate in the shipyards. For every 100 shipyard employees, there were 7.3 injuries in 1943, 5.5 in 1944, and 4.9 in 1945.

The Kaiser Corporation had adopted the 'pre-payment' health care system devised by Doctor Sidney Garfield on an earlier project on the Colorado River Aqueduct. In 1939, he moved his operation to the largest construction site in history – the Grand Coulee Dam – to provide care for the 6500 workers and their families. He recruited a team of doctors and nurses to work in a 'prepaid group practice' in a local hospital that he turned into a state-of-the-art facility. But as the dam neared completion in 1941, it seemed that the grand experiment was reaching the end of its life, until world history intervened. Now, Henry J Kaiser had a far bigger problem: how to provide health care for a workforce that would grow to 30,000 in the first Van-Port yard alone.

Kaiser was convinced that Dr Garfield could scale up his system, but according to the Kaiser Permanente archive, he first had to persuade the US Army to release the good doctor from military service. This may have been the first favour Henry asked of FDR during the war effort, but it was definitely not the last! The Northern Permanente Foundation hospital opened in August 1942 in Vancouver and recruited a staff of 45 physicians, including several who had just completed their medical residency. The most frequent injuries were fractures of the hands, feet, and ribs.

Eleanor Roosevelt was given a grand tour of the new hospital in September 1942 when she visited the Vancouver yard to launch their first escort carrier. A few months later, she wrote about the hospital in her regular newspaper column, *My Day*.

> A little after 9 o'clock Monday morning we were met in Portland, Oregon, by Mr Henry J Kaiser and his son Mr Edgar Kaiser. A group of young Democrats presented me with a lovely bunch of red roses at the airport and then we were whisked off for a busy day.
>
> Our first tour was in the Kaiser shipyard itself. It is certainly busy and businesslike. Everything seems to be in place and moving as quickly as possible along a regular line of production. I was particularly interested in the housing, so I was shown the dormitories and then the hospital, which is run on a species of health cooperative basis costing the employees seven cents a day. It looked to me very well-equipped and much used, but I was told there were few accidents in the shipyards owing to safety devices. The men come in for medical care and some surgery and their families are also cared for.

AWARDS

★ **The Oregon Shipbuilding Corporation has managed to capture every production award that the Maritime Commission could create. Here is the list to date:**

Navy "E" Award (only Maritime yard in U. S. to win Navy "E")	*February 15, 1942*
Maritime "M" Flag	*April 18, 1942*
Second Star Maritime Burgee	*August 17, 1942*
Third Star Maritime Burgee	*September 17, 1942*
Fourth Star Maritime Burgee	*October 22, 1942*
Fifth and Sixth Stars Maritime Burgee	*November 30, 1942*
Seventh, Eighth and Ninth Stars Maritime Burgee	*February 13, 1943*
Gold Eagle Award	*April 4, 1943*
"200" Pennant	*June 12, 1943*
"250 Club" Flag	*September 27, 1943*
Maritime Gold Wreath Award (highest USMC award)	*November 4, 1943*
Maritime "30 Day Club" Award	*November 4, 1943*
*AP-5 Champ Flag**	*September, 1944*

**(Won permanent possession) December, 1944*

Above: Oregon Shipbuilding Corporation, the first yard to receive the M burgee, was again honoured on 19 July 1942 when Rear Admiral Howard L Vickery, vice chairman of the US Maritime Commission, presented the first star of the Maritime burgee to Mrs Mary Carroll, first Oregon Shipbuilding woman welder and mother of a soldier who fought on Bataan. 'This is the yard of firsts,' said Admiral Vickery. 'First to deliver a Liberty ship on the West Coast, first to win the Maritime Commission award, the first to bring women into the yard, first to operate on seven day week in such a way as to rotate launchings.' The full list of OSC's awards is appended.

On this occasion Henry J Kaiser gave public utterance to his proposal that some Maritime Commission yards be converted into yards to build freighters of the air.

FLAGS AND AWARDS

When he turned to shipbuilding, Henry Kaiser had spent twenty years running construction crews, and reporters had noted his ability to motivate his road-building employees by introducing an element of friendly competition between the men doing the same work on different shifts or locations. There was no mention of any reward beyond a short-lived boost to the overall production, but there may have been some small financial incentive. This seemed to create some sort of team spirit among the men, and broke the work down into a series of measurable targets and goals..

On the Grand Coolee Dam, Edgar Kaiser and Clay Bedford were supervising teams doing similar work and used this idea of

SAFETY PAYS
FIRST AID UNIT

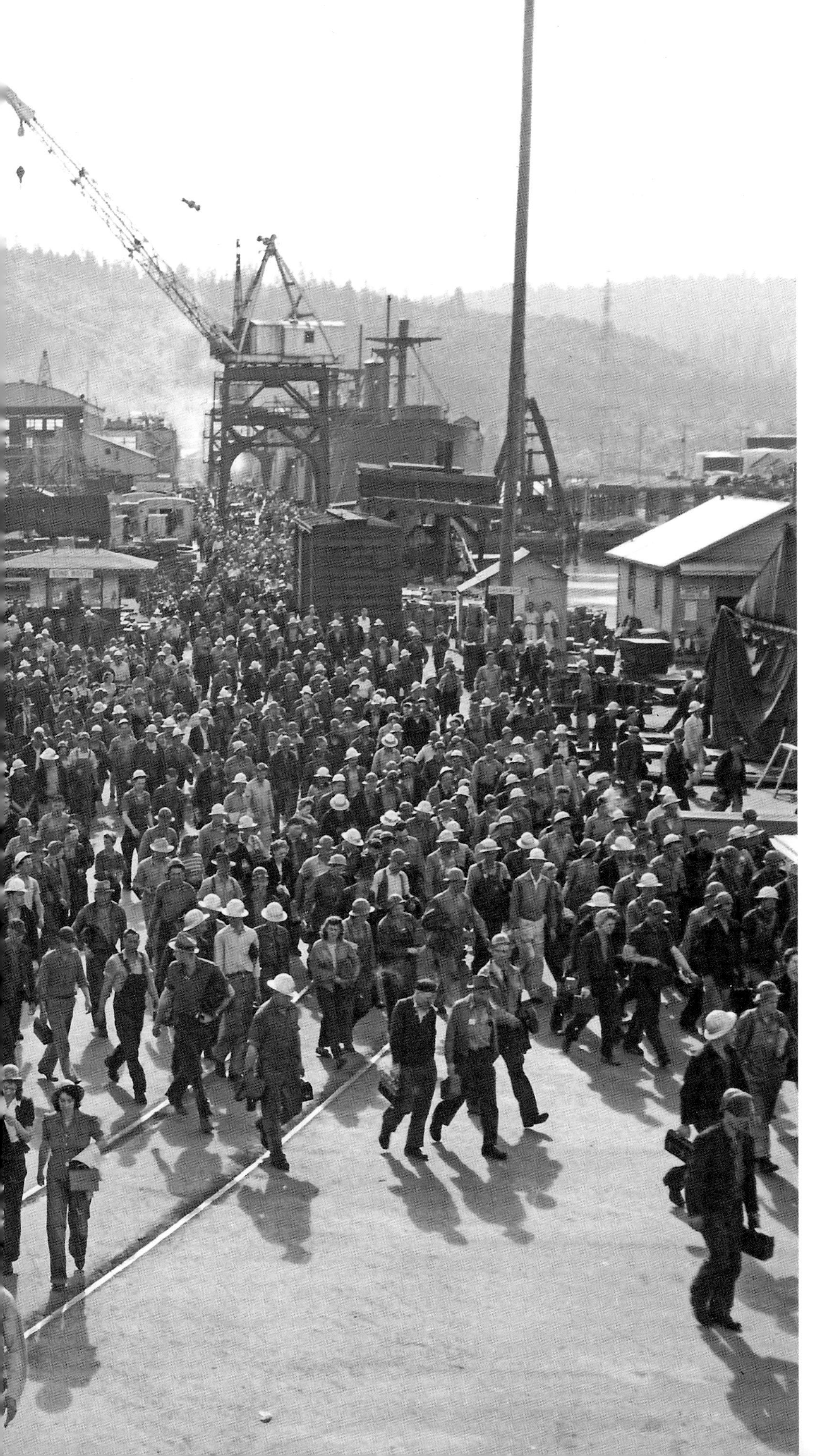

Left: With as many as 10,000 workers changing places at the end of each shift, it was necessary to manage the crowds on foot and in the huge parking lot by staggering the departure times and providing a fleet of shuttle buses.

competition to build a rivalry between them. This was quite successful and they reprised it in 1941 and turned it into a 'major league' contest between Portland and Richmond with the wartime appeal of production records and record breaking. This was picked up by the press and eventually followed by millions of readers all over the west coast.

At the same time, the US Navy had introduced the 'E' (for 'Excellence') flag devised by Vice-Admiral Lewis Strauss, the over-achieving trouble shooter for the Secretary of the Navy. The Army and Navy made about four thousand 'E' awards – the St Johns Woolen Mill was given one – and a few were for very questionable achievements. Strauss himself earned a medal for inventing 'the greatest stimulus to munition production developed during the war.' The Maritime Commission decided to get on the bandwagon and created its own awards for the shipyards, the 'M' awards.

By the end of the war, 35 shipyards – about a third of the Maritime Commission's stable – and 175 factories or workshops had won the 'M' flag and badges for all employees at the time the award was made. These honourees included not only major shipyards but a one-man workshop which turned out spokes for the traditional wooden steering wheels of Liberty ships. The flag system seemed to be working well, but had failed to allow for the ability of the leading yards to exceed every forecast by a huge margin. A response was quickly found: to award stars to the flag for additional improvements in production. The Kaiser yards then competed for the number of stars, which began to fill the background of the flag. Oregonship set so many records that the Maritime Commission ran out of awards and had to invent new ones like the '250 Ship Flag' and the '30 Day Club'. By September, 1944, the yard proudly held all 13 production awards for which it was eligible.

It was said that World War II shipyard managers rivalled baseball fans in their statistical mania. Welding easily lent itself to head-to-head races, quality contests with professional judges, and stunts like most welding in an hour. These competitions offered special opportunities for female workers and a means to assert equality with their male peers, especially in skills that required dexterity or a delicate touch. These breaks from typical shipyard work and life contrast markedly with the absenteeism and staff turnover that characterized the war effort, and begs the question of what effect these diversions actually had. The awards, presentations, launch ceremonies, rivalry with Richmond, war bond drives, and blood donation appeals were sold as ways to improve the employees' morale. Was this what really inspired the biggest shipbuilding program in history, or was it just the window dressing on the mighty industrial and patriotic machine that involved millions of workers all over the USA?

However, it is easy to understand how local contests of more work-related skills could generate genuine enthusiasm. The Albina Engine and Machine Works issued a challenge to find the best ship welders in Portland. Two-man teams from Albina, WISCO and Oregonship agreed to compete for time and quality by undertaking three standard welds before a packed audience at the Victory Center, downtown, in July 1942. The Albina team won handily. Later in the war, champion female welders from the east coast visited Portland on a promotional tour culminating in a welding challenge match with the best local women.

Kaiser's yards competed amongst themselves, as well as with their sister-yards in California in feats of riveting prowess. Also in the summer of 1942, a 26-year-old Portland native, Lloyd Howard Leknes of Oregonship, drove more than 1700 rivets in one shift to break the 'World Record' set just two weeks prior at Calship's Los Angeles yard. His record-breaking feat represented seven percent of the total 26,500 rivets in each Liberty Ship. 'This outstanding record typifies the spirit of Oregon Shipbuilding Corporation men to build ships faster and break more records,' commented Al Bauer, Oregonship's General Manager.

WORKERS WANTED – NO PREVIOUS EXPERIENCE NEEDED!

Tens of thousands of unskilled men and women were recruited to meet the demands of new emergency shipyards. Kaiser paid the highest wage of $1.40 per hour, and provided many notable benefits to encourage the men and women in the yards, like the above-average wages, the canteen serving proper meals at all hours, the Kaiser system of medical care from first aid posts to a complete hospital, and the 24-hour nursery. These were undoubtedly major factors in retaining experienced workers and bringing more women into the yard, despite the shiftwork and industrial conditions. If the shipyards had ever solved the problem of the perpetual shortage of trained workers, they might have produced even more ships.

Finding, training and retaining workers was a significant issue, and the Kaiser Van-Port yards employed as many as 120,000 people at their height – up to one third of them women. Although the shipyards dominated the war effort in Portland, there were still many other industries trying to attract workers. The pace was unrelentingly fast in the shipyards and fatigue sometimes won out over patriotism, especially for mothers with young children. The shipyard newspapers also reported both men and women leaving to join the services.

Years of training and experience necessary to make a journeyman shipyard worker after a traditional long apprenticeship could not be condensed into a matter of days or weeks, yet the war would wait for no one. The solution was to follow the example of Henry Ford and break the complex job of building a ship into a series of small tasks. Classrooms sprang up in the shipyards, schools and even private homes where welding and other crafts were taught. Trade unions objected strenuously to this practice, giving rise to deep conflicts between unions and shipyard management that remained unresolved throughout the war.

Women and minorities entered the workforce in areas previously denied to them. However, they still faced unequal pay, were shunted off into 'auxiliary' unions and still had to deal with day-to-day prejudice and inequities. The perceived frailty of women was also apparent by the portrayal of women in Tihe *Bo's'n's Whistle*, the magazine of the Kaiser shipyards. In earlier volumes the only female employees mentioned were in low-intensity jobs such as nursing or key-punch operating. The deep-seated prejudice against working women meant that when ladies began to funnel into the workplace at the beginning of the war, discrimination was inevitable. This reality was apparent in the shipyards of Portland and Vancouver. Doctor Forest Reike, a physician in the shipyards, summarized the anti-women sentiment when he said 'the old construction people that I know, and that were working there, told me that the minute a woman came in, they were leaving. There was a great male resistance, traditional, deep convictions. These guys had their own ideas about what their wives did, and essentially it was not their work. It was at home, keeping house, raising the kids and watering the grass.' In 1944, though over 25 percent of workers at Kaiser shipyards were women, more than half did clerical work whereas less than 3 percent of the 9755 pipefitters and machinists were female.

In *The Bo's'n's Whistle*, they always appeared well-dressed and attractive; and men were entreated to overcome their inclinations to 'throw your goggles away just to get a chance to meet the capable young ladies who spend their days at the First Aid Station.' This comment belittled the importance of the women's work, making it seem that they were simply potential distractions that would decrease productivity.

The only other women mentioned in the magazine were wives of shipyard workers who led the dedication of the ships, depicted in fashionable dresses and hats. This conformed to the more traditional stereotype that women belonged in the home, a view which had grown in popularity during the Great Depression when any woman who worked was viewed as having stolen a job from a man.

THE KAISER KARAVANS

In his typical direct style, Henry Kaiser, turned his search for employees into a national media event in 1942. Kaiser's eldest son, Edgar, found a responsive official in Anna Rosenberg, the New York regional director of the War Manpower Commission, who authorized the United States Employment Services to support the recruitment of Kaiser's workers in early September 1942. The newspapers announced his intent to hire as many as 20,000 'without lost motions or wasted time'.

Kaiser's hiring representatives said the first 600 men selected from New York would probably be bound for Portland within days aboard a special train – dubbed the 'Kaiser Karavan'. This was headline news in *The Oregonian* just after the launch of the ten-day Liberty ship SS *Joseph N Teal* on 23 September. Larry Barber's next assignment was to catch the first train east to Missoula, Montana, where he was wait for the Kaiser train, ride back with the recruits from New York and get their story first-hand.

Above: One of the Kaiser migrant trains (the 'Kaiser Karavans') stops to give the passengers a break on the route from New York to Vancouver, Washington. The train stopped in Missoula, Montana, where the locals put on a small Wild West show for them. Note the two horse riders in the first photo. The second is dated October 1943.

> This 17-car Northern Pacific train, more than a quarter of a mile long, has been winding and twisting over the plains and mountains for four day and these 490 Portland-bound emigrants are weary but happy. They play cards, sing songs, argue why the Brooklyn Dodgers lost the series … and ask a thousand and one questions of the few westerners aboard the train. Nearly all the men are being accepted as laborers, for

Left and above: On 30 August 1945, as the war in the Pacific was coming to an end, the outfitting dock and adjacent buildings at Oregon Ship burned in the most costly blaze in Portland's history. The fire started by welders closing an opening in the side of a Victory ship. A wooden piling was ignited and the flames reached an acetylene line under the dock. From there, flames spread rapidly upward into the pipe shop, paint shop, tool shop and No 1 dock shop, all built on the landward edge of the dock. The outfitting dock, 2800ft long, was almost entirely consumed. At 8:10 am, when the fire started, according to Hal Babbitt, the yard public relations head, approximately 6000 persons were at work on the pier, with another 6000 scattered through the yard. The loss was unofficially estimated at $3,000,000.

This was even more serious than the yard's previous major fire on 7 November 1944, when the Administration building burned to the ground in a spectacular 45-minute blaze. This was a massive disruption to the 'nerve centre' of the yard, with 900 staff displaced, but the building was entirely reconstructed in ten weeks, and all the crucial administrative departments were fully functioning again by the end of January 1945.

> whom the Kaiser pay is 88 cents an hour for a 48-hour week … The cost of transportation and meals on the way total about $80 a man, financed by the Kaiser Company, but the men repay this from their wages over a period of about ten weeks. – *The Oregonian*, 30 September 1942.

They arrived in Portland on the last day of September. They had filled out paperwork on the train, been given rooms in the on-site dormitories at the three Kaiser shipyards, and were fingerprinted for their ID tags as the train approached the end of its journey so that they could be at work and on the job the following day. Portland's civic leaders struggling with the city's housing issues were less than supportive of this strategy. Undeterred, Kaiser continued his New York hiring, accepting 1800 new workers in just two days and coming under the scrutiny of the federal government who voiced some concern that the company might be draining workers from other essential war industries in the east.

Local interest in the New York group remained high, and

Above: Talented Kaiser employees formed small groups, bands and even orchestras to entertain the workers during lunch hours. This popular band was called 'The Tin Hatters'.

periodic newspaper reports followed the groups 'acclimation' to the western lifestyle and shipyard work. Oregonians compared this sudden influx as something akin to a second Oregon Trail. Newspapers as far away as Abilene, Texas cautioned Kaiser about the implications of importing New Yorkers into Portland, Oregon. 'Have you considered the consequences of turning 20,000 New Yorkers loose on the west coast?' they asked. (Most, ultimately, returned to the east during or after the war.)

Kaiser then directed his search for workers to the South and Midwest. Some papers called these trains 'Magic Carpet Specials' as they carried over 100,000 white people and 20,000 black Americans to the Bay Area and Portland. Most of the recruits hailed from Arkansas, Louisiana, Texas, Oklahoma and Kentucky. Almost overnight, Portlanders were confronted by Americans with accents and attitudes very different from their own. In mid-October, the three Oregon yards announced an agreement with the Oregon Federation of Labor regarding hiring practices and a halt to the costly employee turnover rate that the company sought to improve upon.

Above: 1942 Portland Rose Festival Queen Shirley Louise Fowler christens the Liberty ship *John Harvard* on 4 June 1942. Although the yard was to employ many women workers, this image is closer to what many of the men thought was a suitable role for a woman.

....

12

WOMEN DOING MEN'S WORK

'It's odd that men feel they must protect women, since for the most part they must be protected from men.'

'The young women of today, free to study, to speak, to write, to choose their occupation, should remember that every inch of this freedom was bought for them at a great price. It is for them to show their gratitude by helping onward the reforms of their own times.'

Abigail Scott Duniway (1834–1915),
western pioneer feminist.

Above: Barber: 'First and only Chinese girl welder in Portland is Marguerite Dune. Portland-born daughter of American-born parents, she was a department store employee before taking up welding studies at Kelly school. She likes her new occupation and hopes to make it a career. Her boss says "she's a whiz".' She worked on the record-breaking ten-day ship.

In the summer of 1941 Edgar Kaiser was hiring hundreds of men a month and trying to get the Oregonship yard up and running. But after the Japanese attack on Pearl Harbor on 7 December 1941, the draft began removing his workers aged 20–44 at an alarming rate. To replace them, all the war-related industries found they were competing for the limited number of men who had failed the military's medical exam or were over 44. The Kaiser family was well ahead of the times in worker relations, having recognized and accepted the rights of workers to unionize on the two Columbia River dams, but that really does not explain their ability to lead the nation with the revolutionary idea of hiring women to do manual work in the shipyards.

Historically, the shipyard had always been a workplace dominated by men – a place where women performed 'women's work' but never came into contact with the ships or the tools. But there was a war on and the Kaisers' task was to produce ships – fast. Many researchers have studied Henry Kaiser's career and methods, and the consensus appears to be that he had succeeded in achieving wealth and influence by taking calculated risks and trusting his hand-picked managers. There was no indication that he was interested in changing social values. It may well have been his son Edgar who introduced the idea of teaching women shipyard trades, and it was Edgar who flew to Washington DC to meet with Anne Rosenberg, New York regional director of the War Manpower Commission.

Given the wartime labour crisis, she authorized the United States Employment Service to support the recruitment of women for the new Kaiser yards in Portland and Richmond, and gave the order to issue temporary work permit cards from the Boilermakers Union to the trainees at no cost, pending a referendum on admitting them to full union membership. This was a necessary step, since all the wartime shipyards were closed shops – *ie* they could only employ union members – and this was to be the first large-scale unionization of women in history. This had no effect on the Boilermakers, who were by far the biggest of the shipyard unions with about half the total employees; they were totally opposed to women and blacks joining them.

When the Oregon Shipbuilding Company hired two women welders in April 1942 with temporary union cards, it was the first time a Maritime Commission yard employed female workers to carry out production work. Once the first women welders were shown to be proficient, the precedent was set. Now, the power of the government, unions and the media all made an 'about face': officials at all levels of the state and federal government began a nationwide campaign to recruit women, placing stories and advertisements in publications all over the country.

> 'A shipyard is no place for a woman.' This traditional attitude is yielding to the necessity for employing women in order to increase production in the face of the manpower shortages … Transition from manpower to womanpower on the war production front is not a female problem but an employment problem … In the old days we could have called this a placement and personnel management problem. Today we call it womenpower mobilization.
>
> Charlotte Carr, War Manpower Commission 1942.

Above: Mrs Helen Larkin, wife of Marine Corps General Claude Larkin commanding an air training centre at Cherry Point, North Carolina 3000 miles away, stayed in Vancouver and had been a welder on the swing shift for over a year, partnered with leadman Tilford 'Tillie' Holcomb.

For women whose relatives were in the services, patriotism was an important driver. And when the husband was called up, the wife took on a new responsibility to provide for their family. Almost overnight, women were invited to bypass the traditional barriers to working outside the home and become the breadwinner. (Approximately 12 million women worked in defence industries and support services including shipyards, steel mills, foundries, warehouses, offices, hospitals and daycare centres by the end of the war.)

In Portland, newspapers, radio shows and newsreels celebrated the first daring housewives exchanging their aprons for overalls and welding masks; recruiters went door to door. One of the slogans for this promotion was: 'The More Women at Work the Sooner We Win.' Nonetheless, it was mid-September before the Boilermakers board reluctantly agreed that there was a war on, and voted to accept the members' vote of 12,000 for and 7000 against women members, according to the Kaiser archives.

The key to the participation of women in shipbuilding was mass production, which lowered the skill level needed – for men and women – to the 'semi-skilled' level that was easily attainable with only basic training. This was achieved by attended welding classes held in high school metalwork shops

Above: Mrs Helen Larkin poses with her welding gun in an assembly bay in Vancouver.

Above: Two views of women painters at work on an inverted bow section of a tanker at Swan Island.

where the novices were taught the basic theory, then began hands-on practice after they were shown how to weld horizontal, vertical, and finally overhead seams.

Some ads tried to compare household chores with industrial work in a way that looks simplistic or patronizing today. In a Sperry Corporation recruitment pamphlet the company stated, 'Note the similarity between squeezing orange juice and the operation of a small drill press.' The Ford Company's Willow Run bomber plant publication proclaimed: 'The ladies have shown they can operate drill presses as well as egg beaters.'

The first graduates were assigned to Oregonship as assistants, and started like past generations of apprentices by performing the menial work after the craftsmen had moved on, like chipping the welds clean, sweeping the floor, and collecting tools and supplies from the storeroom. Soon the trickle became a river as thousands of women took wage-earning jobs for the first time in the Kaiser shipyards. While these pioneers were initially referred to by the unwieldy term 'welderesses', it was not long before women-power was considered equal with manpower in doing work previously thought of as 'man's' alone. 'The women came to the school from all walks of life and all parts of town … they expect to go into the welding world as a class of their own, working side-by-side with men who are already engaged in the construction of Liberty ships,' *The Oregonian* wrote on 21 May 1942.

Under the intense pressure to produce, shipyards began to ignore long-held views of workers' gender, and women welders, under no special name, soon became commonplace. The shipyards offered working women a considerable advance in wages, the opportunity to perform skilled labour previously the domain of men, and to make a substantial contribution to the war effort. The other Portland shipyards rapidly followed suit.

'Women in overalls are infiltrating the manly art of shipbuilding. Nearly 12,000 of them now labor in six shipyards in Portland and Vancouver. Sixty percent of them are doing men's work and drawing men's pay as craftsman, helpers, laborers, and sweepers and their numbers are increasing at the rate of more than 2000 per month … the vast majority … are welders, welders' helpers and trainees,' said *The Bo's'n's Whistle* in August 1942.

The women who 'put on their pants and tied up their hair' to go to work in war plants often faced an intimidating workplace with all manner of demeaning comments from male workers. They still faced resistance from the workmen who were too old for the draft or failed the physical, from disapproving husbands who wanted their dinner on time, and even from the early cartoons in *The Bo's'n's Whistle* that would certainly qualify as sexist today. To reassure their male colleagues, women were advised to be feminine but not sensual – a fine line when you are wearing a welder's helmet!

Men often played tricks on women by sending them for tools that did not exist. Men also sexually harassed women by whistling and cat-calling to them as they worked. Most of the resistance and hostility towards women workers disappeared as the novelty of women workers wore off, the labour shortage got worse, and women proved themselves, according to Susan M Hartmann, author of *The Home Front and Beyond: American Women in the 1940s*.

By late November 1942 more than 3000 women at the Kaiser Shipyards in Portland had received their union cards and were helping to build the emergency fleet. Overall, 28,000 women comprised 30 percent of the workforce by 1944, with thousands of others working in the smaller yards along the Columbia and Willamette Rivers. Entire crews of women, some in their mid-60s, worked long hours deep in the bowels of Liberty ships in manual labour, cleaning up scrap metal, grease and oil and otherwise doing what amounted to industrial cleaning. African Americans were usually stuck in lower-wage work once they landed a shipyard job, and were more likely to find better employment in canneries, railroads and military supply facilities, which only paid half the wages of shipyards.

Although women welders tended to get the most attention, women and girls filled many other job categories in the yards from the drafting desks to the painters' shacks. Inside the yards, a non-stop stream of government propaganda persuaded women to 'play their part', while outside, the ethos of the war effort was at odds with a society that reproached them for neglecting their duties as mother and wife. This attitude was rarely articulated, but the women were nonetheless aware of this 'double standard'. This was one of the causes of the high turnover rate and generated another campaign encouraging women to stay on the job 'until the war was won'.

'THE WORLD'S FIRST CHILD SERVICE CENTERS'

The growth of women in the workforce did encounter a notable drawback: despite the draft, or perhaps because of it, the incidence of marriage skyrocketed in the early years of the war and the birth rate in 1943 yielded the greatest birth explosion in United States history. Many of the new wives and mothers

Above: Woman rigger splicing steel cable.

Above: Woman electrician carrying electrical switch and climbing ladder against funnel of a Kaiser ship.

Above: Woman electrician screwing electric cable track to funnel of a Kaiser ship.

Below: Women electricians wiring switch boxes on a Kaiser ship

Above: Woman electrician making welding stingers

Below: Women electricians running overhead wires in the superstructure of a Kaiser ship.

wanted to join the war effort, but soon learned that mothers with children faced a lack of adequate child care. This created a crisis that some critics called the 'War Work Orphans' as young mothers left their children with any caregiver they could find while they worked in the shipyards.

Some desperate women were reported to be leaving their children at home alone or in cinemas. This was naturally causing late arrivals, absenteeism and resignations. The city was running day nurseries for low-income families, but the well-paid women welders were no longer considered in need of publicly-funded support. The mothers of young children working for Kaiser struggled to find adequate arrangements with relatives, friends, or neighbours.

With his pre-paid health care system running successfully, Henry Kaiser was said to have considered the need for child care as a 'production problem', which he solved in typical fashion. He created a department to generate a ground-breaking plan to build large nursery schools at Swan Island and Oregonship, open 24 hours a day. The outcry of complaints by conservatives against the plan required Eleanor Roosevelt to step in and use her authority as First Lady to swing the state's leaders in her favour – a totally unprecedented political step never seen again.

Left: Two female electrician helpers making leads for load centres

Left: Maintaining a safe depth for ship traffic in the Columbia River required continuous inspection by a proficient survey team. When the men who ran the survey boat were called up, women proved perfectly capable of mastering the technical skills needed to chart the river's changing sandbars and shallows. This was an important job in wartime to ensure none of the ships ran aground on their trial run to Astoria and back, or their subsequent delivery down-river to the Pacific Ocean.
The Army Corps of Engineers had three women working on a survey boat operating the electrical equipment that recorded the depth of the Columbia River. 'The work requires intensive teamwork to ensure accuracy and the girls have already proven themselves just as capable, if not more so, than the men who formerly held these positions,' declared F W Rodolf, chief survey engineer of the Corps Portland district in 1942.

With the financial backing of the Maritime Commission, state and federal governments, work began at both sites on a modernist design in the shape of a wheel by Wolf & Phillips Architects of Portland. The 'hub' was a protected open space in the centre with a play area, partitioned by age levels. The 'spokes' held fifteen playrooms with long banks of windows on either side. The facilities – toilets, sinks, lockers, and shelves – were all child-sized.

Teachers with specializations in early childhood education were recruited from all around the United States and were in place when the centres opened in November 1943. They were under the direction of Dr Lois Meek Stolz, former director of the Child Development Institute at Columbia University and a well-known authority on child care and training. Assisting her was James L Hymes, Jr, former assistant state supervisor of nursery schools in New York.

These qualifications give some idea of how important this opportunity was to the group of socially progressive staff who arrived in Portland with the intention to show how modern child care research could be put to good use in the war effort. Despite the fact that the country was at war on two fronts, and they would be aiding the production of emergency ships, Stolz and Hymes faced a barrage of criticism.

'So now Portland is to have three of the nation's largest

Above: Women riveting M-4 aluminium bridge boats (called 'pontons') with pneumatic guns at Oregonship. Over 2000 women were recruited early in 1945 and manufactured 3000 of the 30ft x 7ft craft in four months at the maximum rate of 40 per day. Each boat weighed 1750 lbs and could be carried upside down by a platoon of 20 men to the river bank. Two hulls were fastened transom to transom to form a single 60ft wide bridge unit. OSC fitted two assembly bays with a 35-ton press and industrial routers to cut and bend the plate and drill the thousands of rivet holes. These were the only jobs performed in the Kaiser shipyards that conformed to the famous 'Rosie the Riveter' image.

nursery and child care centers. This means the expenditure of a million dollars, the use of critical materials such as lumber, plumbing, wiring, the employment of scores of workers who are needed elsewhere. Child care standards are brushed aside and great damage will be done if we begin to industrialize six-month old babies. The state committee on child care opposed this plan for the system of child care in Russia; and we don't want it here!' said Saidie Orr Dunbar, chair of the Oregon State Advisory Committee on Child Care, Health and Welfare.

'Real authorities in the field of child care wanted nothing of the kind. They preferred, and rightly, that mothers with small children stay home and take care of their babies, leaving welding and wiring to those without such responsibilities; and if special provision for children was required, that small nurseries close to home be provided,' said another vocal critic.

In fact, every detail of the design and equipment of the centres was the best available, to match the high level of attention the staff were expected to provide. Each classroom had its own bathroom with a personalized touch since 'each child has a low hook for his towel, with his name or picture to mark the hook as his own.' The child-size toilets and sinks made it easier for children to keep clean, to be self-reliant, and to learn how to use the toilet themselves. An infirmary cared for sick children and provided basic medical services.

The routine included a health check, plenty of rest, outside play, and lessons in art and music. There were sleeping rooms for naps and overnight stays, as well as the previously mentioned child-sized sinks and toilets, lockers, and a sick room to isolate ailing students. The teachers took care to make the children's stay educational and stimulating. The importance of food and nutrition were seen as a key component in the program's success. Each centre had a large kitchen that provided all the children with 'all the food they need during their stay, including the daily requirement of cod liver oil.'

Above: The Kaiser Corporation's post-war report on the two Child Service Centers – 'probably the largest nursery school in the world.'

A child nutritionist planned all of the meals including those made for the 'Home Service Food' program, described in *The Bo's'n's Whistle* in February, 1944: 'Time is always tight for

Below: Kaiser Child Center on the man-made land bridge at the head of the Swan Island lagoon. Single men's dormitories on the right.

Left: The Kaiser Child Center was built around a circular playground divided into six areas for children of different ages, with a wading pool at the middle

Right: Kaiser Child Center cooked healthy meals and snacks for the children under the direction of a child nutritionist, eaten with their teachers at the child-size table and chairs.

working parents, so the Kaiser shipyards helped out. An article announced a program of ready-cooked meals for all day-shift workers at the Oregon and Swan Island shipyards. The meals were planned by an expert nutritionist. Upon ordering two days in advance, the meals could be picked up at the Child Care Centers.'

The peak one-day attendance was over 1000 children and the two centres provided a total of just under 250,000 child care days. It was calculated that this made it possible for mothers to work almost two million hours in the shipyards, the amount of time needed to build six Liberty ships. The centres became well known for their innovative approach to early childhood care and education. *Parents' Magazine* awarded the centres its medal for Outstanding Service to Children in 1944. The Office of War Information, through a broadcast, newsreels, and a traveling photo exhibit, shared the story of the centres internationally.

However, although the centres were integrated and open to African American families in theory, in practice the racial prejudice of the white families was so great that most black parents

Left: The Kaiser Child Center playgrounds contained a large variety of equipment including climbing apparatus, sand boxes, wagons etc.

arranged for child care within their own community. When the shipyards began to lay off staff in the spring of 1945, it was clear that the centres' short career would soon come to an end. After only 22 months in existence, the two Portland centres closed when all funding was suspended in September 1945. All vestiges of the public child care facilities throughout the nation disappeared, including the unique circular buildings in Portland that were demolished to make way for the expansion of the roads serving Swan Island when the shipyard was converted to peacetime use and a new industrial estate developed.

The child care system was gone but not forgotten, and remarkably its short history lives on in the twenty-first century in the USA as a utopian example of what government can do for working families in a progressive political era – or a world war! Today, the Kaiser kindergarten experiment continues to be studied, debated and celebrated 75 years later by female educators and politicians.

WOMEN DRIVERS

Approximately 12 million women accepted the challenge of working in traditional occupations like offices, hospitals, dining halls and daycare centres, and in warehouses and transportation. The Oregon State Highway Commission announced plans to train at least 150 'lady juggernaut jockeys', meaning women who would learn 'the ponderous arts of operating Diesel road rollers and heavy gravel trucks' due to the acute shortage of manpower. – *The Oregonian*, February 1943.

'Fourteen girls have replaced men as chauffeurs for the United States Maritime Commission who said they find the girls are excellent drivers and their care has reduced accidents to a minimum,' said *The Oregonian* in January 1943.

The Portland Traction Company, which operated the sorely-needed bus system in Portland, hired its first women driver, one Zada F Pratt on 21 February 1943, and announced plans to hire at least 75 more. Yellow Cab hired its first woman driver, the 'comely Mrs Evelyn Downs' in September 1942.

In coastal timber towns, women were accepted, if not always welcomed, into all-male domains such as millwork and logging. In agriculture, women fieldworkers were critical in bringing in Oregon's harvest during the war, accounting for three out of every four harvest jobs. By 1945 nearly one out of every four married women worked outside the home.

SURVIVING WOMEN WORKERS INTERVIEWED

Starting in the 1970s with the emergence of feminism and women's studies course in colleges, graduate students at coastal universities began interviewing and recording the surviving women who had worked in the defence industries during World War II. This has developed into a new field of study based on women's wartime experiences, and has produced numerous papers, articles and books with a sociological or feminist viewpoint. These accounts by journalists and historians focus on the personal experience, trials and tribulations of the task of women in a 'man's world', and the reluctant post-war return to a traditional role as home maker and mother.*

Miss Bethena Moore of Derrider, Louisiana was one welder interviewed by a *New York Times* reporter who was covering the opening of the national park in Richmond in 2000. She had been a laundry worker and weighed only 110 pounds, so was sent down into the depths of the hull on a narrow steel ladder to finish the welding of the double-bottoms. 'It was dark, scary,' she later recounted. 'It felt sad, because there was a war on. You knew why you were doing it – the men overseas might not get back. There were lives involved, so the welding had to be perfect.'

A former shipyard worker named Phyllis McKey Gould came to the Kaiser yard in Richmond as a welder. 'I'd never worked in my life,' she told a reporter. 'I loved the look of welding, the smell of it ... You'd look through really dark glass and all you'd see was the glow. You moved the welding rod in tiny, circular motions, making half-crescents. If you did it right, it was beautiful. It was like embroidery.'

However, there is a counter-narrative to the well-known image of Rosie the Riveter, the icon of female patriotism during World War II, her fist raised to show her hidden strength. Rosie was an asexual Amazon warrior on the home front, but there were also thousands of young women supporting the troops by providing 'morale-boosting services' to soldiers.

Meghan K Winchell's book *Good Girls, Good Food, Good Fun: The Story of USO Hostesses during World War II* (University of North Carolina Press, 2008) is a study of this aspect of the war effort, focusing on the Saturday nights when hundreds of thousands of 'respectable' volunteer hostesses and servicemen happily forgot the war as they danced and relaxed in United Service Organization clubs. These served as an escape from the reality of war in a time of social and moral separation. She demonstrates that in addition to boosting soldiers' morale, the USO acted as an architect of the gender roles and sexual codes of the time.

Working women lived with less public observation of their social activities during the war, and were often conflated with 'working girls'. (Some of the USO hostesses may also have been welders during their working day.) Young women who appeared to be enjoying themselves a little too visibly in the evening were called 'Victory Girls' and other less flattering terms as rumours about loose morals became a cause for concern among upper class ladies.

This double-standard was accurately summed up by a government official who dubbed these women 'patriotutes' – part patriot, part prostitute – merely for their attendance at USO dances or because they seemed to be offering more open sexual services. Socially active women fell under suspicion as a threat to the sexual health of soldiers; in some states they were even imprisoned for up to a year in disused Civilian Conservation Corps camps.*

* Here are a couple of titles that are typical examinations of this subject:
– *Fleeting Opportunities: Women Shipyard Workers in Portland and Vancouver during World War II and Reconversion* by Amy Vita Kesselman, Albany, NY, 1990.
– 'Women Workers and Child Care during World War II: A Case Study of the Portland, Oregon Shipyards.' Karen Beck Skold, PhD Thesis, University of Oregon, 1981.

* A scholarly examination of the reaction of civil and military leaders to women who used their sexuality – either intentionally or inadvertently – to serve their country is *Victory Girls, Khaki-Wackies, and Patriotutes: The Regulation of Female Sexuality during World War II)* by Marilyn Hegarty (NYU Press, 2007). It points out that a contradictory morals campaign launched by government and social agencies shunned female sexuality while endorsing masculine sexuality.

....

13

DAILY LIFE ON THE HOME FRONT

After Pearl Harbor, the entire USA was mobilized in the war effort in many ways that seemed unimaginable just a year before—and only appear more remarkable in retrospect. The emergency shipbuilding program on the west coast immediately began drawing unemployed people from all over the western states and would eventually create over 1.5 million jobs nation-wide. Throughout the country, the small cities around the new shipyards were completely unprepared for the dramatic changes the war effort would bring,

Between 1940 and 1943 defence employment in the Portland and Vancouver area climbed from a few thousand to 140,000 and the population of Vancouver had doubled by 1942. Portland's population grew by more than 25 percent in less than a year, straining the local community to breaking point in housing, transportation, medical and child care etc. Needing still more workers, Henry Kaiser scoured the country for recruits, finding thousands of willing volunteers in the prairie states where mechanization had displaced thousands of farm workers.

In a modern re-creation of the Oregon Trail of the 1850s, tens of thousands of men and women joined a second great migration to the Willamette Valley, increasing the population of Portland by almost a quarter and transforming it into a major industrial centre. Americans from all walks of life were rapidly retrained as welders and equipment operators, regardless of their previous education or work experience. In a matter of days, they were ready to join the small army building the ships the nation desperately needed.

HARD WORK FOR GOOD PAY

Working in the defence industry, building ships and other products manufactured in the Portland area during World War II, was backbreaking, demanding work. Most workers worked six-days on, one-day off, on one of the three shifts that allowed the yards to operate on 24-hour production schedules. In mid-1942 a welder at Oregonship working on the 'graveyard shift' was pulling in $1.28 an hour, a lot of money at the time and, apparently, a cause of some resentment among those either unable to secure such work or working in other areas of the industry for considerably less.

Journeymen in other trades at the shipyards (pipefitters, sheet metal workers, electricians and others) made $1.12 an hour, with assistants making less. Welders, the 'royalty' of the shipyard, were proud of their status and sensitive to the complaints they were overpaid. 'My husband is a welder … he gets his eyes burned … he gets fumes in his lungs … he squeezes into places one can barely squeeze … [you] get behind an electric arc welder in a confined space sometime and see how you like it!' said one proud wife quoted in *The Oregonian* in May 1942.

One family, the Braukmillers, gained national recognition by combining their living expenses and putting the money they saved into war bonds. Thirteen members of the family moved from Iowa to Portland to work in the yards and save money. 'Today the Braukmillers have staked out a rich claim and are thriving on it. Thirteen adults, all working for Kaiser … the aggregate family payroll is a staggering $996 a week, almost $52,000 a year!' (*Life Magazine*, August 1943).

THE BO'S'N'S WHISTLE

One of the ways to retain workers and keep up morale was to involve them in the daily activity of the shipyard by publishing

Left: *The Bo's'n's Whistle* was the house magazine of the Kaiser yards. A woman welder named Mary Carroll was featured on the cover of the edition for 13 August 1942 as a 'War Mother'.

a news magazine. *The Bo's'n's Whistle* was the name of the Kaiser publication that covered everything from the softball scores to production statistics. Amply illustrated by Kaiser's staff photographers, the *Whistle* chronicled the activities of the three yards and provided workers with information on safety, local events, and other matters of importance to the company's huge workforce.

The publication's reputation in Portland was bolstered in mid-1942 by appointment of a professional editor, Hal Babbitt. The publication quickly developed into a well-written professional journal, expanding to reach Kaiser Vancouver and Swan Island as those yards took shape. Babbit made a consistent effort to educate the workforce on shipbuilding, educational opportunities, housing and transportation and more. A typical issue might include notes of bond winners, production records, or what sort of footwear was most appropriate and comfortable for steel workers. *Whistle* articles, and particularly photographs, were regularly reprinted in *The Oregonian* and *Oregon Journal,* increasing their regional impact.

THE NEVER-ENDING BOND DRIVES

All the defence contractors encouraged their workers to enrol in payroll deductions to purchase bonds with every paycheck and, naturally, they competed against each other for highest percentage committed to the program during periodic drives. The US Treasury encouraged all war workers to donate 10 percent of each paycheck through the purchase of war bonds, the overall goal being '90-10' for each facility, meaning that 90 percent of the worker force donated at least 10 percent toward bonds. It appears that all Portland's yards met or bettered that mark.

The Kaiser yards had full-time war-bond promotional departments and at least one report claims the average Kaiser worker put fourteen cents of every after-tax dollar into savings, contributions or bonds. The Vancouver yard was 'in a league of its own', being the first defence plant in the nation to reach the 18 percent mark. The average monthly bond sales from Kaiser's three Portland shipyards during the war was nearly $3 million dollars—enough to pay for a couple of Liberty ships!

There were numerous special drives that encouraged workers to sign up for payroll deductions, to buy bonds during a particular drive, or to donate to other charitable causes. 'It Takes More than Bullets' was the name of the United War Chest drive that sent monies to war victims in Europe and Asia. 'Back the Attack' was the name given to a 'Third War Loan' drive that hoped to raise $15 billion dollars for Uncle Sam.

The campaigns usually included visits from celebrities or local entertainers. One of the favourites was a talented young singer with an exquisite soprano voice named Suzanne Burce who began entertaining as the 'Oregon Victory Girl' at the tender age of 12. She too was expected to join in the war effort and travelled around the state singing and selling victory bonds for almost two years. The show was performed at war bond rallies, military camps, veterans' homes and so forth. This earned her a slot on two weekly radio shows, where she sang popular war-era songs.

She once performed on a war-bond show with another aspiring local singer named Johnnie Ray. He was two years older than her and went on to become world famous in the 1950s, especially in the UK, where he was one of the first Americans to introduce a new popular musical style and caused a sensation with his theatrics on stage! John Ray was his real name, but 'Suzanne Burce' did not have the same ring to it. She too would find fame, but under a different name.

In 1944, when she was only 15, her mother took the Victory Girl to Hollywood where she hoped to achieve her goal of making her daughter a star. She entered Suzanne in a talent competition on a radio show, and she was soon being auditioned for Louis B Mayer at MGM. Without even taking a screen test, she was signed to a seven-year contract and made her screen debut in *Song of The Open Road* in 1944. Her character was named Jane Powell, and that became her stage name. As Jane Powell, she rose to national fame before she was 20 and starred in a series of MGM musicals for the next decade.

SHORTAGES OF EVERYTHING

Shipyard workers competed with the local population for everything required for daily life: clothes, food, housing, butter, meat, shoes. Under a nationwide ration system, shipbuilders sought high priority for their own production, but recognized that their workers also needed tyres and gasoline for their vehicles in order to get to work every day. This was a constant irritant for many Portlanders during the first year of the war and became everyone's favourite wartime scapegoat. It remained replete with red tape, including coupons, certificates, stamps, stickers, and a changing point system based on availability.

Around twenty essential items were subject to regulation, including household necessities such as canned food, coffee, sugar, meat, butter and gasoline. In order to purchase these goods, citizens were issued books with small square-inch stamps which they were required to use to buy goods rationed by the Office of Price Administration (OPA). They would be passed from the cluttered handbag of the consumer to the retailer, who passed them on to the wholesaler, who sent them to the manufacturer, who had to account for them to the federal government.

The system was a headache for everyone concerned, as billions of stamps changed hands every month. People took the wartime slogan of 'use it up, wear it out, make it do or do without' to heart. They really had no choice since shortages developed in thousands of different items. In addition to rising prices, the incredible demands of building and supplying the

UNITED STATES OF AMERICA OFFICE OF PRICE ADMINISTRATION
MILEAGE RATION—IDENTIFICATION FOLDER
Coupons "B" "C" "D" "E" "R" "T" 26

STATE Non | VALID DATE 6-25-45
LICENSE NUMBER Highway | EXPIRATION DATE
YEAR, MODEL AND MAKE | EARLIEST RENEWAL DATE 9-14-45
FLEET IDENTIFICATION OR CWN NUMBER (IF ANY)
SERIAL NUMBERS OF COUPONS ISSUED FROM 2857518 TO 7943 INCL.

ISSUED TO Lawrence Barber
ADDRESS NUMBER AND STREET 6422 N. Kerby Ave
CITY AND STATE Portland 11, Oreg.

COUPONS MUST BE KEPT WITH THIS FOLDER AT ALL TIMES
Size of folder optional—use entire card, or cut away along lines indicated
16—40576-1
OPA FORM R-577 (REV. 8-44)

FOLD HERE

War Price & Rationing
Board 85.20.7
4501 N. Mississippi
Portland 11, Oregon
BOARD STAMP

GSK
(SIGNATURE OF ISSUING OFFICER)

Any Person Finding Lost Coupons Should Mail or Return Them at Once to the Nearest War Price and Rationing Board

CUT AWAY ALONG THIS LINE

M 2857580 NONHIGHWAY E3h NAME ADDRESS	M 2857579 NONHIGHWAY E3h NAME ADDRESS	M 2857578 NONHIGHWAY E3h NAME ADDRESS	M 2857577 NONHIGHWAY E3h NAME ADDRESS
M 2857575 NONHIGHWAY E3h NAME ADDRESS	M 2857574 NONHIGHWAY E3h NAME ADDRESS	M 2857573 NONHIGHWAY E3h NAME ADDRESS	M 2857572 NONHIGHWAY E3h NAME ADDRESS
M 2857570 NONHIGHWAY E3h NAME ADDRESS	M 2857569 NONHIGHWAY E3h NAME ADDRESS	M 2857568 NONHIGHWAY E3h NAME ADDRESS	M 2857567 NONHIGHWAY E3h NAME ADDRESS
M 2857565 NONHIGHWAY E3h NAME	M 2857564 NONHIGHWAY E3h NAME	M 2857563 NONHIGHWAY E3h NAME	M 2857562 NONHIGHWAY E3h NAME

OPA FORM R-530 E

Above: Lawrence (Larry) Barber's gasoline ration card, along with examples of the ration coupons. As a journalist who covered many miles for work, he was privileged to be rated 'E', so entitled to the maximum allowance.

Above: The historic battleship USS *Oregon*, built 1896, was displayed in downtown Portland between 1925 and 1942. The ship was to become the largest contribution to the scrap drive, and is shown being manoeuvred by two of the Columbia River's venerable sternwheel tow boats.

US war machine led to shortages, black markets, hoarding, and constant calls for conservation. The elaborate system of gasoline rationing caused more problems.

Each driver was assigned a windshield sticker with a letter of priority ranging from A to E. Cars used only for pleasure driving wore an A sticker worth one stamp redeemable for three to five gallons a week, depending on the region and the period. Commuters were assigned B stickers worth a varying amount of fuel depending on their distance from work. Additional systems developed for other rationed products such as car tyres and tubes.

In reality, large and small violations of rationing and price control regulations combined to form a flourishing black market. Typically, this consisted of consumers paying prices above the established limits or buying goods without the required coupons. Many customers, flush with money from high paying defence jobs, were willing to violate the law in order to buy that really good cut of meat for a special occasion or a rare pair of shoes that would go perfectly with a new dress. Retailers found a number of ways to work the system 'under the counter'.

SCRAP DRIVES

Even before America's entry into World War II, a parade of scrap drives kept citizens busy. The drives started by collecting aluminium before moving into a wide range of products such as rubber, paper, tin, household fats, silk stockings, and even coats for Russian refugees. Comparisons also drove home the value of salvaging materials. Thus, the amount of rubber salvaged from one old tyre could provide 20 parachute troopers with boots or make 12 gas masks.

Below: The USS *Oregon* was removed from its permanent berth in downtown Portland in 1943 and the upper works removed prior to scrapping. (The mast can still be seen on display on the waterfront.)

Kitchen fats and greases would seem, on the surface, to be odd materials to be fervently collecting in the midst of a world war, but officials had their reasons. The fats contained a significant amount of glycerine that could be used in explosives. Glycerine was valuable to the war effort in other ways too, including as an antiseptic, a medicinal solvent, in cellophane and glassine packaging, and as treatment for sunburn and other skin irritations. The biggest item donated to the scrap drive in Oregon was the aged battleship USS *Oregon*, a local museum attraction; but the ship was never completely taken to pieces and, ironically, it survived the war as a barge and was finally broken up in Japan.

THE CRITICAL NEED FOR HOUSING

Portland was the only city on the west coast without a public housing authority, so in April 1941 Portland's Mayor, Earl Riley, appointed a 15-member commission to survey available housing units and recommend a system to shelter the expected influx of new workers. Providing quarters for the area's legions of workers was identified as a serious public concern and the council was forced to look for ever-more creative solutions to accommodate the new residents.

They reluctantly began to accept that the war effort was going to take priority in every aspect of city life, and took the first steps to accommodate the housing demands from the shipyards and defence contractors. The simplest, speediest solution was to persuade more Portlanders to rent out rooms to migrant workers. The National Housing Agency launched a campaign titled 'Share Your Home' that explained how homeowners with empty bedrooms could do their part and earn a steady income.

In some cities, surveys were organized to identify potential accommodation and explain how to organize a rooming house. Older women whose family members were in the armed forces – or who had died in action – were encouraged to think of this as their patriotic contribution to the war effort. In November 1941, *The Oregonian* reported that 'Oregon Shipbuilding officials state that there is not a vacant house within six miles of that plant.' Some newly-arrived workers were sleeping in tents, caravans and trailers, and were taking time off to search for proper long-term housing. This led to a lot of absenteeism and turnover if people failed to find tolerable accommodations.

The federal government's Division of Defense Housing began to look for projects it could pursue on its own, with or without the city's involvement. That effort was stymied by local resistance, but four days after Pearl Harbor, the city council finally established the Housing Authority of Portland (HAP). At first, the HAP board was dominated by private realtors; but it would find its feet and begin taking actions like rent control and converting single family homes to house two or more families. Then vacant land was identified and appropriated for the placement of mobile homes and portable buildings.

HAP designed and built several housing estates on the North Portland Peninsula, between the Columbia and the Willamette Rivers close to Oregonship and Swan Island. Within two years, there was enough new affordable housing for 72,000 inhabitants, but this barely met the need of the growing population. In 1942 the War Housing Zoning code was adopted, allowing higher density development for workers in the war industries.

Edgar Kaiser built a camp of long barracks-like buildings across the lagoon from Swan Island for some 7000 single men. That represented one entire shift at the yard, yet it still was not enough with Vancouver coming on line. So the Kaiser organization decided it could do for housing what it was doing for shipbuilding: think big and start from the ground up to create an entirely new town.

VANPORT – SECOND BIGGEST CITY IN OREGON

With the support of the Maritime Commission and the White House, Edgar purchased 650 acres of vacant land on the flood plain between Portland's northern limit and the Columbia River's south channel. The site was well below the river's high-water mark, but was protected by a dyke on the riverbank, the main north-south highway on the east side, and the North Pacific railroad embankment constructed in 1907 on the west side. The site was roughly equidistant between the Kaiser yards at Swan Island, St Johns, and Vancouver.

Portlanders living nearby were surprised when contractors broke ground in August 1942 and a workforce that grew to 5000 men and women was soon swarming all over the site, grading roads and setting foundations. Board members of the HAP grumbled about being left in the dark, but they agreed to take over management of the project, known initially as Kaiserville. The town received its official name of Vanport in November and was completed in just 110 days. The first tenants arrived on 12 December 1942.

They settled into a town of 10,414 apartments and homes – complete with schools, a library, post office, 750-seat theatre and a college – the forerunner of Portland State University. Vanport quickly overtook the state capital, Salem, to become the second biggest city in Oregon and the largest housing development in the United States, At the ribbon cutting in August of 1943, *The Oregonian* heralded it as a symbol of America's wartime ingenuity. 'Vanport City goes beyond providing homes for defense workers,' the article proclaimed. 'It is encouraging all possible conditions of normal living to parallel the hard terms of life in a war community.'

At its peak, Vanport housed as many as 40,000 people – 15,000 of them black (more than in the entire rest of the state). Five overcrowded elementary schools served 4000 children in two shifts of four hours each. The homes were admittedly poorly built because they were supposed to be only temporary.

Above: Kaiser Vancouver barracks-type housing Hudson House with 5000 beds in dormitories.

They lacked insulation and many kitchens were only equipped with electric hot plates and coal-burning stoves for heating. But the new town boasted a cinema, recreational centres and playgrounds and was the forerunner of the vast post-war housing developments like Levittown on Long Island, New York that grew to a population of 82,000.

One failing was clearly visible to anyone who entered the town: Vanport was physically segregated from the rest of North Portland inside the levees. 'The psychological effect of living on the bottom of a relatively small area, diked on all sides to a height of 15 to 25 feet, was vaguely disturbing,' wrote Manly Maben in his 1987 book *Vanport*. 'It was almost impossible to get a view of the horizon from anywhere – at least on the ground or in the lower level apartments, and it was even difficult from upper levels.'

VANCOUVER HOUSING AUTHORITY

Although there was only one shipyard in Vancouver, it was the biggest of Kaiser's seven yards and employed 38,000 people at its peak. That number was double the population of the city in 1940, and many of them arrived with their families, so there was a huge demand for housing across the Columbia in Washington state. The Vancouver Housing Authority was established in 1942 with very little fanfare to respond to the crisis. It had an advantage over Portland because Vancouver was still at the focal point of an agricultural area with many small farms and orchards close to the small urban centre that would be available for housing.

Eight estates capable of housing 55,000 people were quickly planned and constructed on farmland around the city. One of the largest was McLoughlin Heights, which had 60 miles of streets and housed 25,000 people, making it the second largest wartime housing project in the nation. The Vancouver school district went from 200 teachers to 1000, with most schools running double shifts to educate the children whose parents worked in the shipyard and the aluminium plant. Homes rented for $36 to $45 a month.

Recreation centres provided after-school activities for children while their parents worked. Land was set aside for people to plant 'victory gardens' to help feed their families. A bus service was available to take residents to their jobs. This situation of these big new cities appearing in just a few months and facing each other across the river is so unusual one would think it deserved some attention from the press, but there is no record of any. This may be because each of them alone was causing enough consternation in their respective states, that no one felt the need to cover both in one story.

After the war, the people who could afford better housing moved out of Vanport, but many black, minority and poor families moved in, keeping this 'temporary' city half full. In 1948, heavy winter snowfall in the mountains was followed by a warm spring with heavy rainfall that combined to send a raging flood down the Columbia River. Despite reassurances from HAP that Vanport was safe, at 4.15 pm on 30 May, without any warning, the railroad embankment gave way. The water rushed in through this 'side door,' and straight into Vanport, and formed a lake that began to rise inexorably up over the ground floor of every home.

The inhabitants all began running for their lives towards the nearest levee, struggling to hold on to infants or pets or luggage. From a safe height, they looked back to watch the water rise until entire apartment blocks were lifted off their flimsy foundations and floated away. In a couple of hours,

Below: Kaiser Vancouver McLoughlin Heights emergency housing contained 5500 units. The Vancouver Housing Authority built 1000 permanent homes and 11,396 temporary units capable of housing 50,000 people. The development was named after Dr John McLoughlin, a French-Canadian member of the Hudson's Bay Co.

Vanport was no longer the second biggest town in the state; in fact, it no longer existed. The authorities insisted only 15 people died, a number that was never publicly challenged, but the death toll was likely higher.

Portland was again faced with thousands of homeless people and again struggled to find homes for them—especially the black families who now considered Oregon their home. The issue of 'imported' black workers was still a cause of uneasiness for the white community, three years after the war, and was seen through the racial bias that still exists 75 years later. Today, nothing remains of Vanport; in its place stands the Portland International Raceway and Heron Lakes Golf Course.

ABSENTEEISM

Not all workers were entirely dedicated to the war effort with the gruelling six-day shifts and absenteeism was a constant problem for much of the defence industry. Some workers were just shirking responsibility and basking in their new-found wealth for a day or two, others had a serious lack of the work ethic. The yards, which worked so hard to find workers, to train them, and paid them well for their labour, were aggressive in their efforts to reduce unnecessary absenteeism. It was not just a Portland problem, but one that faced plants nationwide, from Seattle to Detroit.

Many employees at factories had migrated from the hard working but more organically paced life of the farm, to find themselves in the middle of a war production line: 'machines whirring, spinning; electric hammers pounding; pulleys moving and giant cranes swinging; tools cutting, punching, polishing to the thousandth of an inch – life and death hanging upon the turn of a hand.' Not surprisingly, many workers were 'still shy of the monstrous machines, the roar of noise, the Vulcan fires of the furnace.' (*Spare Time: A War Asset for War Workers*, Handbook, Federal Security Agency, 1943)

THE UNFIT IN THE SHIPYARDS

During the war many individuals who were considered unfit for duty in the military were able to contributed to the war effort by working in the yards. The Albina Engine Works was praised by Vice-President Wallace for its hiring practices to include the disabled and the 'handicapped', many of whom were returning wounded soldiers. Earlier in the war the Woodlawn Defense Training Center, one of many vocational schools that were established through the Portland School District to pre-train men and women for industrial work, established special course work for blind students, who were taught how to operate drill presses and would work in electrical assembly work upon graduation (*The Oregonian*, May 1942).

'The stresses of war are giving a rude jolt to many preconceived and well-established notions. Not the least of these are generally-accepted ideas about the efficiency of physically-handicapped workers' (*Bo's'n's Whistle*, April 1943). Shipyards found places for amputees, paralyzed workers, the deaf and dumb, the blind and many other individuals who were previously considered unemployable. As the war had done for women, the elderly, and blacks, these workers benefited greatly from a willingness on the part of employers to broaden the labour pool. 'Whatever the reason, industry is making a great discovery and learning a lesson that may mean much for the 'handicapped' worker when the war is over,' commented *The Bo's'n's Whistle*.

COMPETITION

Oregonians augmented national popular culture with more of the local, homegrown variety. They participated in the pageants, contests, concerts, recitals, plays, speeches and other entertainments, many designed to promote war efforts such as selling war bonds or collecting Victory Books. Athletic competitions were considered a wholesome way for workers outside of the yards to exercise. Competition between the various divisions in each yard, and between the yards and community-based workers was a large part of Portland during the war. Kaiser's yards sponsored a series of teams, in softball, bowling and other sports, as did Commercial Iron Works, WISCO and Albina.

RACIAL TENSIONS IN THE SHIPYARDS

Pre-war Portland was known as the 'worst Northern city in racial relations' and had a reputation as the most openly racist city on the west coast, dating back to the pioneer days. The city allowed active discrimination against non-whites in downtown bars and restaurants, and restricted them to living in a small section of the city called Albina. Realtors refused to sell blacks property outside of that run-down neighbourhood, but it had one advantage: it was close to both Kaiser's NE Portland yards, and the intense worker shortage allowed black Americans, to seek more responsibility and higher paying jobs than had previously been open to them. Around 1000 black men were working for Kaiser early in 1942, out of the total of 67,000.

Then a second wave of migration from the southern states brought thousands of poor African-American sharecroppers and domestic workers to Portland, escaping from the school segregation, racial hatred and low wages they had grown up in. The issue of 'imported' black workers was a cause of uneasiness for the white community. The Boilermakers union pushed back, and Lodge 72 refused to hire 30 New York black workers except for menial jobs. They complained, but it was not until 7

Overleaf: Vancouver off shift leaving work. At its peak the yard employed nearly 39,000 people on three shifts, which resulted in vast numbers of pedestrians during shift changes, and traffic jams around the parking areas.

DECK ERECTION

October 1942, that the Portland Kaiser shipyard and the Boilermakers agreed to permit black workers to be employed at the shipyards, '... making use of "their highest skills" in all departments.'

But that interpretation was up to the union. By mid-December 1942, resistance mounted. A representative for 150 black shipyard workers at Kaiser's Vancouver, Washington, yard charged that 'the proposed auxiliary union represented downright open discrimination.' The Oregon Kaiser shipyards were forced to fire more than 300 black workers in July 1943 for refusing to join the auxiliary. The Fair Employment Practices Commission held public hearings and issued a 'cease and desist' order against the union, but with little result.

The alternative was to find better opportunities in canneries, railroads and military supply facilities, which usually paid lower wages. Nonetheless, the black workers were determined to stay, and set about creating their own social circles and services. The growth of a new black community and the resulting housing crisis served to alarm the city leaders, and most Portlanders greeted these new arrivals with disdain and hostility. Despite all this, by 1944, there were about 6000 black shipyard workers in the area.

Six African-American women welders in Vancouver were fired after they complained about unfair treatment and racial slurs. They appealed to the Employment Practice Committee but their case was dismissed. Nevertheless, the war moved many black women out of domestic service – as one woman put it, 'Hitler was the one that got us out of the kitchen.'

To put this in perspective, things were a whole lot worse in the southern shipyards. There were racially-motivated riots at the Alabama Dry Dock and Shipbuilding Company at Mobile in 1943, and another at a yard in Beaumont, Texas, also in 1943. Riots like these happened many times during the war, but by far the worst was in Detroit where a total of 34 people were killed, hundreds were wounded, and there was over $2 million in property damage. The riot threatened war production in the nation's leading industrial supplier, and revealed a level of racial hatred that continues to plague the USA.

THE DAILY STRUGGLE TO GET TO WORK

Three times a day, seven days a week, some 8000 to 10,000 workers left the three Kaiser Van-Port shipyards at the end of their shift, as a similar number were starting their workday. While the company had mastered the art of transporting steel into the yard and turning it into a ship as quickly and efficiently as possible, there was only so much they could do to keep their employees moving as smoothly outside the gates. This issue applied not just to the Kaiser yards, but to the entire war effort in Portland, where every boatyard and factory was also working around the clock.

The irony in this situation was that less than twenty years before, Portland had been at the centre of one of the largest urban rail systems in the west, rated one of the best in the nation for a small city. In the late 1800s, Portland began to build a system of trains and trolleys that connected the downtown with the new suburbs that were appearing outside the city limits. By 1893, it boasted the first inter-urban electric rail service in the nation with sleek modern trains, while smaller municipal trolleys provided inexpensive and efficient local service into the early 1920s.

But the rise of the Automobile Age in the Roaring Twenties caused a sharp drop in demand. Portland's commuter rail lines went out of business and in many cases the track was ripped out completely and scrapped. By 1940, the only public transportation company still operating was the privately-held Portland Traction Company with a fleet of 300 well-worn buses (see endpaper map for its routes).

CARPOOLING SUGGESTED TO EASE TRAFFIC JAMS

In the year before Japan declared war on the USA, Oregonship was growing its workforce by at least 1000 men per month, and paying a decent hourly wage. Many of them could finally afford a new car and anticipated a pleasant commute in the morning. What they actually found was a daily struggle with snarled traffic and long delays to get into the yard's giant parking lot. With the huge increase in the local workforce after Pearl Harbor, and the patriotic urge to increase production, the problem only got worse.

Portland's many war industries were all faced with the same self-inflicted crisis. Many ideas were proposed to solve the city's transit problem, which seemed to be almost as intractable as the housing crunch. Several solutions required the sacrifice of old habits, especially those related to the use of cars. Kaiser and other employers urged employees to form car clubs, where 'members would ride together and rotate daily use of automobiles owned by the group'.

Larry Barber began reporting on this situation early in 1942, when the Oregonship workforce had already reached 20,000.

31 January 1942. 'There is already serious crowding of lines serving industries and there is delay ... in the peak traffic hours of morning and evening.'

1 February. 'Transportation becomes problem; danger of tire and gas shortages seen. Men asked to double up [carpool]. Cooperative bus clubs begin to spring up. First was The Gang club from SE 82nd and Bybee, Working Men's Club from Tigard and others. They get special parking privileges. Highway bottlenecks surveyed; boats and trains seen in future.'

22 February. 'Oregonship begins campaign for more homes within walking distance of yard and better traffic routes. Only

Above: Parking lot rush hour on a winter morning.

5 percent of 23,314 employees live within walking distance. More than half drive more than 10 miles each way.'

15 March. 'Traffic story – full page – 26,200 employees. Tires wearing out under need to drive 900 miles a month and no more rubber in sight; congested access roads; two more yards under construction with prospects of 100,000 workers to be moved daily; dispersal problem in case of bombing; need for trains and ferries; big bus fleet sought for traction company etc.'

By this time, the 8000 parking spots at Oregonship barely accommodated all the buses, trucks and private vehicles that carried each shift; all the roads leading to the plant were regularly jammed to a standstill. Public bus service was clearly the answer, but with only 300 vehicles, the Portland Traction Company was unable to keep up with the demand the plants created and still provide acceptable service to the rest of the community.

The existing bus lines and car clubs could only do so much; individual workers at the various shipyards began to band together and form cooperative 'bus lines', that took the car club a step further. An individual with a truck or large car would build a trailer, fit seats, and offer to haul workers in it daily. Such groups were required to petition the county rationing board for additional tyres, which were strictly rationed.

The extreme shortage of rubber was the result of the Japanese capturing 90 percent of the world's rubber-growing areas. Officials reminded citizens that 'failure to participate in group-riding plans is to waste rubber, and wasting rubber in the light of today's conditions is nothing short of disloyalty to the war effort.' The elaborate system of gasoline rationing caused more headaches.

12 March. 'Oregonship awarded a contract to the Russell Towboat Company to operate a ferry for its employees across the Columbia River.'

26 March. 'The Russell company proposed to employ three large covered barges, each equipped to carry 600 men at a time … [charging] passengers $1.25 for book of seven round trips, including parking.'

9 April. 'Federal government granted the OSHD [Oregon State Highway Department] $185,000 to improve road access to Oregonship, including the construction of temporary viaduct to create a fifth lane next to the existing four-lane viaduct.'

Despite the multi-modal effort to develop and improve public transport, and gas and tyre rationing, many shipyard workers continued to rely on private cars to get to work, continuing to clog the roads in and out of the shipbuilding district. The shipyards began staggering the end of shifts in an effort to reduce the rush hours as workers streamed into and out of the plants.

21 May. Plan announced for two San Francisco Bay ferries to serve OSC and Swan Island, a shuttle train to Vancouver, and 150 additional buses. Ferry terminal planned for downtown riverfront. The ferry operation expanded after the Maritime Commission announced plans to buy two aged ships in San Francisco, the *City of Sacramento* and *the Sierra Nevada*, and use them to establish a ferry line between the local shipyards. They were sizable vessels: the *Sacramento* was 300ft long and capable of carrying some 3500 people on its three decks while the *Sierra Nevada* was somewhat smaller at 218ft long.

The boats, which would operate on the Willamette, between downtown, Swan Island and Oregonship were renamed *Victory V* and the *Liberty Clipper* as the result of a contest sponsored by *The Bo's'n's Whistle*. The ferry service succeeded in moving large numbers of workers efficiently and reduced pressure on the surface transportation systems.

23 July. *The Oregonian* reported the Maritime Commission had announced its plan to requisition two more large ferries from the San Francisco area for use in Portland: the *Hayward* and *San Leandro* were each 225ft long and could carry 3000 passengers. The new ferries arrived in the Portland area by late August. New terminals were constructed at Swan Island and Oregonship, and on the opposite shore of the Willamette.

23 November. The Kaiser shipyards urged its workers to 'lay-up their cars, conserve both gas and rubber, and ride the buses and the ferries provided for them on the 20-minute run.'

Traction Company bus routes were re-designed to converge upon the ferry terminals at the appropriate times, allowing thousands of workers to streamline their commutes, with the ferries making the return trip with those employees going off-shift. Each of the ships was scheduled to make three round-trips every day. The ferries went into full service in January 1943. Men and women workers found the ferry exceedingly comfortable, virtually vibration-free, and a great improvement of the buses. 'I'm going home and jack up my car. It's the ferry for me now,' said one man.

But despite high expectations, the ferry service was not particularly successful. Only 500 workers were on that first boat – probably not the massive take-up that had been anticipated.

Below: A converted goods vehicle and surplus school buses wait outside the shipyard cafeteria for departing workers. These conversions were known as 'Cooperative Buses'.

Modest use of the ferries may have been affected when, less than a month after the big Maritime Commission ferries went into operation, a small, privately operated tug boat carrying passengers across the Columbia capsized, killing ten workers in what *The Oregonian* reported as 'the worst accident in Columbia River history.'

The ferry ride was pleasant but slow; after several months the plan was quietly abandoned and the buses once more brought their loads directly to the yards. The railroads were also called into service to reduce traffic. In early 1943, the Maritime Commission purchased 22 coach cars and laid track south along Front Street in north-west Portland, connecting the ferry terminals with Union Station.

February 1943. 'It is the plan of the commission to run two ten-car trains from both the Portland and Vancouver shipyard terminals for the day, swing and graveyard shifts.' The train was dubbed the 'Vanship Limited' and went into service in March offering a round trip fare of 25 cents, accommodating up to 1500 seated passengers.

30 June. 'Portland Traction Company told it was getting 150 school-type buses for hauling shipyard workers, but they did not arrive for over a year.'

With the announcement of plans for the Swan Island shipyard, the transportation system faced potential collapse under the added volume of its 30,000 workers. Portland Traction Company appealed to the US Maritime Commission for assistance in procuring additional buses, already a scarce commodity. In the meantime, the company decided to re-open the old electric trolley lines that had formed Portland's original mass transit network. In addition to rehabilitating its old rolling stock, the company purchased several new streetcars in mid-1942 from a line in New York, and began to run cars on the long-unused lines it had operated decades earlier.

July. Portland Traction Company receives its first 50 new buses for hauling shipyard workers. To meet the demand for drivers, it turned to women just like so many other industries. There were more complaints about women being incapable of handling a

Below: This steam-powered ferry from San Francisco Bay had also been given a short trial in Seattle, then sent to the run between Portland and Vancouver, where it was no more successful.

Above: One of the school-type buses eventually acquired to transport commuting workers at Swan Island. Note the huge 'hammerhead' crane in the background.

heavy vehicle, deserting their children to flirt with their male passengers etc, but of course they turned out to be as proficient at bus driving as they were at welding.

The Office of Defense Transportation issued a guide to avoid unnecessary travel, giving priority to journeys connected to the war effort.

Necessary

Travel that will help win victory at the front and keep us efficient at home. Necessary travel includes: military travel, including furloughs, official and company business, urgent family business, family emergencies, and trips to doctors, dentists, hospitals.

Permissable

Travel that may sometimes be necessary to keep the life of the country going efficiently. Permissible travel includes: visits to

Left: Female bus drivers were recruited by the Portland Traction Company to run extra buses to the shipyards.

service men, necessary shopping trips, and vacation travel from home to the place where one spends his holiday, and home again.

Non-essential
Travel that cannot in any way help us to win the war. Non-essential travel includes: social visits, trips to sports events, theatres, fairs; unnecessary shopping trips; tours, including vacation excursions; and trips to conventions, trade shows.

At its peak in the winter of 1943–44, the War Manpower Commission estimated there were 140,000 workers in war industries in greater Portland: 92,000 in the Kaiser yards, 23,000 in the smaller shipyards, and 25,000 in all other companies. The population in the area had increased by one third from 500,000 to 660,000.

January 1945. In response to the added strain on the transportation system, and because they were 'compelled to re-emphasize facts about wartime travel,' the Office of Defense Transportation highlighted the 'Vacation at Home' promotional campaign. They urged communities to form Vacation at Home committees consisting of representatives from entities such as municipal government, churches, labour unions, radio stations, theatres and restaurants.

Authorities envisioned local activities that would be limited only by the imagination of the community. But, just in case, they offered suggestions. For example, radio stations could conduct 'Our Town at Home' broadcasts from backyards and porches that highlighted interesting "stay-at-home" families in the community.' One railroad ran advertisements telling potential travellers: 'You'll be more comfortable at home.'

....

Part Three Other Portland A

ea War Industries

14

COMMERCIAL IRON WORKS

Located at the western end of the Ross Island Bridge, south of downtown Portland and on the opposite side of the Willamette River from the Kaiser yards, Commercial Iron Works (CIW) was established in 1916 as a foundry and machine shop in the SW marine-industrial district. It did not take full advantage of its waterfront location until the 1930s when it began building small barges and tugs. In 1938, the company leased property south of the bridge where they laid down a slipway and erected a 250ft by 60ft shed to permit work in all weathers. This remained the first and only covered ways in the region throughout the war years. The *Jean*, one of the last sternwheel steam tugs, was built here, followed by a smaller river tug the *Keith*.

In July 1940 CIW was the first Portland yard to win a pre-war order from the US Navy in response to Japan's war of expansion in SE Asia. CIW secured a contract for four 146ft net tenders (YN) worth $500,000 each. These vessels were heavily-built tugboats that worked the heavy steel anti-submarine nets that closed the entrance to a naval base or enclosed anchorage like Pearl Harbor to secure it from submarine attack.

In September the management followed this success by announcing plans to lengthen this building for a plate and assembly shop and lay out a second ways covered by a 200ft x 75ft building. This was reputed to be the biggest covered building way on the west coast. They continued the expansion by moving the rest of the plant from the north side of the bridge to the south, then took another big step up by starting pile driving in October for an outfitting dock running north from the bridge. Note that this activity took place in the months before Henry Kaiser's arrival and Pearl Harbor.

This was carefully noted by Larry Barber, who began to follow the company's progress more closely. He started to keep a log of activity at the yard, as he did for Oregonship. His entries are reproduced below, with some dates taken from a souvenir booklet published to celebrate the company's 100th launch.

28 February 1941. First net tender, *Catalpa*, launched.

20 March. Second tender, *Chestnut*, launched.

24 March. Defense Secretary Knox announces new awards, including seven *Admirable* class 184ft minesweepers for $4,770,500 for hulls; 650 now employed and 200–400 more will be required. Means spreading material and equipment orders among 50 subcontractors in district.

There were now around 150 men working in the yard on the net tenders and the excavation, which soon exposed the old slipways from World War I. The pilings were found to be sound, so they were cut off and re-capped, and the keels for the first tenders were laid. A monthly paper, *The Port Hole*, was started with Ed Donnelly, safety engineer, as editor, turning out four-page mimeograph of company scuttlebutt.

12 April. *Cottonwood,* third tender launched.

28–29 May. *Catalpa* on builder's trial to mouth of river and return. First trial of a navy vessel here since 1900.

29 June. Acceptance and commissioning ceremony for *Catalpa*.

26 July. *Buckeye,* last tender launched.

The YNs carried a crew of 40 to accomplish the arduous and dangerous work of laying and recovering the heavy steel net. They were equipped with one small deck gun. The prominent steel 'horns' on the bow of a net layer are very distinctive and today are still seen in modern cable-laying ships. All four net layers were delivered before Pearl Harbor, and served through the war, often ferrying troops and cargo around the anchorage after the net was safely set.

The Navy's Bureau of Ships was so impressed that the chief officer signed this letter addressed to employees of Commercial Iron Works:

Previous pages: In early 1945 work is underway at Commercial Iron Works on two LCS(L) with their forward gun tubs to carry dual-purpose 3-inch/50 calibre guns clearly visible. Two more LCS(L), less advanced in construction, can be seen behind. To the right is *PCE-882* and, in camouflage, an *Auk* class minesweeper.

Left: The vessel in the cradle is the *Tawasa* (AT-92), a 205ft *Cherokee* class armed fleet tug. They were also the first large surface vessels in the US Navy to be equipped with a diesel-electric system. It consisted of four General Motors 12-278A 900 hp (2685 kW) engines driving four GM generators that turned a single shaft and propeller.

Chief of the Bureau of Ships

USS *Chestnut* – Jack of All Trades

The important contribution you are making to the war effort is reflected in the following report of the excellent performance of the net tender, YN6, which was built in your yard. The commanding officer of the YN6 wrote: 'In spite of the fact that I have been with ships for almost twenty years, up to the time I became skipper of the YN6 I did not know that any one ship could do so many different jobs, and do them well. We have, in addition to our regular business, ferried water and fuel, transported raiders, salvaged planes, towed targets, picked up broken down ships at sea, laid all kinds of mooring buoys, been used as a pilot vessel, and sundry other jobs. The YN is self-sustaining for a long period and, with intelligent handling, will last a long time.' The Bureau of Ships extends grateful thanks to you who are helping to provide these sturdy and efficient ships for the Navy.

E L Cochrane
Rear Admiral USN

31 July. First minesweeper keel laid for the USS *Adroit*. (The *Admirable* class was one of the largest and most successful classes of minesweeper, with 123 completed around the USA. All seven of this contract were delivered in the autumn of 1942.)

24 September. Contracts for four 174ft subchasers (PC) $640,000 each, and four fleet tugs $1,500,000 each. Plans for two more ways, both covered. Also a mold loft, additional office, restaurant, and warehouse. New buildings about 325ft x 60ft. New sheet metal shop, electrical shop, etc. Railway spurs S500,000 cost. Leased 14 acres of land.

By January the country was at war, there were 430 employees, and the 'Commercialites' as Larry Barber called them, were gaining experience in prefabricating welded assemblies for the subchasers under cover.

8 January 1942. Donnelly reports 1,054,548 man-hours of work with no fatal injuries in 15 months operation.

29 January. Warehousemen discovered hundreds of World War I workers' badges and tool checks in hole for footings of new buildings. Similar to present ones. Scramble.

10 March. Large repair and conversion dock planned, 1500ft long, 30ft into waterway, to be ready in June, says Henry A

Left and below left: *LCI-736* at speed during trials in Portland. It was built in less than one month and launched on 13 February 1944.

White, executive vice-president. Port approved deepening of river below bridge outfitting dock stretching 1500ft under the bridge.

12 June. Office building enlarged for sixth time in three years, with addition of 60ft x 80ft unit. Original office was old steamboat pilot house.

2 August. Centennial 1200 workers out of 2500 sign up for blood donations.

8 August. First subchaser, *PC-596*, launched.

7 September. Marine railway dedicated and two tug keels laid. Two subchasers, *PC-597* and *PC-598*, launched; 20 young men inducted into navy onboard *PC-597* as she slid down ways.

7 December. First anniversary of Pearl Harbor – *PC-779* launched by Mrs A B White, gold star mother. Son killed at Pearl Harbor. Navy gold star mothers attended in group.

Stephens St plant poured 100th set of bed plates of Liberty ship engines, seven tons of metal. Each set weighs 21 tons. Oscar Bowden, foundry supt, proudly announced that only one in 300 huge casts had been rejected. Plant furnished seven sets a month to Oregonship.

24 January 1943. Heavy snows of past week have not slowed Commercial production materially owing to covered ways. *PC-785*, the 25th naval vessel by CIW, launched on schedule.

19 February. Absenteeism combatted by large signs at entrances, picture of Gen MacArthur. Each day the number of man hours lost by absenteeism was posted.

22 February. Mrs Thomas F Sullivan, mother of the 'Five Sullivan Boys' sponsors AT tug *Tawasa* on marine railway. She came here on western tour of navy war plants at request of navy dept. First time railway in operation. Largest side-haul railway yet constructed, according to contractors. Cost given as $2,000,000.

11 March. A PC subchaser hauled out by marine railway, first.

13 March. New jig for cutting and fitting hawse pipes reduces work by 75 percent. Oscar Pfaffle, shipfitter, and Geo Wray, foreman, get credit.

1 April. Fred Thoman, supt of machine shop, absent only eight days in 26 years. Owes it to 'Disgustingly good health'.

27 April. CIW workers oversubscribed war bond quota, buying a subchaser with their $500,000 subscriptions.

11 June. Joe Grebe and Harry Mendenhall resigned to form own company, Northwest Marine Iron Works. (This business outlived CIW and remained active on Swan Island into the 1990s.)

3 July. CIW gives $5000 to the Camel Caravan for cigarettes for servicemen.

(Third and fourth tugs launched: *Yuma* and *Zuni*. The ATs were 205ft long and were built like a small ship to comfortably tow a disabled Liberty ship across an ocean. They were the first large surface vessels in the US Navy to be equipped with diesel-electric drive – a single 3600 hp (2685 kW) diesel-electric propulsion system. Armament was a single 3-inch/50 calibre gun forward, and four machine gun positions, two with twin 40mm and two with twin 20mm gun mountings.

28 July. USS *Adroit* commissioned.

THE NAVY'S PC/MINESWEEPER EXPERIMENT

It took exactly one year to complete the *Adroit* as a minesweeper conversion of a standard PC subchaser hull. CIW delivered seven in 1942, all with twin 1770 bhp Cooper Bessemer diesel engines that delivered a service speed of 16 knots and a range of 3000 miles at 12 knots. The USS *Adroit* served in the Pacific for two years as a convoy escort until the minesweeper experiment was officially declared a failure. All 18 vessels in the class were converted back to a submarine chaser.

Above: USS *Alpine* was a 492ft C3 cargo ship built at Los Angeles, California, by the Western Pipe and Steel Company and commissioned on 30 September 1943 in San Francisco as APA-92 (Auxiliary Personnel, Attack). It arrived in Portland on 4 October where work continued at the Commercial Iron Works to complete the full conversion to an attack transport. The ship departed on 7 May 1944 and eventually earned five battle stars for service against Japan.

On 1 June 1944 the USS *Adroit*'s name was deleted; the ship was given the number *PC-1586*, and it returned to active duty until the end of the war. (The minesweeping role was taken over by the 184ft x 33ft *Admirable* class, which had more room for the gear needed for sweeping ever more sophisticated mines.)

By this time, CIW (like Oregonship) was speeding up the pace of construction:

14 August. *PC-798* launched 18 days after keel laying breaking former record of 26 days in February 1943. Was built up of sub-assemblies set down on ways and welded together. *PC-799* launched same day. Like the Kaiser yards, their paper *The Port*

Hole took pride in reporting Portland 'firsts' and its own production records.

Commercial also outfitted two of the *Bogue* class escort carriers for the Royal Navy: HM Ships *Trouncer, and Trumpeter.* The hulls were built in Tacoma, based on the Maritime Commission's Type C3 cargo ship hull. Four other hulls completed were troop transport ships, APs and APAs.

The carriers were well regarded by their new owners. Larry Barber reported, 'Commercial's Quality of Worksmanship Sensational, Says Skipper.' A surviving letter from one British CO underlines the point:

HMS *TRUMPETER*

Mr Winston W Casey, 22 August 1943.
President, Commercial Iron Works,
Portland, Oregon.3

Dear Mr Casey,

I have tried to thank as many of you as I could, for the excellent job which has been done in turning out the fine ship which I now have the honour to command. I am afraid, however, that there are many whom I may not have met or perhaps even seen.

It is to them that this letter is really addressed, as I wish them to know that their work is appreciated by all on board. As the strength of a cable depends on the strength of its weakest link, so, in a ship, some quite minor fault in work-

Below and right: The *Badoeng Strait* (CVE-116) was laid down on 18 August 1944 at Tacoma, Washington, by the Todd-Pacific Shipyards, Inc; launched on 15 February 1945, the escort carrier was moved to Portland, where she was completed by the Commercial Iron Works; and commissioned at Portland on 14 November 1945.

manship may render the whole complex structure a useless hulk. It is apparent therefore that every man and woman who has helped to build a ship has a share in the success or failure of that ship.

We for our part are going to do our best to use HMS *Trumpeter* to advantage against our common enemies, and if we are lucky enough to win any success then a share in that success will belong to those who built her.

I would be grateful, Mr Casey, if you could convey my feelings and thanks to as many of the staff and employees of C.I.W. as possible – perhaps by inserting this letter in the 'PORTHOLE'.

Yours very sincerely,

K S COLQUHOUN,
Captain, Royal Navy.

On 4 May 1945 aircraft of 846 Naval Air Squadron flew from *Trumpeter* to take part in Operation Judgement, an attack on the U-boat depot at Kilbotn, Norway, contributing eight Grumman Avengers and four Grumman Wildcats to a 44-aircraft strike that destroyed several vessels including the depot ship *Black Watch* and *U 711*.

20 October. Basil Dominc Izzi, navy seaman, tells workers how he was rescued by a PC boat after 83 days on a raft. Urged building fast and well. Lots of other fellows awaiting rescue too, he said.

30 October. *PC-806* launched today, was the 500th steel ocean ship built in Portland during World War II. To date CIW has launched 50 ships. The first ship, YNT *Catalpa,* also launched down same slipway.

10 December. First LCI(L) launched, *LCI(L)-725*

The Landing Craft Infantry was 158ft long with a 23ft beam, and could land up to 200 soldiers directly onto a beach. Over 900 were built in ten American shipyards. Over 200 were provided to the Royal Navy under Lend-Lease.

1944. After the heavy losses during the landings on Tarawa on 20–23 November 1943, 24 LCI landing craft were hurriedly converted into gunboats carrying a wide variety of offensive armament to spearhead the next amphibious assault. They saw action during troop landings in the Marshall Islands early in February 1944, and were so effective that the order was given for a fast-track program to build a new class of heavily-armed landing craft to be called LCS – Landing Craft Support. Two of the three yards chosen to build 130 vessels of this vital new variant were Commercial and Albina, with the third being Lawley & Sons of Boston, Mass.

Over the next nine months, these yards each averaged a ship a week. The first one was launched in Boston on 20 June, the last in March 1945. Armament varied but typically was two twin 40mm guns, four 20mm guns, and four .50 calibre machine guns. Mounted in the bow was one of three guns, either a single 3-inch/50, a single 40mm, or a twin 40mm. Just aft of the bow gun were ten Mark 7 rocket launchers. The main difference with the standard LCI below decks was that all the space allotted to 200 troops and 30 tons of supplies was freed up for large stores of ammunition, and three times as many crew as the typical 24 men. Commercial's workers invented many special tools to help them cut the time it took to get these boat down the ways, and was the top supplier of the LCS with 52 delivered.

3 August 1944. Commercial Iron Works celebrated the launch of its 100th vessel, *PC-799*, with a full ceremony that included the local Coast Guard band, speeches from VIP's, and a large audience of employees and their families. This memorable event was recorded in a souvenir 12-page photo album containing a commendation from the US Navy's Chief of the Bureau of Ships, a progress report on the company's wartime record, and letters of thanks from Royal Navy crews. The book illustrates the seven classes of ship the yard had built: CVE, LCI(L), YN, APA, AT, AM, and PC. Also pictured are 44 senior staff, with half being experienced craftsmen too old for the draft.

CIW's workforce grew to over 9000 working three shifts, and went on to build close to 200 small warships – 7 minesweepers, 40 subchasers (PCs), 58 Landing Craft Infantry (LCI), 52 LCS. The yard continued with seven more net tenders, ten more 100ft yard tugs (YT) in 1945– 46, and a variety of small craft. There is no sign or memorial on the waterfront where this incredible war effort took place. Fortunately, one of Commercial's vessels was saved for posterity – by The Landing Craft Support Museum in the Mare Island Shipyard in Vallejo, California – on the east side of the San Francisco Bay – one of the region's many historic World War II sites.

This is the *LCS-102*, the sole surviving example of the 130 Landing Craft Support, the heavily-armed LCS. Built by Commercial Iron Works, it was launched on 13 February 1945 and commissioned on the 17th. The National Parks Service states that 'this ship built in Portland is eligible for listing in the National Register of Historic Places under Criterion A for its participation in the amphibious invasion of Okinawa and peacekeeping operations following the surrender of Japan, and as the sole intact representative of her class of vessel, at the local level of significance, as a significant example of naval engineering in World War II. Although these smaller ships are seldom mentioned in accounts of that war, they, along with the men that served on them, played an important part in the closing battles of that conflict.'

The boat's official naval designation is listed as: LCS(L)(3)-102 – Landing Craft Support (Large) (Mark 3), hull number 102. After wartime service at Okinawa and the Gunto operation between 18 and 30 June 1945, USS *LCS-102* served as part of the occupation forces in Japan until December 1945. Post-war, a period in reserve was followed by transfer first to the Japanese Maritime Self Defense Force (1953–1965) and then the Royal Thai Navy as NTMS *Nakha* from 1966. In 1997 a veterans group of LCS officers and enlisted men discovered that the last operational Landing Craft Support vessel was in Royal Thai Navy custody. They formed the National Association of USS LCS(L)1–130, and became the official custodians of the vessel in 2007.

SW PORTLAND SITE CONTINUES MARITIME CONNECTION 1946–2016

Commercial Iron Works closed in 1946 and the property was taken over the Zidell Corporation, which soon began dismantling surplus wartime ships, including many that were built within the city limits. Many vessels built in Portland came back to the Rose City for scrapping – from subchasers to Liberties. This became one of the biggest war-surplus ship-dismantling operations in the country, only a few blocks from Portland's city centre, where 336 oceangoing ships were scrapped in 30 years.

Remarkably, the Zidell family then returned the site to its former function when they began building barges in 1962, re-using some of the steel they had stockpiled. The new slipway even included a couple of surplus whirley cranes to move the barge modules into place on the ways. They built 277 barges of all types including the new technologies of double-hull tank barges and articulated couplings (ATB) in the last 20 years. It closed in 2017 with ambitious plans to develop the site into a modern mixed-use project with river access for the public and preservation of the cranes as an outdoor memorial to the site's nautical history.

15

ALBINA ENGINE & MACHINE WORKS

The Albina Engine & Machine Works was founded in 1904 on the east side of the Willamette River close to downtown, to repair the local fleet of steam-powered sternwheelers. It participated in the government's emergency program in 1917 by launching seventeen identical 300ft steel ships of 2865 gross tons in 1918–19. Only six were delivered before the armistice, but all were still afloat in 1941 when they were recalled to serve the nation again.

Albina survived the lean inter-war years with repair work and only an occasional newbuild. The first bright spot came in 1930, when they built three 133ft lightships for the Coast Guard: *Swiftsure Banks* (Straits of Juan de Fuca), *Blunts Reef* (northern California), and *Fire Island* (New York). They were the first US lightships equipped with a diesel-electric system with four 75 kW diesel generator sets powering a 350 hp electric shaft motor.

After this contract, there was nothing but repair work from 1930 to 1938, which was barely enough to keep the business alive. As the economy picked up in 1938, the local towing companies all began replacing their steamers with the new diesel-powered boats. In three years, the yard managed to turn out eleven tugs and three barges from its five building ways – two for ships and three for smaller vessels.

Pearl Harbor changed the situation overnight and Albina was given a second opportunity to serve the nation in wartime. Larry Barber followed its progress in the war years, and wrote a detailed four-page record of the yard's activity in 1944.

In January 1941 the managers learned they had submitted the lowest bid to build five 321ft tankers for the Navy at $1,751,270 each. This order enabled them to option the property they had occupied in 1917, with 600 feet of river front, but it failed to materialize.

25 March. Secretary of the Navy Frank Knox announced contracts for four 165ft subchasers (PC) to Albina.

26 March. First crews began clearing the site for the new plant. Found pilings driven for World War I still sound, tops cut off and new caps installed. Site 600ft by 300ft deep, later enlarged. Construction started on two-storey mold loft and warehouse, plate shop, office, lunch room and rest rooms. Expected to employ 350 men in near future.

2 April. F C Ralph, builder, had crew pouring footings for buildings while Albina Shingle Mill and Floating Marine Ways, and one houseboat moved away.

25 April. Offices moved to new site.

20 June. Electric power installation about completed by NW Electric Co.

16 July. L R Hussa, vice-president, an experienced naval architect, announced that Albina's World War I design for coal-burning boilers and engines for anchor winches and windlasses for coaster-type ships had been adopted by US Maritime Commission for Lend-Lease coasters for Britain. Coal burners were cheaply operated where coal most available. Albina submitted lowest of six bids for nine vessels 250ft long, raked stems, cruiser sterns, 10½ knots. Estimated 900 men would be employed at peak. Albina asked $1,385,500 on fixed price basis.

9 August. Contracts awarded, Albina omitted. Understood that negotiated contracts were sought by USMC.

11 September. First two PC keels laid. Described as 'baby destroyers'. No ceremony, three Navy officers present. 350 men at work.

21 September. Navy announces contracts for five more PCs, $640,000 each for hulls.

27 September. Albina lays two more PC keels.

23 November. Fabricating and assembly plant under construction, 220ft by 54ft. A 220ft machine shop already up.

5 January 1942. *PC-570* launched, first combat ship launch in Portland since Spanish War period. Stiffened grease delayed vessel 20 minutes until 200 workers helped start it moving. 450 employed.

23 January. *PC-569* launched. These were first two PCs in nation, according to local reports. Albina startled the industry by dropping keel sections on ways for next ship right behind *PC-569*.

9 February. Navy E award to Albina, Willamette and Oregonship announced.

12 February. *PC-571* launched. Official presentation of E flag, six more PC contracts received. Mayor Riley spoke. Merit pins awarded to two employees with 20 or more years with company.

(Albina was the first shipyard in Portland's history to win the Navy's 'coveted E pennant' – E for excellence – bearing two stars, which denoted that the shipbuilder had maintained its record for two years.)

30 April. First triple launching in city: *PC-578*, *PC-579*, *PC-580*.

After Kaiser introduced women welders, the other Portland yards quickly followed suit.

4 June. *The Albina Subchaser* newspaper made its first appearance. By this time 2000 employees. Announcement of 'beauty contest' among male employees.

(From the first issue, this bi-weekly began featuring the new female workers on almost every page. It was not as professional as the Kaiser publications, since it was written and edited by the company's own staff.)

9 July. *PC-581* launched. Several delivered by this time. Queen contest in high gear – votes were purchased at the rate of one cent each in war bonds and stamps.

14 July. Curly Goguen, machinist, was crowned 'King of Youth and Beauty', but abdicated in favour of Bill 'Pigsfeet' Moore, boilermaker. Coronation held with robes, crown, staffs, blondes, brunettes. Hussa handed $100 bonus to five principal candidates. Telegram from Frank Knox, newsreels. Total war bond sale $137,000.

29 July. First PCE launched, *PCE-1077*. ('Later named Hell Horn.')

7 August. Welding contest between various yards at Victory Center.

ALBINA – THE SUBCHASER KINGS

The PC, universally known as a subchaser, became a popular symbol of the navy's intention to take on the enemy submarines that had wreaked so much death and destruction on the merchant fleet. Subchasers were narrow and fast steel-hulled ships that were specially designed to attack U-boats and submarines in shallow coastal waters. *The Oregonian* described the design as a 'lean, trim, 175ft speedboat that is death to Axis submarines … a deadly craft that foretells hell for the enemy.' Albina's workers took to referring to the subchasers during construction as 'HellShips,' and started to give each hull a provocative (if unofficial) name that resonated locally, including *Hell for Hitler*, *Hell for Mussolini*, *Hell-A-Plenty*, and *Hell-in-General*.

According to Larry, another was named *Hell Hat* after the perky mink hat often worn by Jean Muir, marine reporter for *The Oregon Journal*, the rival Portland daily to *The Oregonian*. In keeping with the somewhat ribald tone that accompanied much of World War II shipbuilding, the Albina women's bowling team who played in a city-wide league were known as the 'Hell Hussies'. The Albina men played in a Hellships basketball team and a Subchasers soccer team.

The 184ft World War II version of the PC was steel hulled, and armed with a dual-purpose 3-inch/50 and 40mm gun. Later the 3-inch/50 was replaced with a single Bofors 40mm and three single 20mm guns were added. PCs carried a considerable amount of detection and ranging gear for locating submarines. They were capable of a speed of about 18 knots and were highly manoeuvrable. Over 100 were built in Portland by Albina, WISCO and CIW – another local achievement that has never been publicized.

The orders for subchasers kept on coming and Albina expanded its workforce and production, and hired more women to work in its accounting and bookkeeping office. They kept track of employee records, payroll, supplies, contracts, production – all vital information necessary to run the business.

29 August. *PC-1081* '*Hell Harvest*' launched after 27 working days, a new record for this type. 'The job was handled by what is believed to the smallest crew ever to turn out a fast job … which means (the ship) was built in the smallest number of man hours in the history of subchaser building. That is the real record, the record Albina workers take pride in,' said *The Albina Subchaser*. Two other PCs also launched this week.

16 September. New process for shrinking galvanized metal plates without burning off galvanizing, yet eliminating zinc fumes. Five foremen given credit for development.

24 October. 2200 employees now. Hussa says they turn out more steel per man than any other yard in the world.

27 October. Navy Day. Comm Chas Hibbard presenting new army-navy E pennant, declared Albina was building small ships better and faster than any other yard of comparable size.

Left: Albina launched *PC-582* on 2 October,1942. Its twin 2880 bhp Fairbanks Morse diesel engines gave it a top speed of 20 knots. At an economical cruising speed of 10 knots, it had a range of over 3000 miles – enough to escort a convoy across the North Atlantic, although they were never used on such duties.

Left: Over 400 of these 173ft *PC-461* class patrol boats were built for anti-submarine warfare (ASW), convoy escort duty, and coastal patrols. In the US Navy's typology, PC stood for Patrol Coastal, but the class was generally referred to as a 'subchaser'. *PC-580* was launched at Albina *Engine* & Machine Works on 26 September 1942.

(At the same time, the yard was making progress on orders for 24 small oilers (YO) and tankers (YOG); 64 landing craft to the LCC, LCI and LCS variants.)

5 November. *YO-73*, yard oiler, first small tanker, launched.

7 January 1943. Mrs Melva Lillian Cole, widow of subchaser hero, was brought from Fargo, North Dakota, to christen *PC-816*, '*Hell Hornet*'.

16 January. Swing shifters have downtown theatre show at 1.30 am.

5 February. Whole workforce sings pledge against absenteeism, addressed to FDR.

20 February. Second star presented at ceremony with talks by navy battle veterans. 2500 employees now.

10 March. Red Cross drive makes records. Raised 168 percent of quota.

9 April. *Albina Subchaser* announces plan to issue gold merit pins to all employees having good attendance records.

16 July. Campfire Girl leaders sponsor *PCE-876* '*Hell Hooray*'.

8 September. Farmer's Market opened in parking lot; savings for men, profits for farmers.

24 October. 'No Work No Woo' club getting publicity. 350 girls signed up. Absenteeism dropped from 11 percent to 2.85 percent. See 25 October story by G Barteau. (A clipping of this story was placed in the folder. It begins: 'Albina yard is still going strong after the layoffs of some 500 chronic absentees.')

27 October. Three-star army-navy E flag presented, said to be the first for a PC shipyard. Two launching, *PCE-880*, and *YO-123*.

23 November. 'No Work No Woo' club asks city council for Sunday dancing permit.

13 January 1944. New contracts for LCI(L), YO, YW, and YOG announced by Hussa, Albina's vice-president. Sufficient to keep all 5000 workers, and 1400 more too, busy into 1945. More workers sought. New slipways added, now total 10.

(Larry Barber's record ends here.)

Feb–March. Albina fired all its 'late arrivals and miscellaneous deadheads' in this period. (This clearly reveals that not

Left: Albina built 20 of the 158ft LCI(L) – standing for Landing Craft Infantry (Large) – then was selected to produce 30 of the heavily-armed gunboat version, the Landing Craft Support (large) or LCS(L). Commercial Iron Works was also awarded a contract for the LCS(L), which was badly needed to spearhead beach landings on the Japanese-held Pacific islands.

Left: There is no information on this artist sketching the busy scene in the Albina yard, but since this was one of the most efficient US builders of small vessels, so he could be illustrating an official story for the US Navy. The hull marked YO was a Yard Oiler, a self-propelled fuel barge.

everyone was as enthusiastic about the long hours, night work, and hard toil required by the war effort as all the slogans, speeches and awards implied.)

April. A second newspaper clipping is headlined 'Albina's Personnel Policy Pays Off'. Hussa is quoted as saying that the discharge of fully 18 percent of our 4000 employees over the past two months was a drastic attempt to cure growing absenteeism. Despite the layoffs, production at the shipyard had jumped an estimated 20 percent. 'All over the United States, absenteeism has been a headache. Albina took a chance and found that morale jumped and production went up,' he added. 'This will not be tolerated at Albina again.'

Despite these issues, Albina established a record-setting pace for its construction of 36 subchasers in 1942–44, averaging 140 days per hull, plus 30 LCCs, six oilers and one gas tanker. The yard continued building 66 more 158ft landing craft in various configurations until March 1945, giving an overall production of about 100 LC class vessels.

PCs were highly effective in protecting convoys along the Atlantic seaboard, in the Caribbean and South Atlantic during the critical 1942–43 'Battle of the Atlantic' years, filling the gap until the Destroyer Escort (DE) could be built and deployed. Though only a few German U-boats were actually sunk by PCs, their presence, and the threat of depth charge attacks, was a deterrent to the U-boat commanders. With the threat of submarine attacks on the wane, the PCs took on more hazardous duties, serving in virtually every combat theatre around the world.

The PC proved exceptionally adapt as Patrol Control Craft (PCC), controlling and guiding waves of landing craft in every European amphibious landing from Operation Husky, the invasion of Sicily in July 1943, to Operation Overlord, the combined Allied invasion of Normandy on D-Day, 6 June 1944. In the Pacific, the PCCs were assigned to the Seventh Fleet, 'MacArthur's Navy', participating in all island-hopping amphibious landings through Iwo Jima and Okinawa.

A notable aspect of the Albina Engine & Machine Company was its particular efforts to employ disabled veterans and the handicapped. After touring the Albina plant and reviewing its record-setting production practices, US Vice-President Henry Wallace commented, 'The thing that has impressed me most at Albina is the manner in which you are utilizing veterans and civilians who are handicapped … who are unable to hear or speak,' reported *The Albina Subchaser* on 15 February 1944.

After the war, Albina continued to build four 396ft C1 cargo ships for the Maritime Commission, and twenty 177ft coastal freighters (CS) for the US Army that were sold to the Dutch government for service in the Dutch East Indies. Albina went on to build some 190 tugs and barges from 1947 to 1971.

16

WILLAMETTE IRON & STEEL CORPORATION (WISCO)

The Willamette Iron & Steel Corporation or WISCO began in Oregon's pioneer days in 1865, and grew into a general foundry casting a wide variety of industrial products, including thousands of steam winches called 'donkeys' used by logging crews to mechanize the hauling of logs out of the forest. In the early 1900s, they opened a small shipyard in NW Portland that specialized in repairing steam engines on sternwheel boats, and supplied boilers and parts for the short-lived shipping boom in 1917–20.

In the 1920s, the company found a new market as a manufacturer of a steam locomotive driven by a crankshaft, used in the NW lumber industry to transport logs on very steep terrain. Building on that tradition of engineering, WISCO became an

Below: A Baldwin steam locomotive is loaded onto a Soviet cargo ship at specially-built dock on the WISCO property.

essential part of the region's arsenal of democracy in World War II, and a valuable resource for all the yards in Portland. WISCO's experience in steam power was recognized by the Maritime Commission and the company was one of the three local foundries chosen for the vital work of mass producing the triple-expansion steam engine for the Liberty ships that the Kaiser company was building at Oregonship.

> After the award of a $6 million order for 56 of these engines, the company proudly announced: 'Willamette Iron and Steel is building 71 engines for the commission under previous contracts, bringing the total ordered from this firm to 127 units.' The final total by 1944 was 222 engines. Their experience with railways and ships led to WISCO winning the most unusual contract in Portland's war effort: loading Russian ships with steam locomotives under Lend-Lease, starting late in 1943. The three biggest locomotive factories in the north-east were contracted to manufacture them, including Baldwin in Eddystone, Pennsylvania, the biggest in the world.

These E-class locos were relatively small coal-burners originally designed by the Russian government during World War I. Like the Liberty ships, they were very basic transportation, suitable for the desperate wartime conditions in the Soviet Union where the deteriorating rail system could not handle heavy axle

Below: A lorry fitted with a mobile power unit is loaded into the hold of a Soviet ship

Above: A Soviet ship with full holds and a deck cargo of locomotives bound for Vladivostok.

loads. They were notable for having ten drive wheels to reduce the individual axle weight, resulting in a 2–10–0 wheel pattern.

Because the Russian rail standard was wider than the 4ft 8½in adopted in the rest of the world, it was impossible to send these trains across country under their own power. Instead, the locomotives were shipped in kit form on railcars that carried a single boiler or a load of axles, and were all assembled in Portland. WISCO gathered an experienced crew of 150 men for this task, and laid down a short stretch of Russian standard gauge line (5ft wide) to roll the completed engines out to the new loading dock equipped with a 100-ton derrick.

Barber reckoned over 1200 locomotives and 300 power-generation cars went through the workshop.

'Russian ships came and went around the clock, as many as 30 a month. Five were converted into train carriers, each capable of carrying 18 locomotives and tenders,' Larry wrote twenty years after the war ended. 'They made 45 round trips each before they cleaned up the backlog of rolling stock provided by a generous America.' Train shipments constituted almost half the count of 550 Lend-Lease ship visits in 1943–45 from vessels flying the USSR's hammer-and-sickle flag. They all faced a 5000-mile crossing of the North Pacific to Vladivostok, where they were unloaded and driven east on the Trans-Siberian railway towards the eastern front.

Starting in 1940, WISCO was equally busy with a variety of marine work for the navy, fitting out ships at its long dock, and starting new construction on its hurriedly extended ways with an order for ten lightering (covered) barges 100ft x 32ft. The

Above: WISCO had experience building steam-driven logging equipment, so was able to put together a team of around 45 men to assemble the Baldwin locomotives that arrived in dismantled form on freight cars. Note that only two of them look under 45, the maximum age for conscription.

first contract for conversion work involved two 507ft cargo ships built in 1918–19 by the Bethlehem Steel Corp, Alameda, California. They worked in the 1930s as the *City of Norfolk* and the *City of Baltimore*, which ran from New York to San Francisco for the Panama Pacific Lines throughout the 1930s. They were acquired by the US Navy in October 1940 for service as troop carriers and were converted to the *Heywood* class (APA-6) attack transport, and were commissioned in November 1940.

Then the workforce increased from 4000 to 6000 and must have been proud to learn they were going to build the first two vehicle-landing ships of the *Catskill* class. The 453ft *Catskill* and its sister, the *Ozark*, were laid down on 12 July 1941. But this was not destined to be a full-speed ahead project; indeed it may have set a record for the length of time taken to completion – three years – and multiple changes in role. Starting off as a Coastal Minelayer (CM 6), the *Catskill* was launched almost a year later in May 1942, followed by the *Ozark*.

Fitting out slowed down when WISCO won a contract for two 184ft *Admirable* class minesweepers (AM), the USS *Concise* and USS *Compel*, in that month. The cost was estimated at $12,000,000 and *The Oregonian* reported that it 'constituted a ship building contract of the first order, and a fine one for Portland because it means steady work for many men.' This was the first order for US Navy ships in the Portland area after Pearl Harbor, and the management realized they needed some advice on how to meet the Navy's specifications and performance goals as efficiently as possible.

Fortunately, WISCO had already been chosen by the US Navy's Bureau of Ships at the start of 1942 as the base of the Supervisor of Shipbuilding for the 13th Naval District, so the chief officer was able to arrange for 29 WISCO foremen and supervisors to spend a weekend at the Puget Sound Naval Shipyard where they were each assigned to a department that specialized in their type of work. This short course was the first of many interactions with the Bureau of Ships, which inspected the navy work in progress in Portland throughout the war, plus the Astoria and Coos Bay operations building wooden minesweepers on the coast.

Generally speaking, the US Maritime Commission oversaw the three Kaiser Yards, which produced merchant ships under a different Federal funding and review system. However, this separation seems to have been less than absolute. Many hulls produced by the three Kaiser yards, like the *Haskell* class, were based on Victory hulls that were inspected, received (and presumably paid for) by the Maritime Commission, but were ultimately delivered to the US Navy and accepted by the Supervisor of Shipbuilding.

With 15,000 employees working around the clock, WISCO went on to record 14 AM minesweepers launched in 1943–44.

Left: *PCE-891* (Patrol Craft Escort) was larger than the PC-type subchaser. At 184.5ft overall, it had more than twice the displacement of the PC, and proved to be an inexpensive substitute for larger and more valuable convoy-escort ships. There was a minesweeper (AM) version on the same hull, known as the *Admirable* class, one of which is inboard of *PCE-891*.

Left: This photo clearly shows the PCE's larger size, which gave it a range of 8500 nautical miles with a lower top speed of 14 knots.

That was a superb performance, but it was just another aspect of the company's many achievements. The Todd Pacific Shipyard in Tacoma, Washington was also breaking records by building the hulls of escort carriers (CVEs) faster than they could be completed. (They launched 36 hulls in about 18 months.) The first hull was finished up to the flight deck with a few bulkheads for stiffness and only the basic machinery installed, and launched in March 1942. Then it was immediately towed around Washington state and up the Columbia River to WISCO, where the pre-fabricated control centre/bridge was installed and the interior was fitted out with all the accommodations to house the crew and systems to handle the aircraft.

With the outfitting completed by the end of 1942, the ship could carry a maximum of 20–24 planes at a service speed of 16.5 knots. Propulsion was by two boilers connected to a 9350 shp (6970 kW) steam turbine, which drove a single shaft. It was transferred to the Royal Navy in January 1943, and renamed HMS *Tracker*. This enabled WISCO's in-house bi-weekly newspaper *Stem to Stern* to claim to have commissioned 'the first aircraft carrier ever built in Oregon'.

HMS *Tracker* served as an escort carrier during 1943–44 for North Atlantic and Arctic convoys and its pilots were credited with sinking one U-boat. It took part in D-Day and was returned to the USA in December 1944. It was used as an aircraft transport, and spent the remainder of the war in the Pacific. WISCO finished and delivered nine more CVEs to Britain – HMS *Ravager*, *Tracker*, *Searcher*, *Slinger*, *Speaker*, *Rajah*, *Ruler*, *Arbiter*, *Smiter* – plus several auxiliary vessels and patrol craft to the US Navy.

WISCO received letters of appreciation from the Royal Navy officers who took delivery of their ships in Portland. But Captain R S D Armour, Royal Navy, went one better by passing on a script about HMS *Rajah* written by Paymaster Sub-Lieut Eric Williams, Royal Navy Reserve, about his visit to Oregon to join the crew, before the ship was commissioned on 17 January 1944. This was broadcast over the BBC radio in England and parts of the script were published in *Stem to Stern*.

> In the bright sunshine of a west coast American shipyard (Willamette, Portland, Oregon) one day early last summer a welder's torch stabbed at a long bar of steel and a ship began to grow. A 'Baby Flat Top' or escort carrier, though she did not know it at the time. And there she lay all late summer, through autumn and into winter and the new year. And men swarmed over her, crawled around inside her, helmeted figures fingered her with torches and smeared her with welding, putting pieces together, slicing off waste with butter-knife ease.
>
> Below in the engine-room, in the workshops and storerooms, through the messes, decks and accommodation, working in the galleys and offices, making washrooms and living spaces up higher in the hangar deck; then as she reared robustly up, welding, riveting, drilling and

hammering in the offices and operations rooms under the flight deck. Then on to the flight deck itself over the sprouting bridge.

What a cacophony. All the discord of Babel directed and amplified at this monstrous carcass, as she lay gaunt and gawky under the Oregon sky. And so she grew, not from eight till five, not from six till midnight – but all the time, overtime. Then Lend-Lease came up the gangway with the morning shift. She was going to be H.M.S., not U.S.S! They picked a commander, told him what was wanted and sent him out to be ready to take her over when the US Navy had finished with her. A handful of officers suddenly got orders and steamed across the Atlantic to find their new job. A batch of naval ratings got a draft chit.

Gradually her 'slaves' began to know her, to find out where they were to sleep, where to eat, where to wash, where to ask about their pay, where to tell the doctor about their aches and mistakes, where to muster when the pipe sounded through the relay system. Stores began to arrive. Food to eat, clothes to wear, pots and pans for the galleys, nuts and bolts to mend her with, fittings and furniture, spares and suchlike – all these things were swung and 'humped' aboard and somehow stowed.

And when they finished work, the hands mustered for 'Liberty men – fall in'. And this west coast shipyard town opened its arms to them (at times quite literally, I believe). It certainly threw open its doors and turned out its pockets. There was great fraternizing, undreamed of and overwhelming hospitality, and friendliness everywhere. The American way. No need even to thumb for a car ride – drivers simply honked lift offers. And the food and the beer and the entertainment – and the girls! But that would be telling …

It was another fortnight or so before she went to sea because she had to fit special apparatus. By this time most of the ship's company had arrived and began to find excuses for sustained farewells ashore. There was a ship's company dance, among other events. She reached a Canadian port and stayed there for several weeks, completing her storing, getting finished off inside, having alterations made, collecting the remainder of her company.

It was here that her captain took over. When the ship was ready for him the Admiralty sent him out in a hurry. A new ship, a new ship's company, settling down and learning its job, ready to punch its mark on the page of history, preparing for its part to get the war over and ensure a peace in which we can all hopefully return having done our duty, to enjoy the blessings of the land and the fruits of our labours.

The carrier survived the war and was returned to the USA in 1947. It was sold to Waterman Steamship Corporation, who stripped off all the naval additions and converted it back to the 493ft, C3 cargo carrier it was originally designed to be. It was scrapped in Taiwan in 1975.

By 1943, the future mission of the two *Catskill* class ships was still not clear, two years after work began. In May 1943 the hull was reclassified to AP-106 (Troopship), but it was changed again to LSV-1 (Landing Ship Vehicle) in 1944 and finally commissioned on 30 June. The *Ozark* followed the same course but a couple of months behind. The USS *Catskill* sailed from San Diego on 12 August 1944 for Hawaii, where she embarked marines, and joined the transport group of the Southern Attack Force for the assault on Leyte in the Philippines. The landing was successful, and *Catskill* departed before the start of the bloody battle for Leyte Gulf in which five CVEs were sunk, two of them built by Kaiser Vancouver.

Catskill's varied career continued after the war. She was reclassified as mine countermeasures support ship MCS-1 on 18 October 1956, then struck from the register in 1961, reinstated in 1964, underwent a long modernization to 1967, and then served in Vietnam until 1970. It was scrapped soon after.

In 1944–45 WISCO built 14 subchasers (PC), taking over where Albina, their neighbours across the Willamette, left off. By the end of the war, the three Portland yards had delivered around 120 vessels, more than any other region. WISCO could also boast of another unexpected achievement, revealed in the *Stem to Stern* for May 1945. The company had 3000 women on staff and the paper liked to feature their hard-working young ladies on the cover. It was not shy about announcing new couples, engagements and weddings, and this issue included what may have been the most surprising story ever printed in a wartime shipyard newspaper.

It was titled 'Phyllis Dunnuck Thrilled By Queen's Command Letter To Her.' Writer Anne Dooley explained that Phyllis was a senior clerk in accounting, who was the proud possessor of a letter written to her by a wing commander of the Royal Air Force at the command of the Queen of England!

'It all started when Phyllis began to follow the career of Wing Commander J E (Johnny) Johnson, RAF ace of World War II, just as a hobby. She faithfully watched newspapers for any word of the current heroic activities of Johnson, and managed to get a few clippings. The last report she saw was under date of September 28, 1944 telling of his downing his 38th German aircraft, and from that time until she received the letter from Buckingham Palace, she found no trace of the flyer. Taking a long chance, she decided the best way to find out was to write to someone in the 'know,' and get the facts. Following are the two letters; first, Phyllis' to Her Majesty, then the reply.'

Your Majesty:

My co-workers and I have been following with interest the career of Wing Commander J E (Johnny) Johnson, an

English boy who was leading a Canadian Spitfire squadron. Our interest was evoked at the time his picture appeared in an Associated Press Wire photo after he became the leading Allied ace in the European theater when he downed his 33rd plane on June 30, 1944. Our last news report under date of September 28, 1944 told of downing his 38th German aircraft, but since that time we have found no further reports.

To many of us Johnny Johnson has assumed a personality closely allied with the boys of our own families who are now overseas. It is with heartfelt concern that we inquire of his safety and further progress since last September.

Perhaps it would be of interest to you to know that we are employees of Willamette Iron and Steel Corporation, a firm that has constructed a number of vessels for the British Royal Navy. We are grateful to have had a share in this program and in the knowledge that we have helped in a small way to further our common cause. With best wishes for you and your family and a quick, successful end to the war, I remain
Sincerely yours,
Phyllis Dunnuck.

Buckingham Palace
20th March, 1945

Dear Miss Dunnuck:
I am commanded by Her Majesty the Queen to write and thank you for your kind enquiry about Wing-Commander J.E. Johnson, D.S.O., D.F.C. This Officer has held an appointment on the staff of a Wing Headquarters of the Second Tactical Air Force since July, 1944, and, as far as is known, is in the best of health.

Her Majesty commands me to say how touched she is to hear of your concern at the welfare of so distinguished an Englishman, and that you feel his personality has so much in common with your own fighting men, our allies. Her Majesty is proud to learn that you and your co-workers of the Willamette Iron and Steel Corporation have shared so importantly in the ubiquitous victories of the Royal Navy which, now alone, now in concert with the United States Navy, has consistently outmatched our enemies.

The Queen is grateful for your kind wishes for the Royal Family, and joins with you in praying that an early victory may, by continuous effort, develop into a strong and lasting peace.

Yours very truly,
Peter Townsend,
Wing Commander, Royal Air Force.
Equerry-in-Waiting.

(Group Captain Peter Wooldridge Townsend, CVO, DSO, DFC & Bar (1914–1995) was also a flying ace in the Battle of Britain, and also a courtier and author. He was equerry to King George VI from 1944 to his death in 1952. Townsend held the same position for Queen Elizabeth II from 1952 to 1953. He had a famous romance with the Queen's sister, Princess Margaret, which was frowned on by the British aristocracy because he had been married and divorced his wife in 1952.)

On 2 May 1945 Larry Barber was invited to ride along on the sea trials of the USS *Kula Gulf* (CVE-108), the first of three escort carriers to be completed at WISCO for the US Navy. The keel was laid by Todd-Pacific Shipyard in Tacoma, Washington on 16 December 1943. The program for the builder's trials described the ship in these words:

> This vessel was launched in Tacoma, Washington on 16 August, 1944 and was towed to Portland. As received, on 21 August, the vessel was a bare hull with no structure above the main deck and with only that machinery aboard that

Below: The invitation for Larry Barber to join the escort carrier USS *Kula Gulf* for the builders' trial run to Astoria and back. The hull was built in Tacoma but the ship was completely fitted out by WISCO.

was necessary prior to launching. The vessel as completed embodies all of the latest refinements and equipment for efficiency in combat and for the comfort and safety of the crew that have been developed though combat experience in the Pacific.

The trial was to Tongue Point (Astoria) and back, a distance of about 200 miles. Visitors were given a full 11-page schedule describing the ship and the program for the various tests, as follows:

0630 All hands to be aboard and at proper station

0700 Leave WISCO dock. Start gyro-compass tests and fathometer.

0840 Start measured mile, record speed; downstream.

1000 Pass under Longview Bridge.

1020 Conduct steering test, hard right to hard left and back at flank speed.

1210 Off Tongue Point. Turn around. Conduct steering test,

1355 Start measured mile, record speed; upstream.

1450 Pass under Longview Bridge. Hoist both anchors together and record hoisting speed.

1645 Crash Stop. Engines Full Astern, Record Time.

1500 Stop for Anchor Tests. Let Port Anchor out 60 fathoms, starboard 30 fathoms.

1930 Arrive at WISCO dock, trial concluded.

The contractor's Port Captain, assisted by the River Pilots, will be in full charge of, and responsible for, the safe and efficient navigation of the vessel

The *Kula Gulf* departed San Diego on 5 August 1944 with a full complement of aircraft for operations with the 7th Fleet in the Western Pacific. After the surrender of Japan on 29 August, the ship was engaged in shuttling planes and men back to the USA until January 1946. The *Kula Gulf* was decommissioned in Boston and entered the Atlantic Reserve Fleet. It was recommissioned in 1951 to serve as a training ship during the Korean War. From 1953 to 1955, *Kula Gulf* participated in the development of improved anti-submarine tactics with ships of the Atlantic Fleet. The carrier was transferred to Military Sealift Command on 30 June 1965 for use as an aircraft, helicopter and troop ferry in the Vietnam conflict. The *Kula Gulf* was decommissioned for the last time on 6 October 1969, struck from the Naval Vessel Register in 1970, and sold for scrap in 1971.

The yard's small boat division continued production on a run of ten 184ft Patrol Craft Escort (PCE) derived from the 180ft *Admirable* class hull, before the demand for small fighting ships began to subside. The last military order was for six barracks barges. WISCO continued as a repair yard for 45 years, performing major ship repairs and upgrades at the Port of Portland's repair yard on Swan Island until 1990.

....

17

THE OREGON WAR INDUSTRIES COLLECTIVE

Portland's place in the shipbuilding sector of the arsenal of democracy rested on the output of the three Kaiser shipyards and three smaller yards that supplied hundreds of small warships, landing craft and support vessels for the US Navy and to a small extent for Britain's Royal Navy via Lend-Lease. These highly productive yards sat on top of a huge pyramid of suppliers from all over the nation. They included a vast network of machine shops, pattern works, small foundries, plus other specialized fabricators experienced in precision machine tooling and structural steel assembly.

In January 1942, six weeks after America's entry into the war, President Roosevelt appointed Donald M Nelson as the head of the War Production Board. 'He will be the big boss, the wartime czar, empowered to tell American industry what to do, and to expect its ready compliance. His only superior officer is President Roosevelt himself,' explained *The Oregonian*. The paper reported regularly on the dozens of smaller local companies that converted to defence-related work and helped supply many of the components that kept the big shipyards on schedule.

Henry Kaiser used his own network of companies to take this system a step further: he built his own steel mill in Fontana in southern California. Iron Fireman built steam engines for Kaiser's Liberty ships in Oregon and California. Some complex parts for the steam engines were mass produced by specialist machine shops thousands of miles away. To improve their chances of participating in the war effort, twenty of the smaller manufacturers in the Portland area formed the Oregon War Industries (OWI) collective under the leadership of Iron Fireman, whose crucial contribution to the supply of Liberty ship engines has already been highlighted in Chapter 8.

This entity handled the vast military bureaucracy and streamlined the local bidding and billing processes associated with large government contracts. The OWI companies covered almost every type of product that could be needed by the military – even the grey paint for the hull could also be mixed locally. *The Oregonian* noted that the Pacific Chain and Manufacturing Company was expanding its operation to quadruple the output of anchor chains and propellers for Liberty ships. This enabled Kaiser to source much of its needs locally, saving on time and transportation.

BUCKLER-CHAPMAN SHIP JOINERS

The Chapman Lumber Co was founded in 1901 and grew to become the major supplier of lumber for the building of the Hoover Dam, Bonneville Dam, Grand Coulee Dam, and the San Francisco Bay bridges. Chapman also ran a planer mill where huge amounts of local Douglas fir was turned into dimensional timber to supply the joiner plant where skilled carpenters, manufactured wooden furnishings, doors, and even truck bodies. This property was located in North Portland at the intersection of North Columbia Blvd, south of the Columbia River flood plain.

One of the great skills of the Kaiser organization was the ability to delegate, and Edgar Kaiser recognized the Chapman and Buckler companies from their connection to the dam building projects. He realized that they had experience to take on the huge task of 'ship fitting', the process of turning bare steel hulls into seagoing ships to ready them for the war at sea. They responded by forming the Buckler-Chapman partnership to increase the capacity of their mills and plants, and quickly built an independent team that could satisfy the anticipated demand for woodwork on all Kaiser's ships. They employed around 2500 workers – carpenters, joiners, painters etc – who could turn a bare hull into an inhabitable vessel for a crew of 40–45 and a Navy Armed Guard of 12–25 men in a matter of weeks with galleys, mess rooms, cabins, refrigerated food storage etc.

According to contemporary records, the partnership did not extend into the shipyards: Buckler had the contract for Swan Island and Vancouver, and Chapman was responsible for Oregonship. They formed a small army of woodworkers in each yard that numbered many hundreds, and the Kaiser employees called them all 'Bucklerites'. In fact, it was Chapman who sent the first crew into OSC, where they built their own warehouse for their tools and storage and began pre-fabricating furnishings for the first Liberty ship. As soon as the welders had completed a compartment, the Bucklerites started learning the unexpected ways in which a ship differed from a building.

It took 96 days to fit it out the SS *Star of Oregon* with a vast amount of wooden equipment: around 100 pieces of furniture, 80 doors, mess tables and benches, numerous ladders and stairways. One ship required 67,500 board feet of lumber and 12,300 square feet of plywood to panel the walls and ceilings. They found that fitting out the freezer room was a specialized job requiring truckloads of insulation, tons of cement and lead sheet, and hanging a 600 lbs wooden door to seal the entrance. On deck, they installed deck gratings, hatches, handrails and the circular wooden foundations for the guns on the bow and stern.

The Buckler-Chapman mill looked down onto the lowland where they supplied much of the lumber and manpower to build the short-lived town of Vanport. When it was completed, the carpenters were sent to the shipyards where they quickly became 'ship fitters.' As ship production took off, the superintendents hired and trained over a thousand people as carpenters and ship fitters, including many women. This increased the workforce to over 2000 spread over three yards, the mills and workshops.

Below: A ship fitters crew in a Kaiser yard. To Kaiser employees, the woodworkers were known as 'Bucklerites' as they were usually contract workers from the Buckler-Chapman partnership.

In Vancouver, the Bucklerites also took on the task of laying the flight decks on all fifty of the escort carriers. It took 74,000 feet (14 miles) of 3in by 6in fir to cover the 477ft x 80ft flight deck of a CVE, each ship requiring five railcar loads of planking. As the time to produce a Liberty ship dropped, so did the time to fit it out. The company reduced that to just a week in 1943 as it became an essential and reliable part of the record-beating production team at the Kaiser yards. Buckler-Chapman emphasized its status and success by producing its own glossy publication *The Challenger*, which rivalled the *Bosun's Whistle* for quality and won a national award for excellence under the direction of Nan Selleck, one of the handful of women running a department in a large firm. She also produced special hard covered albums detailing the work performed on each class of Kaiser ships.

In the 23 May 1945 issue of *The Challenger*, a skilled carpenter and welder named Dale Holmes was quoted as an enthusiastic champion of women welders in the shipyard. 'Those girls come to work in the morning all spic and span, all neat and clean,' he told the reporter. 'Then they work around these ships, and crawl around through the dirt and grease and mess, and when they are ready to go home, you cannot tell one girl from another, they're all so dirty. I tell you, it takes a lot of nerve for a girl to go through that day after day, and do a good job. And I'm telling you, those girls really work.'

Other lesser-known and smaller scale industries related to the war effort came from Oregon's traditional lumber industry. Mills sawed Douglas fir into planks for use in manufacturing army truck beds to replace valuable steel. With practically every business on the waterfront involved in the war effort, there was a shortage of contractors to handle the needs of civilian ships that continued to call on the west coast ports.

NORTHWEST MARINE IRON WORKS

In May 1943, Joe Grebe, and his son George, recruited a group of experienced shipyard professionals and formed Northwest Marine Iron Works to supply mobile ship repair services to visiting ships. They began with a small staff and soon had 75 men on the job. By 1944, they had a staff of over 1000 to meet the demands for ship maintenance and repairs, and were available if newly launched ships had mechanical problems.

In 1947, they constructed the last sterrnwheel steam-tug built in North America, the 210ft *Portland*, for use by the Port of Portland. It replaced an earlier wooden sternwheeler that handled Kaiser's ships after the launch ceremony. The 'new' *Portland* was steel and worked until 1990. It has been preserved as a historic vessel and still runs on the Willamette River every summer powered by its original pair of single-cylinder 900 hp horizontal beam engines and is the only steam vessel built in Portland that is still in operation.

ELECTRIC STEEL FOUNDRY COMPANY (ESCO)

The Electric Steel Foundry Company (ESCO) was founded in 1913 with an imported electric furnace from Europe – first of its kind in the western United States. It stood on low land recently reclaimed from the Willamette River for the Lewis & Clark Exposition of 1905 – a western version of a world fair. In the 1930s ESCO began to specialize in hardened steel parts for use in mining and excavating equipment. It also backed a new business called Willamette-Ersted Company, specializing in log and lumber equipment. This firm became Hyster, the world-famous producer of lift trucks and materials-handling equipment.

During World War II, hundreds of ESCO dragline buckets went to war with the US Army and Navy to dredge ship channels, build airstrips etc. The company also produced anchor chain and valves for ships, and many cast components were supplied for tanks and aircraft. The ESCO foundry prospered in the post-war construction boom, but eventually closed in 2017, after it was purchased for $1.3 billion by The Weir Group, a Scottish maker of equipment for mining and oil and gas drilling industries.

HESSE-ERSTED IRON WORKS

The Hesse-Ersted Iron Works opened in SE Portland a few blocks from the Willamette River in 1918 to cast and machine

Below: These Hesse-Ersted employees pouring molten steel into a mould appear to know exactly what they are doing and probably never thought of this as hazardous work, as we do today. The overhead crane operator has the best view looking down on the scene, while another seven men are visible in the background taking a break from the daily grind.

Above: These men are moving an assembled winch out of the workshop to a test bed. The small drum is for hemp rope or hawser; the large drums are for wire rope. Note the steam engine on the base of the winch.

steel parts. In World War II, the company manufactured its own brand of anchor windlasses and cargo winches powered by electric motors manufactured by General Electric Co, Schenectady, NY. These were supplied to the Kaiser Swan Island yard for T2 tankers, and to the Victory ships on the west coast.

In January 1944 Hesse-Ersted bought the bankrupt Oregon Electric Steel Mill, Portland's only steel rolling mill. They were able to resume operations, turning out 100 tons of steel in a single shift with a staff of 70 to 100 employees. (The Victory ship SS *Red Oak Victory* in San Francisco Bay is equipped with a standard Hesse-Ersted anchor winch, capable of raising two 9500 lb cast-steel anchors simultaneously. Anchors like these were also cast in Portland.) The buildings that housed Hesse-Ersted and Iron Fireman are still in use. Both have been converted into multi-use urban centres with tenants like coffee bars and brew pubs.

COLUMBIA STEEL CASTING

Columbia Steel Casting was founded in 1901 to cast machine parts for logging, mining and agriculture using coal-fired Bessemer furnaces. By 1910, the company had expanded its foundry in NW Portland to pour large castings for the railways, shipping and gold dredging. 1923 saw the opening of the first three-phase arc furnace in the western states, which produced parts up to ten tons like gears, jaws and wear parts for dredges and crushers for rock mills using steel alloys. The Wall Street crash of 1929 seriously impacted many of its customers, but fortunately, the gold dredging industry stayed active and kept Columbia afloat until Pearl Harbor.

After the first Kaiser yard arrived in 1941, the managers of

Above: A large anchor windlass with warping drums on each side on its way to the Newport News naval base on the east coast. In the summer of 1945, Hesse Ersted changed its name to Western Machinery, as seen on the building in the background.

Columbia Steel recognized the need to expand their capacity and purchased the vacant Pacific Car & Foundry plant on the central east side of the city. This had four times the furnace capacity to allow them to pour huge castings for Liberty ships like propellers, anchors and stern frames. This frame was the most complex part, combining the rudder post and lower pivot with the aft bearing for the propeller shaft, which saved the shipbuilders many hours of work.

There was very little automation during these years. The work was hard and the hours long to produce a frame every day of the week. All the moulding sand was hand-rammed and parts cleaned with hand tools. To speed up production, ladles of molten steel were trucked the four miles from the East Side to the old plant in the NW – with a police escort! The company was awarded the Navy 'E' flag for excellence and the US Maritime Commission 'M' flag for production.

Columbia Steel continued in business at its original plant until 1962, surviving a serious fire in 1957. It settled in a new location in North Portland at the very edge of the city on the south side of the Columbia Slough wetlands, and only a mile west of the site of Vanport. Here it successfully weathered the changes in the industries it serves, and incorporated modern technology like electronic analysis and computer-aided design. The company celebrated its centenary in 2001, and they have continued the tradition of innovation and quality into the twenty-first century. Columbia Steel has the distinction of being one of the oldest industrial companies in Oregon, and the only major supplier to the Portland shipyards still manufacturing the same type of products.

Operations like these competed for workers with the big shipyards and aluminum plants, all creating more new jobs and putting additional pressure on the city's housing supply, transportation network and daily life. Federal involvement played an important role in defence manufacturing due to the increasing shortages of a wide variety of critical materials. Soon steel, rubber, copper, electricity and virtually everything else associated with manufacturing was allocated on a priority basis, with critical industries like shipbuilding taking preference over all peacetime manufacturing of cars, appliances, furnishings etc.

CHEMICAL PLANTS

In addition to manufacturing, Portland-area firms with defence-related contracts included a wide variety of chemical plants. 'Portland has two carbide plants, ... two soap plants, a sodium chlorate plant, a Ferro-alloy plant, a half dozen oxygen and acetylene plants, and several other specialty chemical plants,' said the Portland Chamber of Commerce in 1945. The Electro Metallurgical Company, a division of Union Carbide, purchased a 100-acre tract north of St Johns In March 1941, and announced plans to produce calcium carbide and acetylene gas, and ferro-silicon – used to make metal alloys. 'About 300 men will be employed at the outset and the original plant investment will be about $2,500,000.'

The electrical output of the Bonneville Power Administration (BPA) provided a major element in making Portland a defence centre from the start of hostilities. The most notable example was the aluminium plants along the Columbia River that relied on the abundant and inexpensive electric power. Aluminium demand during the war skyrocketed because of its introduction into aircraft construction. The first aluminium reduction mill in the region was built by Alcoa at Vancouver, Washington, and a second line was added in February 1940.

The Alcoa plant expanded to a 164,000-ton annual output of aluminium, equal to the capacity of the rest of the nation's plants. Most of this metal went to the Boeing Aircraft Company's sprawling bomber factory in south Seattle. (Coincidentally, Vancouver was also the main supplier of high-quality wood for the biplanes of World War I. The world's largest spruce mill was erected there in 1917 specifically to supply top-quality stringers to US and French aircraft plants.)

To further increase capacity and avoid a monopoly, the Reconstruction Finance Corporation was prodded by the War Department to provide the funds for a Reynolds Metal Corporation aluminium plant at Longview, Washington that went into production in August 1941. Defense Plants Corporation, in cooperation with Alcoa, built the Portland area's third aluminium mill at Troutdale, Oregon within the year. After the war Reynolds Aluminum purchased the Troutdale plant and continued to operate it. These three plants were responsible for a large share of the national production of aluminium and manufactured all the plate, sheet, and extruded shapes required by Boeing.

A year end summary in 1941 reported that 'Portland's dreams of centring an aluminium and chemical empire were translated from hopes into actualities in 1941,' and elaborated upon the millions of dollars in new investment in the area from not only Alcoa and Reynolds, but also the Pennsylvania Salt Manufacturing Company, United Engineering and Foundry, of Pittsburgh, Pacific Carbide and Alloy, General Chemical and many others. The Portland DP Corp then built an aluminium plant in Spokane in NE Washington with government help – because it was close to the Grand Coolee and far enough inland to be safe from even the most determined of Japanese bomber pilots. In 1946, this plant was taken over by an industry newcomer, none other than Henry Kaiser.

All of these companies worked in partnership with a series of federal agencies, both civilian and military, for the duration of the conflict, allowing them to meet tight production schedules, secure scarce resources and develop improved designs to improve the nation's military capacity. Near the end of the war, OWI reported having been awarded nearly 200 separate contracts from various federal agencies, with a total value of estimated at more than $50 million.

The nuts and bolts and sub-assemblies, and a thousand other parts and supplies furnished for the Victory Fleet by plants both large and small, were an important part of a national effort. As Admiral Land wrote to one manufacturer: 'The products you make are component parts of these vessels ... You are important members of the great shipbuilding team which is achieving an almost unbelievable production and thereby helping win this war ... We are confidently counting on every man and woman to stand by, as you always have, until the last shot is fired.' And Admiral Vickery told a group of plant workers, 'I know it's not very exciting bevelling plates all day, or turning out castings, or bending pipe. However, that's the way we get ships built. Without you, we would be lost ...'

The big shipyards did not hesitate to acknowledge their debt to their many suppliers. These tributes, from the US Maritime Commission archives, come from outside the Portland area but are equally valid for the local yards.

'There are 15 sub-contractors at Marinship, all real specialists in their lines of work ... Our combined sub-contractors in the yard do 60,000 manhours of work on each ship. The sub-contractor is tremendously vital to the success of our production.'

'The Bethlehem Steel Co has over 6000 individual sub-contractors, many of whom in turn are served by other firms, so that a total of more than 30,000 enterprises are at work on Bethlehem's ship and other war programs.'

18

PORTLAND SHIPBUILDING COMPANY

By the time of the D-Day landings in France in 1944 and as the USA began to push the Japanese forces out of the western Pacific islands, every boatyard on the west coast had been enlisted to aid the war effort by producing some type of craft that could be used by the military. This included many wooden boats that ranged from the Higgins 36ft plywood landing craft to the 136ft YMS double-planked minesweeper. However, there is one type of vessel built in Portland during the war years that you will be hard-pressed to find in the official

Below: A team of barge builders eases another baulk onto the side of a wooden barge under construction at Portland Shipbuilding. The long bevel amidships is a scarf joint.

Left: Each heavy timber is stacked on the one below and secured with long galvanized steel rods driven tightly into the holes.

Below: A finished 110ft wooden barge ready to be side-launched into the Willamette River.

lists of World War II ships – the 110ft wooden barges built for the US Army and Navy on the Willamette River by the Portland Shipbuilding Company. This business claimed the title of 'the oldest boat-building operation in Oregon' into the 1960s, when it disappeared leaving only the faintest trace.

Although the name sounds impressive, this modest yard a mile upstream of the city centre stayed faithful to wood construction long after the rest of the marine industry had converted to steel in the 1920s. The Portland Shipbuilding Company had been founded in 1885 by Charles M Nelson, a Norwegian immigrant who became one of the pioneers in the construction of wooden sternwheel riverboats. These fine steam-powered craft provided the only form of reliable transportation between the Willamette Valley farming towns and Portland from the late 1800s to the 1930s, travelling as far upstream as the state capitol in Salem, 50 miles south when the river was high. Nelson built 25 of them before the highways captured all the freight traffic.

Nelson's son Albert took over the yard in the 1930s when steel construction was becoming more accepted by the inland boatmen, but to convert the yard from wood to steel during the Depression was not feasible, and the yard had built its reputation on its expertise with big wooden hulls. Fortunately, there were still a handful of wooden sternwheel steam tugs moving ships around in the Port of Portland that needed regular maintenance and repair, which helped keep the yard afloat until Pearl Harbor.

The company continued to find customers for their traditional wooden barges because their solid bottoms could withstand heavy impacts and groundings better than steel, and the changes in water level on the local rivers meant skippers often had to navigate in very shallow water that made contact with the bottom more likely. Albert Nelson began producing these sturdy cargo carriers in a standard 110ft size with a combination of traditional craftsmanship and production-line methods. Much of the work was still done by hand on their side-haul marine railway, but the heavy baulks of timber were hoisted with the aid of a 10-ton steam crane equipped with a 55ft boom, running along the shore on a narrow-gauge track.

Early in World War II, barges were desperately needed to haul military supplies along the west coast and to the forward bases in Alaska and Hawaii. With steel in short supply and all the coastal shipyards busy with wooden minesweepers and small craft, the Army and Navy looked for a yard with empty ways

Left: Two caulkers fill the seams between the planks of a wooden barge. They use the traditional tools and caulking cotton to create a flexible watertight seam filler.

Left: Five of the veteran shipwrights pose for Barber's camera, four of them holding the traditional axes and adzes that have been used in wooden shipyards since medieval times.

that could supply barges. There must have been some eyebrows raised when it was suggested they consider wooden hulls, but they sent representatives to Portland Shipbuilding to examine some of the yard's products that had seen a lot of hard use.

They were surprised and impressed by the construction method perfected locally using the plentiful supplies of lumber. It involved stacking large Douglas fir baulks to form the sides, drilling through the assembly, and driving long vertical bolts from top to bottom to create an incredibly solid hull. Portland Shipbuilding was given a military contract and went straight to work, joining the numerous marine industries on the Willamette already in the war effort.

'We had 68 men on the job and built 68 barges,' Nelson told *The Oregonian*'s marine editor Larry Barber in 1969. In 16 months, the yard turned out well over 'a mile of barges' for the Army, Navy, and maritime commissions, said Nelson proudly. That meant about one per week! Good craftsmen were scarce at the time, he recalled, so he promoted half a dozen experienced shipwrights and carpenters to serve as leadmen, directing the work of the scores of men who joined the crew after being rejected by the draft.

Like all the other shipyards in the vicinity, they started work cautiously, but soon began to speed up production until they could complete a barge ready for launch in 6–8 days. The traditional art of caulking the seams was not something you could pick up in a few days, and there were less than 30 experienced caulkers available in Portland for all the wooden boats being constructed. Luckily the barges were easier to make watertight than thinly-planked vessels, and Nelson managed to keep eight to ten caulkers busy, he explained. However, the navy insisted they use heavy powered caulking machines on the deck to speed up the work. To protect the bottom from rot caused by pools of freshwater from rain and spray collecting in the bottom, five tons of rock salt was usually spread out in each barge to 'pickle' the wood.

The company continued to maintain and repair the remaining wooden barges and tugs on the Willamette and lower Columbia Rivers until 1964, when a big flood destroyed the slipway. In 1969, Nelson sold the property to the city to convert into a new waterfront park. At that time, some of the company's pre-war barges built with high-quality lumber were still working locally, Barber noted in his article.

19

GUNDERSON BROTHERS

Although Kaiser's yards ultimately grabbed most of the attention during World War II, and the three mid-size yards (Albina, CIW and WISCO) built small fighting ships like subchasers and minesweepers, many other Portland companies would create their own impressive production records.

Gunderson Brothers Company was another established Portland engineering firm, founded in 1919, and noted for its experience in steel fabrication of various types, including trailers, wire wheels and truck bodies, before it re-tooled for war work in a property directly across the Willamette River from Swan Island.

In 1939 the company developed and constructed the worlds' first resin-pressed laminated plywood lifeboats, using modern manufacturing techniques to produce compound curved panels.

Below: Half a dozen landing craft are under construction in one bay of the big assembly building. This production line shows how Gunderson was able to turn out LCMs at a very rapid pace.

Left: Gunderson also built thousands of laminated wooden lifeboats, and countless Carley floats, which were the crew's last resort if a ship was sunk. They also trained and employed a large number of women workers.

Below: Gunderson called the LCM (officially a Landing Craft Mechanized) a 'tank lighter' because it could carry a medium-size 13.5-ton tank, 15 tons of cargo, or 100 troops.

The Maritime Commission was satisfied after testing Gunderson's prototypes and ordered 1000 moulded wood lifeboats in July 1942. 'From a downtown garage in Linnton, the concern has expanded into one of the Pacific Coast's finest all-covered waterfront boat-building plants in NW Portland. Payroll has jumped within a comparatively few months from 30 or 40 workers to a factory crew of 500 men,' said *The Oregonian* in August 1942.

In its search for ways around the growing metal shortages that were hampering boat building nationally, Gunderson continued building lifeboats and other wooden craft, and turned out more than 3600 craft – lifeboats, landing craft mechanized (LCM) and rafts. Their name was often mentioned in national news stories about the production of the famed wooden PT Boats (Patrol Torpedo) and the plywood Higgins Landing Craft as one of the other major builders of wooden boats in the war effort.

In addition, Gunderson also built a large number of welded steel landing craft (LCM-3), which they called 'tank lighters'. They were 50ft long, 14ft beam, and powered by twin GM diesel engines. They were used by the Navy to land Sherman tanks weighing 30 tons, or construction machinery and other equipment on beaches all over the Pacific theatre. These hulls, essentially barges, were simple but rugged enough to operate in exposed waters. The company created an exhibit featuring a tank lighter and two lifeboats for the 'Portland Invasion Exposition' in the summer of 1943.

The GUNDERSON GUNNER

Volume 1 Number 18 September 23, 1943 GB Published Every Second Thursday by and for Employees of Gunderson Brothers, Portland, Oregon, U. S. A.

Tank Lighter, Life Boats, Attract Many Thousands

"Definitely the hit of the show!" was the verdict of thousands of Portlanders who crowded around, into, over and under the Gunderson Brothers exhibit of their invasion products at this week's Invasion Exposition along the seawall between the Burnside and Morrison bridges.

"Golly," said one wide-eyed youngster, "my brother's out in the South Pacific and he wrote us that he'd landed on an island in one of these invasion barges. Now I can tell him he's not the only one whose been on one. They're plenty keen!"

Nor were the youngsters the only ones to be impressed by the Gunderson exhibit. Thousands of grown-ups crowded aboard the craft, ignored the fact that on opening day no steps were built to take them up to the main deck and wheel house, swarmed up the ladders for a glimpse of what makes the wheels go 'round. Fearing someone might get pushed off the deck, a burly policeman sat astride the wheelhouse, warned visitors not to go near the edge.

Meanwhile, during the hours when crowds are at their peak along the exposition wall, a Gunderson tank lighter churns the Willamette in a series of maneuvers designed to show off what she can do. And what she can do and does is plenty.

Gunderson men and women who have not yet inspected the big show are urged to attend during the day or evening. Badges issued at Gunderson's when extra invasion bonds are purchased will admit the wearer and his family to the exposition for the season which closes Sunday night.

Friday is to be "Gunderson Day" at the mammoth exhibit, with Gunderson-sponsored entertainment slated throughout the day and evening.

☆ ☆ ☆

Back the Attack!
Buy More Invasion War Bonds NOW!

Above: *The Gunderson Gunner* was the company's bi-weekly newspaper that reported nautical and social happenings in the yard. This copy described their exhibit at Portland's 'Invasion Exposition' In September 1943.

This was very popular because they had the only exhibit that allowed the public to stand in the boats by walking up the ramp. 'The tank lighter was almost invisible beneath the hundreds of visitors,' said the company publication the *Gunderson Gunner*. They also offered rides on the river as a way to raise their profile. Although the lighter was basically a bare hull, management still encouraged the workers to suggest ways to simplify construction. They dedicated an entire page of the *Gunner* to listing the latest crop of ideas – identified by number only – plus the standard appeal to buy more war bonds.

This may have convinced the Navy that they could be relied on to step up deliveries of tank lighters by recruiting enough new workers to man a third shift. 'This number one priority means that promiscuous issuing of "quit slips" must stop because unless we retain persons who are qualified to perform the work of building this craft, we cannot expect assistance from the government agencies in getting us more manpower,' the 'Gaffer' warned in the next issue of the *Gunderson Gunner*. 'Henceforth, no quit slips will be issued until full circumstances of every case have been fully investigated. All the Victory bonds and ballyhoo about winning the war will not do the job unless all of us stay on the job. I am sure that none of us here at Gunderson wants to let the boys down on the firing line.' Apparently, that did the trick, because before the war ended the company went on to build many more lighters for a total of 442, five YTL 66ft tugs and ten YTN 170ft barges.

Gunderson has the distinction of being the only one of the seven local shipbuilders to remain in business. They acquired a complete fabrication plant and a slipway on NW Front Avenue where construction of commercial vessels such as tugs, barges, and trawlers began in 1947. By the 1970s the company was building vessels as long as 650ft (200m) and as wide as 100ft (30m) on a side-launch ramp, and became one of the premier barge builders on the west coast after the *Exxon Valdez* oil spill in 1989, when all new barges and tankers were required to have full double hulls.

20

ASTORIA MARINE CONSTRUCTION COMPANY (AMCCO)

By the late 1930s the historic port of Astoria at the mouth of the Columbia River already had several established military posts. There were three gun batteries dating from the Civil War, originally intended to guard against naval attack by Confederate raiders, although they were not completed until 1865 after that war had ended. The US Life-Saving Service had a fully-manned station at Point Adams west of Astoria in 1889. The USLSS became the Coast Guard in 1915, which ran lifeboat stations on both sides of the river until the 1930s and opened an 'aids to navigation' base on the downstream side of Tongue Point east of Astoria in 1939. That year also saw a naval air station commissioned on the upstream side of Tongue Point. This made the Lower Columbia River the best defended area on the NW coast, before it became the guardian of some of the most productive shipyards in the world – 100 miles upstream in the Van-Port area.

Within hours of the attack on Pearl Harbor, all three artillery sites were put on alert to guard against a Japanese invasion force entering the Columbia River, a squadron of PBY Catalina seaplanes were transferred to the Tongue Point air station where they began patrolling the northwest coast looking for enemy submarines that were rumoured to be carrying seaplanes or commando units. Defensive positions and patrols were organized along the entire NW coast, stretching over 800 nautical miles from Neah Bay, Washington to San Francisco Bay, California.

The Oregon coast was the most likely target of a Japanese attack – anything from putting a spy in a dinghy to a full-on

Below: YMS plans show some of the construction details of the sturdy wooden hull that had to withstand the shock wave from swept mines that were detonated by rifle fire. The round bilge hull shape produced severe rolling in big waves.

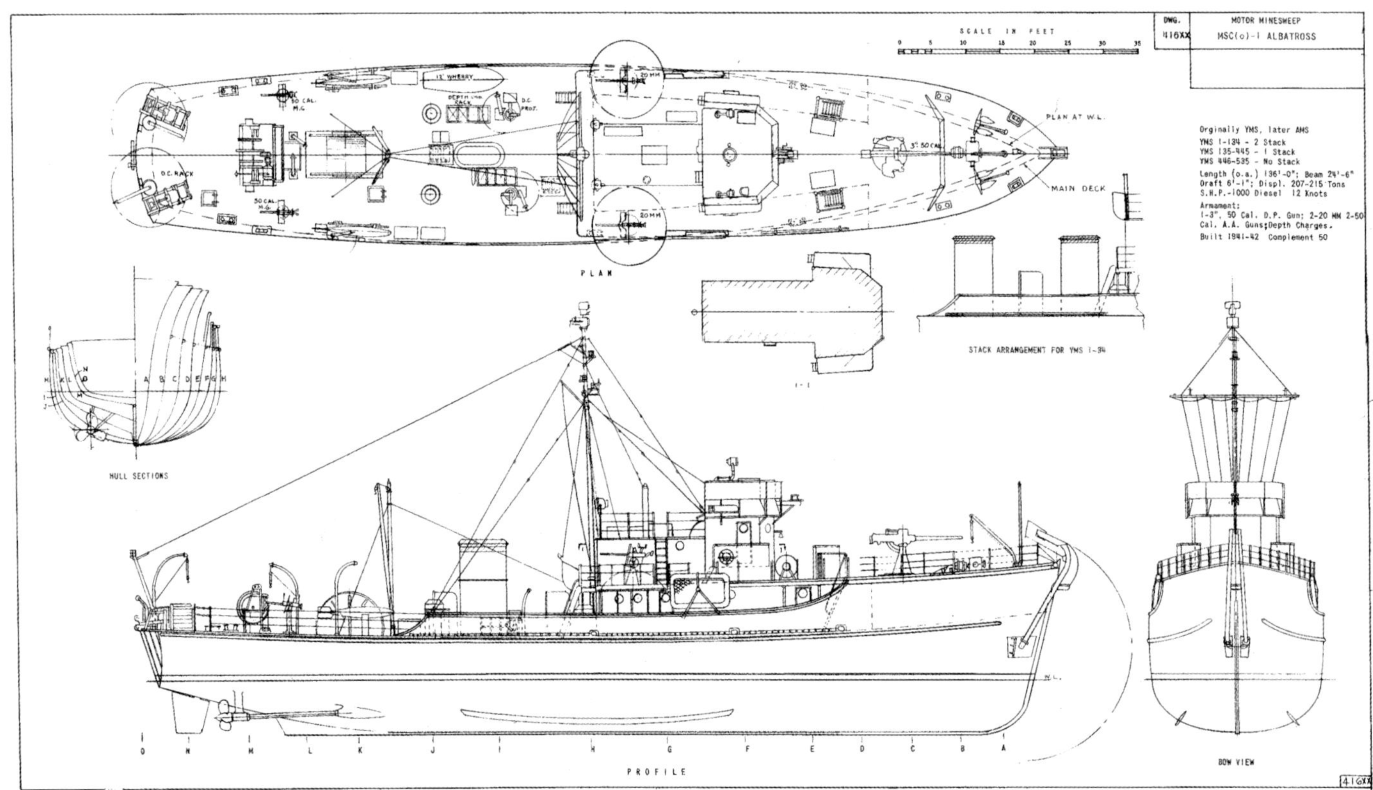

D-Day type amphibious landing. The beaches were absolutely off-limits and were covered in barbed wire, and the Oregon Shore Patrol was organized by American Legion posts in coastal counties in December 1941. They were replaced by improved Coast Guard patrols and Army installations. This was not unlike the measures already adopted on the English coast with aircraft spotters and patrols by foot or on horseback.

However, there was one civilian operation that had already been swept up for nine months in the first national mobilization. Astoria Marine Construction Company (AMCCO) was one of the small shipyards that were awarded contracts to build the first 'emergency ships' for the US Navy and the British Royal Navy. By 1941 America's naval shipyards were already working at capacity to strengthen the US Navy's fleets and the war planners also wanted more small vessels including wooden minesweepers.

On 4 March 1941 the Henry Nevins shipyard in New York laid the keel for its new design of a 136ft wooden inshore minesweeper classified as a YMS (Yard Mine Sweeper – for clearing harbours and anchorages). A week later, on 11 March, FDR signed the Lend-Lease program and by the end of the month the US Navy was inspecting the best wooden shipbuilders all over the US to decide who could start work on the YMS type on an emergency footing. This began a short-lived revival in traditional marine construction skills as boatyards all around the country responded to the government's invitation to submit bids.

Oregon's wooden shipbuilders in Astoria and Coos Bay won initial approval, with more on Puget Sound and northern California for a total of nineteen west coast yards ready to leap into action. Since the British were desperately in need of these vessels and the US was technically 'neutral', eighty minesweepers designated 'BYMS' were promised to the Royal Navy as soon as possible. The US Navy sent inspectors out to the west coast to inspect all these facilities and were probably a little suspicious of the operations that intended to use high-quality softwood instead of the hardwood that was available to the east coast builders.

Once they were shown the company records, the surveyors were able to verify the quality of the local timber, and on 1 April 1941, the Navy awarded AMCCO a $1,312,000 contract to build four minesweepers for Britain. These little ships were double-planked to withstand the shock wave when mines were swept up and deliberately detonated by rifle or deck

Left: AMCCO craftsmen cutting notches in the keelson of a YMS before attaching the laminated ribs.

Above: *YMS-136* ready for launch after a year of highly skilled work by AMCCO.

Left: *YMS-109* on sea trials flying the US flag.

gun fire. The inner planking was to be 2in Douglas fir, the outer layer over 1ft thick. The design was to be powered by a pair of GM 400 hp diesels – a big step beyond the fine wooden yachts, ferries and fishing boats the yard had built since 1922. The yard owner Joseph Dyer intended to pre-fabricate parts for all four boats simultaneously using jigs and patterns to laminate heavier timbers, but was not sure how to finance this ambitious plan.

Fortunately, the Navy had anticipated situations like AMCCO's, and allowed a 10 percent progress payment when the keels were laid. Dyer bought some adjoining tideland pasture, where he laid down four 110ft Douglas fir keels sawn at the big mill in Westport, upriver, then drew up plans for sheds, building ways, and workshops to be built when the money was paid. As soon as the new buildings were roofed and the saws and planers set up, Dyer found more skilled carpenters and shipwrights who came out of retirement and started the pre-fabrication of parts for all four vessels. Then the crew began attaching oak frames on the second keel.

After Pearl Harbor, a wartime mentality set in at the coast, as residents were commanded to black out their homes at night by covering windows with shades and blankets. Block wardens patrolled neighbourhoods, looking for tell-tale lights and reprimanding offenders. K-Series 251ft blimps from Tillamook Air Station kept watch from the sky, and all shipping in and out of the river had to wait for an escort through the minefields,

It had taken almost one year to finish the first hull since the contract was signed; the company's records state that the first vessel, *YMS-100*, was launched on 12 April 1942. But the next three boats were all well on the way and methods of pre-fabricating the ribs from multiple layers of wood and resin glue on a 24ft-wide adjustable steel jig was working well. The propulsion was by twin Cleveland GM 8-268 two-stroke 8-cylinder diesels rated at 500 hp each; the bore was 8 inches and stroke 7 inches.

On the night of 21 June 1942, a Japanese submarine fired seventeen shells at Fort Stevens – now Oregon's largest state park and campground. Most of the shells landed in a swampy area at the edge of the fort, and some exploded on the beach or failed and buried themselves in the sand. Many people expected the invasion would be next, and the volunteer coast watchers were on high alert, but that was the second and last time that the west coast was shelled in World War II.

The new boat shop complex was carefully organized to speed up production and the second minesweeper was delivered on 17 July. *YMS-102* was sent out into the Columbia a month later, followed by *YMS-103* on September 18. They were all commissioned as British Yard Minesweepers (BYMS) and were manned by crews from Britain. This was an outstanding achievement, and the building team of over 400 were able to celebrate their delivery of the second pair only six months after the keels were laid.

Left: Royal Navy officers of *YMS-137* ready for departure in April 1943. In British service the ship was re-numbered *BYMS-2137*.

Left: *YMS-137* departs the Columbia River en route for the Panama Canal, flying the Royal Navy's White Ensign and commanded by J Cramer Perry.

The same spirit that developed in the Portland yards kept the big AMCCO shop in the Lewis and Clark River humming around the clock. Kaiser was already employing thousands of women, and Dyer brought in the first women in April of 1943. They were assigned to the sweeping crew, but soon they were training as drill press operators, light joinery workers, gluers, sanders, pipe-threading machine operators, light deck caulkers, and lead and plugging workers. A total of about 70 women and 400 men ended up working at AMCCO by the summer of 1943. That year, three sweepers were delivered to the Royal Navy. They also won the Treasury T-flag for full participation in the year-long bond drive, paid with 10 percent of their annual wages.

In 1944 the yard's weekly newspaper, the *AMCCO Log*, reported that two welders, Garnet Verschuren and Harold Johnson, stopped work and held a wedding ceremony still wearing their welding masks and overalls and attended by their workmates. (That would be considered 'progressive' even today.) In the three-year period from the spring of 1942 through December 1944, AMCCO built sixteen identical 136ft minesweepers and two 128ft hulls as subchasers/patrol craft. Over 80 of these American-built boats were used by the British Navy, many participating in D-Day. AMCCO also built six 70ft YTs (Yard Tug) and fifteen 46ft MTLs (Motor Towboat Large).

At the Port of Astoria, they had a workforce of up to 1000 to complete finishing work on many of the ships that had been released from their builders upstream. This included the 50 escort aircraft carriers built in Vancouver and 33 attack transports from Oregonship – an astonishing accomplishment for this small port. In 1944, the company proudly announced: '201 Ships Built, Outfitted or Repaired!' The time to complete a YMS was reduced dramatically and they delivered number twelve by the end of 1944.

The amazing total of 561 wooden minesweepers would be built at thirty-five US yards around the US coast and the Great Lakes in a three-year period. This was another great achievement for the war effort, especially because there was no way to modernize many of the traditional skills needed in wooden ship construction. Surprisingly, the most prolific region for YMS launches was New York state, where well over 100 were built. The YMS proved to be one of the US Navy's more durable and versatile types through a quarter-century of service, filling a variety of roles for a number of navies.

A handful of the YMS class from the west coast survived the war and subsequent naval use, and found work in a wide variety of civilian tasks all over the world. One of the most famous was Jacques Cousteau's research vessel *Calypso*, converted from *BYMS-26* built in Seattle. Several became private yachts, including *YMS-328* which as *Wild Goose*, was owned by the movie star John Wayne for seventeen years, and *Calisto* (ex-*YMS-137*) which was originally converted for Thomas Loel Guinness and provides luxurious charters even today. In more mundane employment, *YMS-123* built in Coos Bay remains active as the ferry *Uchuck III* on the west coast of Vancouver Island, Canada and is still powered by a pair of 1940s Cleveland engines.

In 2018 AMCCO was given notice to cease operations because of environmental issues that actually dated back to the war effort, when toxic waste like paint and oil was often spilled and settled into the topsoil. Many of the old woodworking machines and slipways were still in use until 2020, and the yard was listed on the National Register of Historic Places. But that was not enough to save it from the wrecking crew.

TAILPIECE

Left and below: Two of Larry Barber's photos of USS *Carteret* (APA-70) bringing home service personnel to Portland after the end of the war.

OPERATION MAGIC CARPET 1945–46

'Victory over Japan Day' on 14 August 1945 marked the end of the Pacific war, but there remained the huge logistical challenge of repatriating the millions of US military personnel scattered across the western hemisphere. This major operation was named 'Magic Carpet'; it utilised every available naval vessel including aircraft carriers, with every vacant space hurriedly filled with bunks up to five tiers high. Over the next year, an average of 100,000 military personnel were landed in the USA every week. (Even luxury liners like the *Queen Mary* had been converted to troopships. It routinely carried 1000 crew and 15,000 American troops across the Atlantic – seven times the peacetime capacity.)

Many troopships returned to Portland loaded with soldiers in 1945–46; Larry Barber's best shot was of the 426ft USS *Carteret* (APA-70) steaming upriver with men lining the rails. This *Gilliam* class attack transport was designed to carry troops right up to a beach-head using an array of boats and landing craft carried on board. All 32 vessels of the class were built by the Consolidated Steel Corporation of Wilmington, California in 1944–45. The *Carteret* was commissioned in December 1944 and carried troops to the battles on Iwo Jima and Okinawa. Its official capacity was 850 officers and men, but it was probably carrying well over 1000 in these photos.

The *Carteret* ended its short career in the Operation Crossroads fleet of outmoded ships used to test the effects of the atom bomb at Bikini atoll between 28 May and 27 August 1946. It was then towed to Kwajalein for study of radiation effects, and was sunk in deep water by gunfire from the heavy cruiser USS *Toledo* (CA-133) on 19 April 1948.

SOURCES AND FURTHER READING

SOURCES

Lawrence Barber (1901–1996): personal photo archive and papers in the author's possession.

The Oregonian. One of two daily papers in Portland, Oregon during the war years, and the oldest continuously published newspaper on the US west coast, founded in 1850 and published daily from 1861 to 2013. By 2020 *The Oregonian* had drastically cut its staff and printing schedule in favour of its website oregonlive.com.

George Kramer, *It Takes More Than Bullets: The WWII Homefront in Portland, Oregon*. This is a definitive history of Portland's wartime housing estates commissioned by the Housing Authority of Portland, and completed in December 2006. It is available online at https://efiles.portlandoregon.gov/Record/13950134/

The Bo's'n's Whistle, the Kaiser shipyards' newspaper. The entire run has been digitised by The Oregon Historical Society and is available online at https://digitalcollections.ohs.org/the-bosns-whistle

Kaiser Permanente's extensive history archive covers many aspects of the Kaiser corporation's wartime activities. It is available online at https://about.kaiserpermanente.org/our-story/our-history

Kaiser company publications: A *Parent's Guide to the Child Care Centers*,1943; Oregon Shipyard Corporation souvenir booklet *Record Breakers*, 1945; and the company history *Kaiser Story*, published in 1968. Kaiser produced but never released the film *We Build Tankers*, a 21-minute 16mm colour documentary about Kaiser's Swan Island shipyard, made in 1945; from the Leonard Delano Film Collection at the Oregon Historical Society, available online.

Gus Bourneuf Jr, *Workhorse of the Fleet. A History of the Liberty Ships* on American Bureau of Shipping website. https://ww2.eagle.org/content/dam/eagle/publications/company-information/workhorse-of-the-fleet-2019.pdf

The City of Portland Archives & Records Center provided the 1942 Trolley Map of Portland and other historic documents for reference. https://www.portlandoregon.gov/archives/

Oregon Secretary of State's online history archive: World War II. Life on the Home Front: with over 400 printed pages of commentary by notable local authors. https://sos.oregon.gov/archives/exhibits/ww2/Pages/default.aspx

Rosie the Riveter/World War II Home Front National Historic Park in Richmond, California https://www.nps.gov/rori/index.htm

The Log was the west coast's monthly maritime magazine during the 1930s and 1940s with much reporting on wartime shipbuilding. The Log archive is accessible online at Google Books – search for a World War II yard or manufacturer's name like 'Albina' or 'Hesse-Ersted'.

Shipbuilding History website. This extensive online database compiled by Tim Colton gives construction records of US and Canadian shipbuilders and boatbuilders, including building dates and fate of each ship. https://www.shipbuildinghistory.com/

Pages of particular relevance to this book are as follows:

Index to Emergency Shipbuilders in World War II
http://www.shipbuildinghistory.com/shipyards/emergencylarge.htm

Details of ships built by Kaiser Oregonship
http://shipbuildinghistory.com/shipyards/emergencylarge/koregon.htm

Details of ships built by Kaiser Vancouver
http://shipbuildinghistory.com/shipyards/emergencylarge/kvancouver.htm

Details of ships built by Kaiser Swan Island
http://shipbuildinghistory.com/shipyards/emergencylarge/kswanisland.htm

The Men Who Sailed the Liberty Ships, TV documentary, 57 minutes. Produced, directed and written by Maria Brooks, 1994.

FURTHER READING

Peter Elphick, *Liberty: The Ships That Won the War* (Rochester 2001)
By a retired Master Mariner, this book is based on both documentary sources and information obtained from interviews with men who had first-hand knowledge of the design, build and operation of the Liberties.

Mark S Foster, *Henry J Kaiser: Builder in the Modern American West* (Austin TX 1989)
A comprehensive academic account of the life and activities of Henry J Kaiser in all their variety. A paperback version was published in 2012.

Albert P Heiner, *Henry J Kaiser, American Empire Builder: An Insider's View* (New York 1989)
Heiner was a public relations officer at Kaiser Steel so he was undoubtedly close to the events he describes, but his objectivity might be questioned.

Albert P Heiner, *Henry J Kaiser: Western Colossus* (San Francisco 1991)
Another account of Henry J Kaiser's career concentrating more on his business activities than his private life.

John Henshaw, *Liberty's Provenance: The Evolution of the Liberty Ship from its Sunderland Origins* (Barnsley 2019)
A closely argued, and well illustrated, book claiming that the development of the Liberty design is more complicated than usually presented.

Frederic Chapin Lane, *Ships for Victory: A History of Shipbuilding under the US Maritime Commission in World War II* (Baltimore MD 1951). Reprinted 2001 with comments from modern scholars filling 944 pages.
Ships for Victory chronicles this remarkable wartime program in magisterial detail: the development of revolutionary construction methods; the upheavals in management, awarding of contracts, and allocation of materials; the recruitment, training, housing, and union activities of the workers; the crises, confusions, and scandals that arose; and the role of shipbuilding within the total war effort.

Herman E Melton (edited by Will Melton), *Liberty's War: An Engineer's Memoir of the Merchant Marine, 1942–1945* (Annapolis 2017).
Graduating from the US Merchant Marine Academy at Kings Point, New York as an engineer, Melton shipped out to the Pacific Theatre, where he survived the sinking of the Liberty ship SS *Antoine Saugrain*. Melton's son Will edited his father's notes and recollections to produce this memoir.

SOURCES OF PHOTOGRAPHS

Larry Barber was a very capable news photographer, using a large Speed Graphic camera and developing and printing his plates in his own darkroom at home. He identified some of his important photos with his own rubber stamp, but most of his duplicate prints have no stamp or hand-written information on the back. Fortunately, the professional agencies that Kaiser hired to cover particular events or subjects stamped their photos to ensure they were credited.

All of these also have a Kaiser stamp and some have a signature from Hal Babbit, editor of *The Bo's'un's Whistle* or other approval. In Vancouver, Louis Lee served as the staff photographer and his photographs are now part of the Fort Vancouver National Historic Site museum collection. I have endeavoured to attribute every photo in this book to the correct author, and identify the location, to the best of my ability.

AMCCO 245, 246, 247, 248

Barber 19, 25, 29-30, 30, 31, 32, 34-35, 36, 39, 42, 43, 45, 47, 48, 49, 52, 54, 55, 58, 59, 60, 62, 63, 67, 70, 75, 77, 81, 85, 86, 87, 91-92, 94, 95, 98, 100-101, 102, 103, 105, 106, 108, 109, 110, 111, 112, 113, 114, 115, 118, 119, 120, 121, 122, 123, 125, 126, 133, 134-35, 139, 140-41, 142, 144, 145, 146, 147, 148, 154, 156, 161, 162, 163, 164, 165, 166, 173, 177, 178, 179, 180 lower, 181, 182, 183, 186 lower, 187, 194, 195, 203, 204, 205, 206, 209-10, 211, 214, 215, 221, 222, 223, 224, 225, 230, 237, 238, 239, 240,

Commercial 212 bottom

Gunderson 241, 242

Peter J. Hall 233, 234, 235

Jerry Scanlan for Kaiser 80, 88

Kaiser OSC 33

Kaiser Swan Is 116-117

Kaiser Vancouver (Louis Lee) 22, 71-72, 79, 82-83, 84, 90, 201-202

Photo Art for OSC 22-23, 38, 50-51, 61, 64-65, 69, 96, 124, 126, 128, 129, 130, 168-69, 170, 188, 189, 190, 197-98

Peterson-Schon Engraving Co 41, 55, 158, 174-75 (Jerry Scanlan)

OSC PR 24, 26, 61, 69, 136, 138, 143, 151, 152, 153, 157, 158, 159, 160, 172, 180 top, 184, 185, 186 top

US Library of Congress 20

US Navy archive 89

INDEX

All ship names are followed by a brief definition, except for Victory ships whose names all included the suffix *Victory*. Page references to illustrations are in *italics*.

....

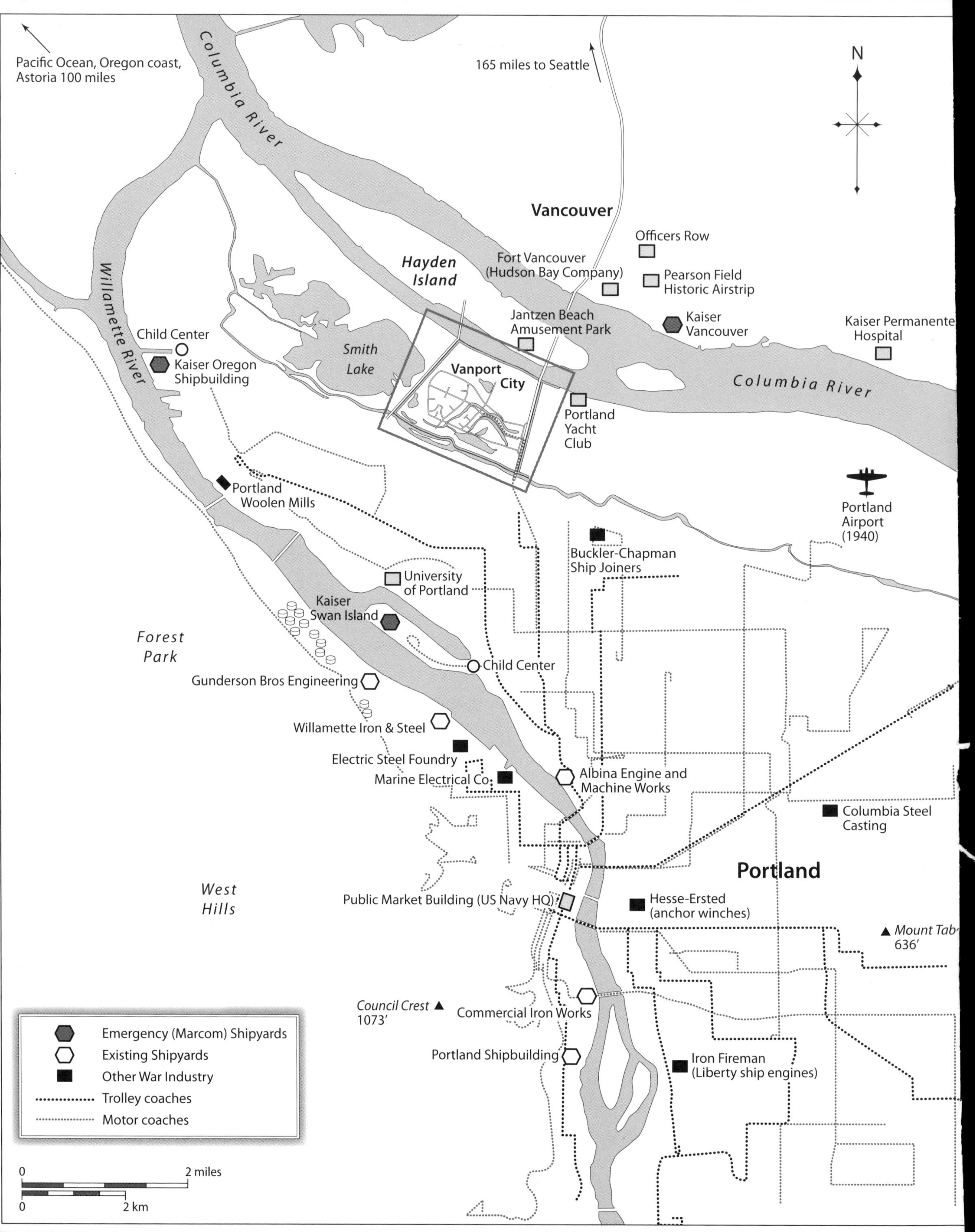

Pacific Ocean, Oregon coast,
Astoria 100 miles
Columbia River
165 miles to Seattle
N
Vancouver
Officers Row
Fort Vancouver
(Hudson Bay Company)
Pearson Field
Historic Airstrip
Hayden
Island
Jantzen Beach
Amusement Park
Kaiser
Vancouver
Kaiser Permanente
Hospital
Willamette River
Child Center
Kaiser Oregon
Shipbuilding
Smith
Lake
Vanport
City
Columbia River
Portland
Yacht
Club
Portland
Woolen Mills
Portland
Airport
(1940)
Buckler-Chapman
Ship Joiners
University
of Portland
Kaiser
Swan Island
Forest
Park
Child Center
Gunderson Bros Engineering
Willamette Iron & Steel
Electric Steel Foundry
Marine Electrical Co.
Albina Engine and
Machine Works
Columbia Steel
Casting
Portland
West
Hills
Public Market Building (US Navy HQ)
Hesse-Ersted
(anchor winches)
Mount Tab
636′
Council Crest
1073′
Commercial Iron Works
Portland Shipbuilding
Iron Fireman
(Liberty ship engines)
Emergency (Marcom) Shipyards
Existing Shipyards
Other War Industry
Trolley coaches
Motor coaches
0
2 miles
0
2 km